David Foster Wallace and "The Long Thing"

David Foster Wallace and "The Long Thing"

New Essays on the Novels

Edited by
Marshall Boswell

BLOOMSBURY
NEW YORK · LONDON · NEW DELHI · SYDNEY

Bloomsbury Academic

An imprint of Bloomsbury Publishing Inc

1385 Broadway	50 Bedford Square
New York	London
NY 10018	WC1B 3DP
USA	UK

www.bloomsbury.com

Bloomsbury is a registered trade mark of Bloomsbury Publishing Plc

First published 2014

Library of Congress Cataloging-in-Publication Data
David Foster Wallace and "The Long Thing": new essays on the novels /
edited by Marshall Boswell. – First edition.
pages cm
Includes bibliographical references and index.
ISBN 978-1-62892-063-5 (hardback) – ISBN 978-1-62892-453-4 (paperback) –
ISBN 978-1-62892-800-6 (ePub) – ISBN 978-1-62892-891-4 (ePDF)
1. Wallace, David Foster–Criticism and interpretation. I. Boswell, Marshall,
1965- editor of compilation. II. Boswell, Marshall, 1965- author.
PS3573.A425635Z662 2014
813'.54–dc23
2014006807

ISBN: HB: 978-1-6289-2063-5
PB: 978-1-6289-2453-4
ePub: 978-1-6289-2800-6
ePDF: 978-1-6289-2891-4

Typeset by Newgen Knowledge Works (P) Ltd., Chennai, India
Printed and bound in the United States of America

Contents

Preface: David Foster Wallace and "The Long Thing"

At the time of his death in September 2008, David Foster Wallace had published nine books. Three were story collections (*Girl with Curious Hair, Brief Interviews with Hideous Men*, and *Oblivion*) and four were works of nonfiction, either collections of journalism and reviews (*A Supposedly Fun Thing I'll Never Do Again* and *Consider the Lobster*) or book-length works focusing on a single topic (*Signifying Rappers*, which he cowrote with his friend Mark Costello, and *Everything and More*, a study of Georg Cantor and infinity). The remaining two books were novels. Wallace's posthumous publishing record is very similar, with the 2011 publication of his unfinished novel *The Pale King* flanked on one end by the chapbook edition of his Kenyon Commencement Address, *This Is Water*, and, on the other, by a posthumous book of thus-far uncollected essays titled *Both Flesh and Not* (2012). All told, he published as many story collections, essay collections, and works of nonfiction as he did novels, which constitute merely one-fourth of his published output.

So why devote an entire collection solely to essays focusing on Wallace as novelist? Given these numbers—as well as the fact that he never finished *The Pale King*—it is reasonable to wonder why critics and readers don't regard Wallace as primarily a short story writer, or perhaps a journalist and story writer who also published novels, similar to the way one might view, say, his contemporary Lorrie Moore, whose ratio of story collections to novels matches Wallace's exactly.

The obvious explanation is because one of those two-and-a-half novels is the 1079-page encyclopedic behemoth *Infinite Jest*, the bulwark atop which so much of his burgeoning reputation rests. But the centrality of *Infinite Jest* in Wallace's published oeuvre also obscures the degree to which Wallace thought of *himself* as primarily a novelist, and not a jack-of-all-trades who happened to have produced one big, generation-defining classic, though he was certainly haunted by this latter possibility. Unlike the vast majority of his contemporaries, most of whom honed their craft by subjecting streams of apprentice short fiction to nitpicking critique in undergraduate and graduate writing workshops, Wallace started out as a novelist. He wrote his sprawling debut novel, *The Broom of the System*, in more or less total isolation while still an undergraduate at Amherst College. In 1985, at the age of 23, he submitted the 500-page manuscript as one of his 2 undergraduate honors theses, resulting in a double *summa cum laude*. Only then did he turn to short fiction. Most of the stories that make up *Girl with Curious Hair* he produced while pursuing his MFA at the University of Arizona in Tucson, where he earned both the ire of his professors, owing to his refusal to kowtow to the then prevailing ethos of Raymond-Carver realism, and the envy of his classmates, due to his having secured a publisher for his undergraduate creative-writing thesis before completing his first year at the program (see Max, *Every Love Story* 39–71, concerting this crucial period in Wallace's life). While his peers were still gearing up for the arduous task of producing a competent debut novel, Wallace was merely taking a breather before his next big book.

From 1989, when *Girl with Curious Hair* first appeared, to his final days, Wallace was buried in a novel project. The stories he produced during those tumultuous two decades were either diversions from the novel-in-progress, exercises undertaken to overcome writer's block, or test runs for themes and techniques that he was developing for the novel project occupying him at the time. In a private letter to me dated May 2002,[1] he explains that he began writing *Infinite Jest*, "or something like it," as early as 1986, and returned to it again in 1988 and 1989. "None of it worked, or was alive," he explains. But then "in '91–'92 all of a sudden it did." Similarly, Michael Pietsch, Wallace's long-time editor at Little, Brown, explains in his "Editor's Note" to *The Pale King* that Wallace began work on that novel almost immediately after finishing *Infinite Jest* in 1994 (see *TPK* v). In letters to Pietsch, Jonathan Franzen, Don DeLillo, and others dating from these years, Wallace repeatedly refers to *The Pale King* as "the Long Thing," while characterizing the various stories and journalistic assignments he undertook during this period as "playing hooky from a certain Larger Thing" (Max, *Every Love Story* 262, 276).

In addition to regarding himself first and foremost as a novelist, Wallace was also a specific *kind* of novelist, devoted to producing a specific kind of novel, namely the omnivorous, culture-consuming "encyclopedic" novel, as described in 1976 by Edward Mendelson in a ground-breaking essay on Thomas Pynchon's *Gravity's Rainbow*. According to Mendelson, encyclopedic narratives "attempt to render the full range of knowledge and beliefs of a national culture, while identifying the ideological perspectives from which that culture shapes and interprets its knowledge." What's more, "[b]ecause they are the products of an epoch in which the world's knowledge

---

[1] Unfortunately, I do not know the exact date of his letter, as his letter was a response to a series of questions I sent him on May 18. Rather than send a cover letter with his answers, he simply returned my letter, which he footnoted in red and black felt tip. The responses to my questions he wrote out in cramped cursive on yellow legal pad paper.

is larger than any one person can encompass, they necessarily make extensive use of synecdoche" (Mendelson 30). Additionally, encyclopedic narratives "include the full account of at least one technology or science" while also embracing "an encyclopedia of literary styles, ranging from the most primitive and anonymous levels . . . to the most esoteric of high styles" (Mendelson 31). Mendelson goes on to list the *Divine Comedy, Don Quixote, War and Peace,* and *Moby Dick* as just a few of the genre's key precursors before singling out *Ulysses* and *Gravity's Rainbow* as the genre's most accomplished modern examples.

All three of Wallace's novels fall firmly within this category. For all its youthful exuberance and slapstick comedy, *The Broom of the System,* with its sprawling treatment of such heterodox themes as language, pop culture, information theory, poststructuralism, and Wittgensteinean philosophy, amply meets Mendelson's definition, while *Infinite Jest,* a novel that both diagnoses and exemplifies the information overload that is twenty-first-century existence, might very well be the genre's most widely read contemporary exemplar. *The Pale King,* which clocks in at a dense 536 pages even in its unfinished state, uses the IRS as a synecdoche for a wide range of urgent issues, including the ethics of citizenship, the concrete effects of supply-side economics, US tax policy, and post-Reagan political history, just to name a few. All three novels also feature a wide range of literary and technical discourses, including standard third-person narratives, first-person monologues, video and audio transcripts, academic bibliographies, magazine articles, *curriculum vitae,* technical manuals, and the like. Unlike Pynchon, however, Wallace wrote his encyclopedias with Mendelson's definition firmly in mind. As such, his novels not only epitomize the form but also interrogate and parody it.

At the time of his death, Wallace had already secured his place as one of the most gifted, important, and influential writers of his generation largely on the basis of a single novel, *Infinite Jest,* a reputation that was burnished by the steady appearance in print of a stream of well-received essays and journalistic pieces. In this respect, his career bears instructive similarities to that of Ralph Ellison. Like Wallace, Ellison vaulted to the top ranks of the literary establishment via a huge, era-defining novel, in this case *Invisible Man,* only to struggle for the rest of his career to complete a commensurate follow-up. Also like Wallace, Ellison saw his stature grow rather than diminish during those long years of frustrating labor, thanks in part to the unshakable greatness of the novel that had defined him but also to the nonfiction, essays, and lectures he continued to produce, work that clarified, enhanced, and built upon the rich and inexhaustible storehouse of themes and ideas he had already addressed in that career-making novel. Of course, Ellison's unfinished follow-up has since been published, not once but twice, first as *Juneteenth* (1999), edited by John H. Callahan, and constituting a self-contained portion of the 2,000 pages Ellison produced during the 4 decades following the 1952 appearance of *Invisible Man*, and again as *Three Days Before the Shooting . . .* (2011), which encompasses all of *Juneteenth* as well as early and late sections and fragments, totaling more than 1,000 published pages.

It is tempting, then, to regard *The Pale King* in much the same light as Ellison's unfinished behemoth. According to Pietsch, Wallace compiled a neat stack of 250 manuscript pages on his desk before he took his life. These pages he hoped to send to Little, Brown by way of securing an advance (*TPK* vi). Wallace's agent Bonnie Nadel and his wife Karen Green subsequently unearthed "hundreds and hundreds of pages" of the novel in progress. To all outward appearances, Wallace had prepared neither an outline nor a plot summary. As a guide, all Pietsch had to work with were "a few broad notes about the novel's trajectory" and various "directions" Wallace had written to himself indicating "where a character came from or where he or she might be headed" (vii). In contrast to the Ellison archive, *The Pale King* papers did not feature a more or less self-contained novel within the plethora of scenes and set pieces. In fact, Pietsch freely admits that the "novel's central story does not have a clear ending," which raises the obvious question, raised by Pietsch himself: "How unfinished is this novel?" (viii). Although Pietsch declares the issue "unknowable," he insists that Wallace had "written deep into" the book and that the notes and set pieces in and of themselves constitute "an astonishingly full novel" (vii, vi). The version he put together, then, is neither a self-contained portion of the whole designed for a general readership, like *Juneteenth*, nor a clearinghouse of manuscript pages and notes targeted at scholars and specialists, like *Three Days Before the Shooting . . .* , but rather something close to a mixture of both.

What is most remarkable about *The Pale King*, as the essays in this issue amply confirm, is how rich it is, even in its unfinished state. Part of this richness, I submit, can be attributed both to Wallace's method of composition and to his approach to novelistic structure writ large, particularly as regards his attitude toward plot. Wallace's longer work achieves its effect through accumulation and collage. For instance, *Infinite Jest* does not proceed in a linear fashion; rather, Wallace arranged the book's various set pieces out of sequence in keeping with his desire, as he explained in 1993 to Larry McCaffery (in reference to an earlier story), "to prohibit the reader from forgetting that she's receiving heavily mediated data, that this process is a relationship between the writer's consciousness and her own, and that in order for it to be anything like a real full human relationship, she's going to have to put in her own share of the linguistic work" (*CW* 34). Similarly, Mark Nechtr, the novelist-to-be hero of Wallace's 1989 novella "Westward the Course of Empire Takes Its Way," hopes one day to write a novel whose narrative momentum would invoke "both the dreamer's unmoving sprint and the disco-moonwalker's glide"; to compensate for this static forward-and-backward movement, Nechtr will make sure that "the stuff the [novel] is *made* of would make it Fun" (Wallace, *Girl* 332). On more than one occasion, Wallace revealed that he structured *Infinite Jest* like a Sierpinski gasket, which Max describes as "a geometrical figure that can be subdivided into an infinite number of identical geometrical figures" (183). The finished version of *The Pale King* was to possess a similarly unorthodox, nonlinear structure. Pietsch reports that Wallace repeatedly referred to the book's design as "'tornadic' or having a 'tornado feeling,'" while in the "Notes and Asides" included as an appendix to *The Pale King*, Wallace describes the plot as "a series of set-ups for stuff happening, but nothing actually happens" (viii, 546). So although *The Pale King* never reaches a conclusion per se, it is clear that Wallace always intended to deny his readers any such satisfying sense of closure in any case.

That resistance to closure speaks to one of the novel's central themes, which Wallace lists as the first of the book's "2 Broad Arcs," namely "Paying attention, boredom, ADD, Machines vs people at performing aimless jobs" (545). As readers, we must pay attention to what is in front of us without expecting such traditional readerly enticements as resolution of suspense or disclosure of secrets, in much the same way that the novel's ragtag band of IRS agents must locate meaning and fulfillment amid the mind-numbing tedium of their work as tax-return examiners. All of this might explain why *The Pale King*'s pleasures and rewards are not contingent upon the book's reaching an ending. Rather, as Nechtr puts it, the stuff the book is made of makes it Fun, and interesting, and compelling. And, as Pietsch correctly intuits, even without reaching a conclusion, or at any rate an end to his novel, Wallace had already "written deep into the book," such that the existing text both touches upon and, in many respects, thoroughly develops a wide range of themes, intertextual engagements, and provocative lines of inquiry. Wallace knew what he wanted to say in this book, and largely said it. What he had not yet discovered was a narrative structure via which to organize all the richly developed character sketches, set pieces, and episodes he had already drafted.

These essays were originally published, in slightly different form, across two issues of *Studies in the Novel* (vol. 44, nos 3 and 4 respectively) devoted to Wallace's work as a novelist, for which I served as editor. Whereas in those volumes I placed all the essays devoted to Wallace's first two novels in one issue and the all the essays touching up on *The Pale King* in the second issue, I have arranged the essays in this collection in a slightly different, but I hope more helpful, way. As such, the essays fall into two larger groupings.

The first section features four essays that treat a motif, pattern, or trend found in two or three of the novels. The second section features essays devoted to a single work or period of Wallace's career; as such, this section is subdivided into three additional sections.

In the collection's opening piece, Adam Kelly provides an important overture to the Wallace corpus as a whole. By comparing key scenes of dialogue in all three novels, Kelly explores the degree to which Wallace might be understood as a novelist of ideas. Drawing upon the work of Mikhail Bakhtin, Kelly argues that Wallace's dialogue owes a debt both to Socratic inquiry and to Dostoevsky's heteroglossia. His essay also explores the degree to which the three novels are in dialogue with one another, each novel addressing conceptual questions remaining behind from the novel before. In "Wallace and Empathy: A Narrative Approach," Toon Staes addresses the numerous ways in which Wallace sets up an empathetic relationship between author, narrator, and text. Allard den Dulk provides a thorough and rigorous account of Wallace's indebtedness to the work of Søren Kierkegaard, paying particular attention to Kierkegaard's concept of irony and its relevance for Wallace's career-long critique of the same. And Andrew Warren, in "Modeling Community and Narative in *The Pale King* and *Infinite Jest*," discloses a quartet of narrative models at work in both of Wallace's major novels, arguing that the coexistence of these overlapping and perhaps incompatible narrative modes prompts a continual negotiation among the communities posited or contested in the novels themselves.

Bradley J. Fest opens the next section with "'Then Out of the Rubble': David Foster Wallace's Early Fiction," which takes on both *The Broom of the System* and its novella-length follow up, "Westward the Course of Empire Takes Its Way," the concluding piece from *Girl with Curious Hair*. Fest argues that both texts seek to exhaust metafiction in order to prepare the ground for *Infinite Jest*. *The Broom of the System* stages what Fest depicts as an apocalyptic battle between two linguistic and narrative teleological poles, that of Ludwig Wittgenstein and Jacques Derrida, while "Westward" confronts the dangers of irony in the postmodern literature via a close dialogue with Paul de Man's "The Rhetoric of Temporality."

The following two essays survey the vast terrain that is *Infinite Jest*. In "Encyclopedic Novels and the Cruft of Fiction," David Letzler looks at Wallace's use of endnotes to argue that *Infinite Jest* challenges the traditional view of the encyclopedic novel as either a source of knowledge or a critique of totalized systems. Rather, Wallace loads his texts, and the endnotes in particular, with "cruft"—that is, excessive, pointless text—to both test, and provide a tool for building, the reader's ability to manage information. Philip Sayers focuses on the lethally entertaining fictional film that gives *Infinite Jest* its title. Drawing on the work of Roland Barthes, Jacques Lacan, and Louis Althusser, Sayers explores not only the fictional purpose of the Entertainment itself but also Wallace's treatment of film in general. Sayers also addresses Wallace's use of ekphrasis in the context of representing film. Drawing on the work of W. J. T. Mitchell and others, Sayers analyzes the way in which Wallace's descriptions of films in the novel suggest similarities and differences between the two media.

The remaining four pieces represent some of the earliest scholarship on Wallace's unfinished third novel. Much of the work included here originated as papers or keynote addresses delivered at a September 2011 conference held in Antwerp, Belgium titled "Work in Process: Reading David Foster Wallace's *The Pale King*" and organized by Toon Staes. Fellow contributor Stephen Burn and I had the honor of delivering a pair of keynote addresses that opened and closed the conference. Adam Kelly's essay originated at that conference, as did three of the essays included in this final subsection. Drawing upon his own keynote, Stephen Burn explores Wallace's abiding focus on the workings of consciousness writ large, while also disclosing a wide range of intriguing fictional analogs for the novel's portrait of the bureaucratic workspace. In "What Am I, a Machine?": Humans and Information in *The Pale King*," Conley Wouters lays out the complex and ambiguous ways in which Wallace dramatizes the conflict between humans and machines, and between organisms and data. My own essay, which is also a revision of my keynote address, examines the novel's treatment of civic responsibility and taxation by way of William James's *Varieties of Religious Experience*. These three essays are joined by Ralph Clare's lucid and rigorous analysis of one of *The Pale King*'s central themes, boredom, and the related issue of *paying attention*.

I wish to express my sincerest thanks to Toon Staes for organizing the 2011 Wallace conference in Belgium, and for allowing me to "poach" some of the essays from that conference. I am also grateful to everyone at *Studies in the Novel*, particularly Tim Boswell (no relation) and Jacqueline Foertsch, for all the hard work they did preparing these essays for their periodical appearance. And hearty thanks also to Haaris Naqvi, Laura Murray, and everyone else at Bloomsbury for their help and patience throughout this process. Thanks also to Scott Garner for his eagle-eyed proofreading and thorough work on the index. Finally, I wish to lift a foamy mug of mead to all my contributors, all of whom hit every deadline and responded to every nagging email request in record time.

Abbreviations

Quotations from Wallace's books are from the following editions, and are cited parenthetically with the abbreviations listed below:

BOS   *The Broom of the System.* New York: Viking Penguin, 1987.

GCH   *Girl with Curious Hair.* New York: W. W. Norton, 1989.

IJ   *Infinite Jest.* Boston: Little, Brown & Co., 1997.

SFT   *A Supposedly Fun Thing I'll Never Do Again.* Boston: Little, Brown & Co., 1997.

BI   *Brief Interviews with Hideous Men.* Boston: Little, Brown & Co., 1999.

CL   *Consider the Lobster.* New York: Little, Brown & Co., 2005.

OB   *Oblivion.* New York: Little, Brown & Co., 2006.

TPK   *The Pale King.* Ed. Michael Pietsch. New York: Little, Brown & Co., 2011.

TIW   *This Is Water.* New York: Little, Brown & Co., 2009.

BFN   *Both Flesh and Not.* New York: Little, Brown & Co., 2012.

CW   *Conversations with David Foster Wallace.* Ed. Stephen J. Burn. Jackson, MS: University of Mississippi Press, 2012.

Part One

Wallace as Novelist

David Foster Wallace and the Novel of Ideas

Adam Kelly

If there do exist such things as novelists of ideas, then David Foster Wallace was surely one. To begin with the obvious, Wallace's novels consistently show specific ideas wielding formative dramatic power in the minds of principal characters. In *The Broom of the System* (1987), Lenore Beadsman fears that she is no more than a linguistic construct, a character in a novel. In *Infinite Jest* (1996), Don Gately commits to praying to a Higher Power of which he cannot conceive, but which mysteriously enables his recovery. In *The Pale King* (2011), Chris Fogle's life is changed by a series of insights into the nature of freedom, which turn him from "wastoid" into self-contented tax accountant. But ideas do not shape only the minds of these characters: the very fictional worlds they inhabit have themselves been constructed through Wallace's close engagement with abstract ideas—logical, political, historical—that are made concrete in the linguistic registers and plot dynamics of his novels. It is this second mode of engagement with ideas that makes Wallace an unusual figure in the modern American literary tradition, at least as that tradition has often been characterized. Philip Rahv, in perhaps the most influential statement on this theme, chastised American authors in "The Cult of Experience in American Writing" (1940) for their "unique indifference . . . to ideas generally, to theories of value, to the wit of the speculative and problematical" (360). With Henry James as chief culprit, modern American fiction, according to Rahv, always privileges psychology over philosophy, and ideas are commonly portrayed by American writers in ways that make them wholly subservient to their dramatic role in the mind, sensibility and experience of the character thinking them. While the first mode of Wallace's engagement with ideas described above could potentially conform to Rahv's characterization, the second could not. One of Wallace's innovations was therefore to insist on the centrality of ideas, and especially of abstract structures that transcend the individual's psychology, to "the art of the novel," in James's own much-cited phrase.[1]

Equally important is the fact that the particular sets of ideas that underpin Wallace's novels changed and developed over the course of his career. This is something thus far under-acknowledged in the published criticism on his fiction, which has tended either to treat an individual work—most often *Infinite Jest*—in isolation, or to reduce Wallace's ideas to a set of tenets drawn mainly from what I have referred to elsewhere as the "essay-interview nexus," namely Wallace's essay "E Unibus Pluram: Television and U.S. Fiction" and his interview with Larry McCaffery, texts paired together in a 1993 issue of *The Review of Contemporary Fiction* (Kelly, "Death of the Author"). This tendency among critics to prioritize Wallace's early-career statements on his artistic practice is certainly understandable, as Wallace was from the beginning a provocative literary critic and sociologist as well as an artist. In particular, his revisionist reading of American metafiction in those early critical statements would prove highly influential, making it henceforth difficult to regard the landscape of postwar US fiction and the phenomenon of literary postmodernism in ways that ignored Wallace's powerful reconstruction of the field.[2] Equally, the critical focus on *Infinite Jest* makes eminent sense, so rich is that novel's engagement with contemporary culture and the literary tradition. But with the publication of his unfinished novel *The Pale King* in 2011, along with the appearance of a first biography and the opening of his archive at the Harry Ransom Center at the University of Texas-Austin, scholars of Wallace's fiction have been presented with a fairly comprehensive overview of his trajectory as an artist and novelist over the course of a two-decade career. At the same time—and as the present volume attests—the study of Wallace's work is reaching a point of critical mass at which it should no longer be necessary to argue for Wallace's place in the literary canon by attempting to encapsulate his various ideas with reference to a single key text or set of unchanging principles.

In this essay, I will examine Wallace's development as a writer with reference to the ideas that shape his novels. I will argue that those novels can be read in dialogue with one another, with each novel addressing conceptual questions remaining behind from the novel before. To make this broad task manageable, I will structure the essay around a comparison of three key scenes of dialogue within the novels themselves: the conversation between LaVache and Lenore Beadsman on an Amherst hill in *The Broom of the System*; the Rémy Marathe-Hugh Steeply dialogue atop an Arizona mountain in *Infinite Jest*; and the multi-character debate that takes place in an elevator in §19 of *The Pale King*. Considering these three examples together, what is immediately noteworthy is the importance of physical elevation in those scenes in Wallace's novels that address wider thematic concerns through dialogue. It is as if such elevation allows the characters a survey of the territory, which in turn permits the consideration of more abstract or "elevated" ideas in each novel. But the other important characteristic of these scenes is precisely that they are dialogues, and I will begin with a treatment of this point. Wallace's heavy reliance on scenes of dialogue between characters as a means of exploring structuring ideas was an aspect of his fiction that remained consistent, though not entirely unchanging, over the course of his writing career.[3]

Dialogic dialogue

In a mundane sense, of course, dialogue is a common aspect of almost all fiction, so there is nothing remarkable about the fact that Wallace makes substantial use of it. Nevertheless, there are noteworthy reasons for its extensive prominence in important strands of his novels. For one thing, passages of dialogue provide Wallace with potential relief from the dominance of his own distinctive narrative voice. Wallace's uncanny ear for American speech, speech usually presented in a slightly exaggerated yet recognizably realistic manner in his dialogues, often allows him to undermine the habituation of his characteristic prose rhythms. That Wallace became increasingly concerned about the overbearing quality of his "self-consciously maximalist style" of narration is suggested by D. T. Max (50), and it is an anxiety likewise indicated by Wallace's experimentation with pseudonyms in his post-*Infinite Jest* work, whether in submitting his story "Mister Squishy" to *McSweeney's* under the pen-name Elizabeth Klemm, or in inventing interlocutors in "Big Red Son" and publishing the essay "bi-pseudonymously" (as he puts in on the copyright page of *Consider the Lobster*). More importantly, by bringing a range of voices into his texts, Wallace can also make those texts a forum for competing ideas, and can explore these ideas in a dialogic context. There are a number of influential models for this practice in literary and philosophical history: among those discussed to date in relation to Wallace are William Gaddis's unattributed dialogue, where a lack of contextual description forces the reader to imaginatively intervene in constructing a scene, and the Wittgenstein of the *Philosophical Investigations*, who explores logic as a language game involving more than one voice.[4]

While acknowledging the importance of these influences, I want to highlight here the relevance to Wallace's work of two other models of dialogue—the Socratic and the Dostoevskian—with reference to their characterization in the work of Mikhail Bakhtin. In *Problems of Dostoevsky's Poetics*, Bakhtin distinguishes between forms of speech that seek to embody prior truth and persuade others of the validity of that truth—Bakhtin calls this the rhetorical or monologic speech genre—and forms of speech that emphasize responsivity and open communication with others in the joint pursuit of truth—Bakhtin usually calls this dialogism.[5] "The dialogic means of seeking truth," as he puts it, "is counterposed to *official* monologism, which pretends to *possess a ready-made truth*" (110). Bakhtin clarifies this opposition between the dialogic and the monologic through a comparison between the early and late Socratic dialogues of Plato. The early dialogues are constructed on the assumption that "[t]ruth is not born nor is it to be found inside the head of an individual person, it is born *between people* collectively searching for truth, in the process of their dialogic interaction" (110). In Bakthin's view, this conception of truth-seeking is organic to the genre of the dialogue itself, and Socrates remains a participant in the process rather than a teacher. In the later Platonic dialogues, by contrast, Socrates has become the teacherly fount of truth and wisdom, and "the monologism of the content begins to destroy the form of the Socratic dialogue" (110). These later dialogues correspond to Aristotelian ideas of rhetoric as logical persuasion, which shore up the monologic notion of truth as existing prior to the interaction between interlocutors.

This monologic conception of truth has been the dominant one since ancient times, underlying the worldviews of religion, philosophy and modern science, but it does find itself challenged at particular moments in history. One such challenge comes with Dostoevsky's "polyphonic" novel, which Bakhtin calls "an entirely new type of artistic thinking" (3). Here written dialogue is used not only to portray the openness of truth-seeking between characters, but also to show how a character can challenge the truth embodied by the novel's author, thus remaining "ideologically authoritative and independent" (5), unpredictable and free in a radical way. This has an impact in turn on how ideas are negotiated in the novels, because "[t]he polyphonic project is incompatible with a mono-ideational framework of the ordinary sort" (78). What Bakhtin means by this is that ideas emerge in Dostoevsky's work through characters who do not simply embody aspects of the author's own ideological beliefs, beliefs which exist apart from the work. Instead, Dostoevsky's characters are themselves involved in internal and external dialogues regarding ideas, which are never finalized into a single truth. "Dostoevsky was capable of *representing someone else's idea*, preserving its full capacity to signify as an idea," Bakthin writes, "while at the same time also preserving a distance, neither confirming the idea nor merging it with his own expressed ideology" (85). But this happens only when characters are convincingly rendered as thinking, self-conscious beings: "the idea itself can preserve its power to mean, its full integrity as an idea, only when self-consciousness is the dominant in the artistic representation of the hero" (79). In order to preserve this process, self-consciousness in Dostoevsky never resolves itself into a unity, regardless of how inward-looking his characters can be. Instead, "[a] character's self-consciousness in Dostoevsky is thoroughly dialogized: in its every aspect it is turned outward, intensely addressing itself, another, a third person" (251).

At first blush, David Foster Wallace's fiction appears similar to this Dostoevskian model, with Wallace's self-conscious characters shown to be prone to internal division and constantly engaged in dialogue with themselves and with others. But Wallace adds an extra element to the mix, which rests in the anticipatory anxiety his characters feel when addressing others. Speakers in Wallace's fiction are often depicted as desperate for genuine reciprocal dialogue, but find that their overwhelming need to predict in advance the other's response blocks the possibility of finding the language to get outside themselves and truly reach out to the other.[6] In the shadow of such anxiety of anticipation, the difficulty of generating reciprocal dialogue means that the stakes are heightened in those scenes in Wallace's novels where two characters do exchange ideas through dialogue. When this process becomes genuinely dialogic in Bakhtin's sense—when truth appears to be generated "*between people*"—something important has occurred in Wallace's ethical world: the means have become the ends. "It is fully understandable," writes Bakhtin, "that at the center of Dostoevsky's artistic world must lie dialogue, and dialogue not as a means but as an end in itself" (252). This notion of dialogue as an end in itself connects to Wallace's view, stated to McCaffery and repeated on many later occasions, that "what makes good fiction sort of magical" is the way the separate agendas of reader and writer can be mediated "by the fact that language and linguistic intercourse is, in and of itself, redeeming, remedy-ing" (*CW* 32–3). As we know from his own essay on Dostoevsky, Wallace deeply admired the "morally passionate, passionately moral fiction" produced by the Russian writer (*CL* 274). The negotiation with ideas that happens in his own novels thus owes a debt to the techniques developed by Dostoevsky, and especially to the value the latter places on the redeeming event of dialogue itself.[7]

Broom logic

Viewed in Bakhtinian terms, however, *The Broom of the System*, Wallace's debut novel, is characterized by the overwhelmingly monologic nature of its dialogue. This is exemplified by the scenes between Rick Vigorous and Lenore Beadsman, where Rick's voice dominates through his lengthy storytelling and his repeated wish to absorb and possess Lenore according to a fixed ontology of self and other. Similarly, the scenes between Rick or Lenore and Dr Curtis Jay are also monologic, in that Jay subsumes everything his patients tell him to an already formed hermeneutic theory of truth drawn from the writings of his imagined mentor Dr Blentner. This monologism is presented parodically by Wallace, of course, in line with what Patrick O'Donnell identifies as the novel's debt to the genre of Menippean satire (8).[8] But what makes *The Broom of the System* monologic in a more fundamental sense is the way the novel is constructed with reference to the ideas of philosophical logic itself.

To highlight this feature of *Broom*, I will examine aspects of the scene of dialogue between Lenore and her brother LaVache that takes place on a hill in Amherst College. This scene is significant for a number of structural reasons: it is the final scene of the novel's longest chapter, the 11th chapter of 21; it is the scene that brings to an end part one of a two-part novel; and it is the scene in which the problems Lenore is experiencing regarding her identity are most clearly explained to her and to the reader. LaVache's explanation runs as follows:

> [Gramma] Lenore has you believing, with your complicity, circumstantially speaking, that you're not really real, or that you're only real insofar as you're told about, so that to the extent that you're real you're controlled, and thus not in control, so that you're more like a sort of character than a person, really—and of course Lenore would say the two are the same, now, wouldn't she? (*BOS* 249)

As convoluted as it may sound out of context, LaVache's explanation of this paradox arrives as a clarifying moment in the text for Lenore (and for the reader). Nevertheless it does not, and cannot, solve Lenore's problem, precisely because of the form it takes as an *explanation*. Lenore's reply makes this evident: "'How about if we just spontaneously abort this line of conversation, Stoney, OK? Since, if I were maybe to ask you to help me out with respect to this evil-and-reality-as-opposed-to-telling problem, what you'd do is obviously just *tell* me something'" (249). Telling is thus established as part of the problem that afflicts Lenore, rather than any kind of solution to it. Here we have, in fact, an early iteration of an idea that would in time become familiar to readers of Wallace, particularly through his discussion of irony in "E Unibus Pluram": it is mistaken to assume that diagnosis automatically leads to cure, that a revelation of imprisonment results in freedom (*SFT* 65).[9] LaVache appears to recognize the difficulty of this situation when he observes, "Well, now, seeing as you're *you*. . . . I can't speak for you, but only for me, regardless of what I might say *about* you" (*BOS* 250).

This remark by LaVache certainly seems designed to provoke Lenore to exploratory dialogue as a necessary requirement for seeking truth, and in the most influential critical reading of the novel published to date, Marshall Boswell argues that this openness to dialogue also defines *The Broom of the System* more generally. According to Boswell, the novel counteracts the "hermetic, enclosed, and self-referencing fictional structures" that characterized earlier American metafiction, in favor of embodying "an open system of communication . . . between two equal and interactive participants, a dynamic carried over onto the novel's relationship with its own reader" (22). On this innovative model, "meaning is achieved through functional and constructive interaction with others rather than through the referential connecting of words to their objects" (34). Although Boswell's explicit point of reference for this new model is the later Wittgenstein—who claimed in *Philosophical Investigations* that when considering language we "must do away with all *explanations*" (qtd. Boswell 25)—Boswell's description of Wallace's open system also resonates with a Bakhtinian account of dialogue, especially when one adds Bakhtin's rejection of Saussurian linguistics to his critique of monologic truth (see Morris 25–37).

However, as Boswell's own analyses of many strands of the novel palpably demonstrate, Wallace's technique in *Broom* actually requires less a creative dialogue with the reader, than the reader simply being willing and able to work out what Wallace is consciously intending with each part of the novel's structure. In other words, readers have only to learn the rules of the (language) game, and apply them. "[J]ust as no cipher can be carved in stone," Boswell avers, "so can there never be one simple interpretation of a story" (39). Yet as Boswell himself shows, the allegorical level, or "second-order significance" (39), suggested by details in the novel is rarely ambiguous. The reason Boswell's reading of *The Broom of the System* is so thorough and convincing is that it demonstrates how curiously studied and clear-cut certain features of the novel are, how their meaning in the textual system can be virtually exhausted.[10] Despite what Boswell calls Wallace's "affirmation of communicative disorder" (59), these transparent features of the text display its affinities with the methods of philosophical logic, which according to Clare Hayes-Brady appealed to the young Wallace as "a way to refine ambiguity out of human communication" (24).[11] Such a position is, in Bakhtinian terms, a monologic one, where truth is preexisting and does not require dialogue to generate it. No point in *Broom* demonstrates this better than the novel's final line, a piece of dialogue spoken by Rick Vigorous to Mindy Metalman: "'You can trust me,' R. V. says, watching her hand. 'I'm a man of my '" (467). Boswell's reading is that "[t]he novel ends with a blank space. The system remains open" (63). But I would argue instead that because there is no real ambiguity concerning the next word in this closing sentence, the reader's agency is in fact negated. There is thus a gesture toward an open system and a readerly dialogue, rather than an achievement of it.[12] This desire to control meaning and the reader's agency is something that Wallace would fight against in later work—a battle made explicit in his writerly allegory "Octet," from *Brief Interviews with Hideous Men* (1999)— and it is this feature of *The Broom of the System*, I would suggest, that most encouraged Wallace later to dismiss the book as a failure. *Broom* is in the end what Wallace elsewhere calls an "INTERPRET-ME" fiction (*BFN* 75), and a monologic one, concerned to tell rather than cocreate, unable to establish fully the open system it craves. Gramma Lenore may disappear in theory, but the monologic modality of truth that she embodies remains firmly in place.

The dead end to which this kind of logical focus can lead is symbolized by an awkward structural feature of the novel, in which a year-date appears at the heading of every chapter, and yet all but two of these chapters are dated 1990. This insistence on constantly repeating the same year adds to the static quality of the narrative, so that history is not allowed truly to enter the story, and despite being set mostly in the future the novel retains a thoroughly presentist focus throughout. One side effect of this focus is that while it critiques the intellectual dead ends of postmodernist metafiction, as the readings of Boswell and O'Donnell both make clear, *The Broom of the System* risks participating in the end of history that pervades postmodernism understood on a wider cultural level. As Fredric Jameson has demonstrated most influentially in a postmodern context, truly dialectical thinking requires that the artist address his or her moment as part of a constantly shifting history, rather than as embodying an endless present.[13] One way to advance this dialectical project is to widen the context of inquiry—culturally, politically, and particularly historically—and this is what Wallace would increasingly do as his career developed. Wallace once described *Broom* as "a conversation between Wittgenstein and Derrida" (qtd. Lipsky 35), and while he would never leave behind the core linguistic and philosophical questions that these two thinkers articulated—as testified to by his continued fondness for abstract moral dilemmas and double-bind structures in his fiction—neither would he fully embrace the ahistorical facets of their thought. Indeed, a critique of such ahistoricism emerges at one moment in the LaVache-Lenore dialogue, when LaVache remarks to Lenore that in constructing his famous antinomy of the man on a hill, Wittgenstein never considered the possibility of a helicopter dropping the man in place. "Technology does affect interpretation, after all," LaVache concludes (*BOS* 251), and this idea is also a central one in the dialogue to which I now turn, between Rémy Marathe and Hugh Steeply in *Infinite Jest*.

Infinite politics

The primary thing to note about the Marathe-Steeply dialogue is that the terms that shape it are drawn not from the language game of logical philosophy, as in *Broom*, but rather from the discourse of political philosophy. Boswell has suggested the importance of William James's utilitarianism for reading this strand of the novel (135–6), but at least as significant is that on the level of ideas the debate can be understood as playing out the terms of Isaiah Berlin's famous 1958 lecture "Two Concepts of Liberty." In this lecture, Berlin distinguishes between negative liberty, which refers to the absence of external constraints on the individual agent, and positive liberty, where the agent possesses internal control and self-mastery in pursuit of his/her goals. An emphasis on negative liberty is associated with classic liberal and libertarian thinkers—Berlin cites Locke and Mill in England, and Constant and de Tocqueville in France (124)—for whom freedom from interference is valuable as an end in itself, and who argue that the state should allow the individual to pursue his or her own ends as long as these do not impinge upon the freedoms of others. In *Infinite Jest*, Hugh Steeply defends this conception of liberty as paradigmatically American: "'The United States: a community of sacred individuals which reveres the sacredness of the individual choice. The individual's right to pursue his own vision of the best ratio of pleasure to pain: utterly sacrosanct. Defended with teeth and bared claws all through our history'" (424). Rémy Marathe agrees with Steeply that such a defense of negative liberty defines the American mindset, but counters with a powerful argument for positive liberty, a tradition embodied by thinkers such as Rousseau, Hegel, and Marx. Here the individual's goals of self-realization and self-determination are assumed to require support from their connection to larger communal goals, goals which Marathe thinks have been lost in an American context. To make this point to Steeply, Marathe reiterates Berlin's distinction between "freedom from" (or negative liberty) and "freedom to" (or positive liberty):

> Your freedom is the freedom-*from*: no one tells your precious individual U.S.A. selves what they must do. It is the meaning only, this freedom

from constraint and forced duress. [. . .] But what of the freedom-*to*? Not just free-*from*. Not all compulsion comes from without. You pretend you do not see this. What of freedom-*to*. How for the person to freely choose? How to choose any but a child's greedy choices if there is no loving-filled father to guide, inform, teach the person how to choose? How is there freedom to choose if one does not learn how to choose? (320)

The Quebecois spy's sentiments here chime with certain views Wallace expressed in his nonfiction. In particular, Marathe's language of temples and worshipping—"'All other of our you say *free* choices follow from this: what is our temple?'" (107)—clearly resonates with positions set out in *This Is Water,* Wallace's Kenyon Commencement Address: "There is no such thing as not worshipping. Everybody worships. The only choice we get is *what* to worship" (*TIW* 99–101). However, the advantage of the novel over the essay form, as Bakhtin would tell us, is that the novel provides a dialogic context in which both sides of the argument can be offered to the reader, without a clear authorial conclusion drawn. Steeply's defense of negative liberty throughout his debate with Marathe is certainly a strong one, and even though Wallace the philosopher or ethicist might not agree with the argument, Wallace the novelist gives it its full due. The classic precursor here is *The Brothers Karamazov* (1880), in which Dostoevsky renders Ivan Karamazov's argument for atheism so powerfully that the writer became worried that it could convince his readers of the nonexistence of God, even though Dostoevsky himself was a believer.[14] In *Infinite Jest,* the importance of giving Steeply's argument its fullest articulation is that the faults readers may find in it as a prescription for the present day will only serve to place greater emphasis on the technologically dystopian world Wallace is depicting throughout the novel. Jonathan Franzen, in his essay on Wallace's suicide and the history of the novel, captures this dystopia well: "as the novel has transformed the cultural environment, species of humanity have given way to a universal crowd of individuals whose most salient characteristic is their being identically entertained. This was the monocultural specter that David had envisioned and set out to resist in his epic *Infinite Jest*" (87). If Wallace and Franzen are right, then the earlier historical context in which Steeply's traditional liberal argument was developed, a context in which individuals were free to follow a plurality of goals, no longer applies.[15] If, as LaVache claims, "technology does affect interpretation," then in the monocultural America (or ONAN) of *Infinite Jest* it seems inarguable that, as Boswell puts it, "bloodless utilitarianism is a recipe for disaster" (136). By allowing the reader to engage afresh with a classic debate in the realm of political philosophy, Wallace throws into starker relief the challenges posed by the altered historical and technological America he depicts.

Yet while the ideas of political philosophy underpin the debate between Steeply and Marathe, the contrast between the United States and Quebec that the agents embody and espouse remains vaguely cultural rather than specifically historical. *Infinite Jest* is clearly not a historical novel. It is set, like *The Broom of the System*, a few years into the future, and, as Stephen Burn has shown in his chronology of the novel, the only incident referred to before the tennis training of James Incandenza in 1960 is his father's career-ending knee injury in 1933 (Burn 91). There are few allusions to a real-world historical context in the novel, and even these apply mainly to Europe rather than America; Wallace writes, for instance, of Enfield tennis director Gerhardt Schtitt, "like most Europeans of his generation, [he has been] anchored from infancy to certain permanent values, [. . .] Old World patriarchal stuff like honor and discipline and fidelity to some larger unit" (*Infinite* 82). These are values also espoused by Marathe, and he contrasts them with the utilitarianism of America, which he sees as coming back to bite the United States through the kind of unconscious death-wish that Jacques Derrida has dubbed "autoimmunity" ("Autoimmunity" 95). As Marathe points out: "'This is a U.S.A. production, this Entertainment cartridge. Made by an American man in the U.S.A. The appetite for the appeal of it: this also is U.S.A. The U.S.A. drive for spectation, which your culture teaches'" (318). But how has it come about that American culture teaches this drive for spectation, and espouses the utilitarianism that underlies it? Marathe and Steeply are both hazy on this point. Marathe remarks that "'[s]omeone or some people among your own history sometime killed your U.S.A. nation already, Hugh. Someone who had authority, or should have had authority and did not exercise authority. I do not know'" (319). Steeply is equally vague. "'The American genius,'" he will only suggest, "'is that someplace along the line back there in American history them realizing that each American seeking to pursue his maximum good results together in maximizing *everyone's* good'" (424).

One important effect of this vagueness about American intellectual history in *Infinite Jest* is that the ideological differences that separate Marathe and Steeply end up depending upon the policing of cultural borders that remain necessarily weak and permeable, open to contradiction by empirical historical realities. One such contradiction emerges when Steeply challenges Marathe's claim to cultural superiority by pointing out that it was in Canada rather than the United States that the first experiments in stimulating pleasure sensors were undertaken. This led to a stampede of young people ready to sacrifice their autonomy for the chance to continually pull a lever and experience lethal bliss: "'This was a totally Canadian show, this little neuroelectric adventure'" (472). What this implies, in effect, is that the cultural distinctions that Marathe and Steeply have been setting out so stridently will have little bearing in the world of "The Entertainment," when pleasure unto death becomes a dystopian possibility attractive to all. But it also means that Wallace's project to write something distinctively American, as opposed to Western-industrial (the broader term he uses in the McCaffery interview [*CW* 23]), ends up requiring further elaboration. In *Infinite Jest*, Wallace is happy to cite, through Steeply, what Greg Phipps refers to in his essay on the novel as "the sentimentalized narratives of the American ethos" (75). In *The Pale King*, by contrast, Wallace takes a more focused approach to exploring these cultural narratives, putting into play ideas that also emerge in his later essays, ideas that are not only overtly political but also importantly historical.

Pale history

I am referring here primarily to §19 of *The Pale King*, in which a number of characters carry on a lengthy and unattributed dialogue that focuses on the issue of civic responsibility in the United States circa 1980. Upon close examination of the text, there appear to be four interlocutors involved in this elevator discussion: DeWitt Glendenning, Stuart Nichols, a man named Gaines, and a character simply named X. In addition, an "I said" also appears at one point in the dialogue, coming out of nowhere and not being referred to again (139). Although in his published fiction Wallace often introduced first-person narrators at unexpected moments—for example in his long story "Mister Squishy" (*Oblivion* 14)—here the inclusion of the "I," as well as the character X, seem only to point to the unfinished nature of this particular chapter of *The Pale King*.[16] Nonetheless, an important observation that can be made is that the specific identities of the characters involved in this chapter—and whether they number three or four or five— are in many ways beside the point. If we compare this elevated dialogue to the ones in *The Broom of the System* and *Infinite Jest* already discussed, we can see a movement increasingly away from the individual characteristics of those articulating the ideas and toward the broader significance of the ideas themselves. In *Broom*, we read the LaVache and Lenore dialogue with specific regard to how the logical ideas expressed in it apply to Lenore, who is the novel's main protagonist. In *Infinite Jest*, by contrast, Marathe and Steeply exist in the novel primarily so that they can undertake their conversation on the mountaintop overlooking Arizona. Their dialogue is a chorus for some of the major themes of the novel, yet Wallace still goes to some lengths to humanize both characters through providing them with personal history and motivation, and by focusing much of his prose on the evocation of their comic movements and the general atmosphere of the scene.

In the corresponding elevated scene in *The Pale King*, however, there is none of this, and the movement is away from the importance of individual psychology and toward the primacy of ideas themselves. This is a dialogue of fine distinctions and complex arguments, and Wallace refuses to obscure it unduly by importing personal characteristics and impressions from other areas of the novel. We are aware, for instance, that DeWitt Glendenning, who can be identified as the main speaker in the first half of §19, is a senior figure in the IRS, and is probably the most powerful individual in the conversation. Yet unlike Marathe, who dabbles in psychological games with Steeply, or Rick Vigorous, for whom conversation with Lenore is an all-out exercise in power and dominance, Glendenning in this scene seems unconcerned to wield power over others. Instead, his interest is focused on what he and others are saying, he is dialogically responsive in Bakhtin's sense, and his tone is generally a humble one, admitting confusion about the accuracy and tightness of his arguments. Something similar can be said for Stuart Nichols, the other participant in the conversation who speaks at most length. The two remaining characters, Gaines and X, are more familiarly cynical, though intelligent types, milder versions of the kind of men we meet in *Brief Interviews*. Taken as a pair, they also provide something of the voice of the radical Sixties as against Glendenning's republican conservatism, with Nichols's liberalism sitting somewhere in the middle.

As the unattributed quality of the dialogue suggests, however, Wallace is not particularly interested in dividing the positions of his characters into traditional liberal/conservative or left/right binaries. Moreover, a number of his late essays offer evidence that a damaging breakdown in dialogue between opposing ideological positions was the largest challenge that Wallace saw defining twenty-first-century US political culture.[17] In this regard, of course, things have gone from bad to worse since Wallace's death, as the debt ceiling crisis of 2011 and the federal shutdown of 2013 (to cite only two instances of many) recently reminded US citizens. Against such a bleak background, §19 of *The Pale King* can be read as Wallace's depiction of what an informed and open conversation about American political and intellectual history might look like. In the context of the novel, the particular premise of the debate lies in Glendenning's remark that "'attitudes about paying taxes seem like one of the places where a man's civic sense gets revealed in the starkest sorts of terms'" (141). But taxation is here really only a vehicle for Wallace to explore the development of American democratic society more generally, with particular reference to how things have changed since the upheavals of the 1960s. In a recent essay, Adam Kirsch opines that "[h]ostility to the 1960s has been a constant in [Wallace's] work" (25), but this position does not give enough credit to the subtlety of Wallace's political reading of that period and its aftermath, a reading which reaches its culmination in this polyphonic section of *The Pale King*.

In discussing the content of the dialogue, I will make two main observations. The first is that Wallace here explores more deeply than in *Infinite Jest* the historical character of American society, by concentrating much of the debate on the period of the American Revolution, the aims of the Founding Fathers, and how well those aims still apply in the altered context of the late twentieth century. Once again he offers the reader two broadly contrasting views. In Glendenning's opinion, the founding fathers were heroes, whose sense of honor and moral fabric were unfortunately not matched by the generations that followed them. Their "'enfranchisement of only wealthy landed educated males'" was rationally motivated, according to Glendenning: "'They believed in rationality—they believed that persons of privilege, literacy, education, and moral sophistication would be able to emulate them, to make judicious and self-disciplined decisions for the good of the nation and not just advance their own interests'" (134). X responds sarcastically to this: "'It's certainly an imaginative and ingenious rationalization of racism and male chauvinism, that's for sure'" (134). And how can the reader of *The Pale King*, sharing the post-Sixties air with X, disagree with him? How can that reader not, for example, join X in criticizing Thomas Jefferson for his hypocrisy in preaching equal human dignity while "'boinking his slaves and having whole litters of mulatto children'" (133)?[18] Yet the question Wallace seems to be exploring through this dialogue is what gets lost when such an easy cynicism about human motivation pervades our assessments of history. If the expressed ideals of the American founding fathers can be so easily dismissed on the grounds of their less than ideal behavior, then where are later generations to receive their moral education from? While fully acknowledging the difficulties with the proposition—by reminding us through X and Gaines that hypocrisy should rightfully suffer interrogation and exposure—Wallace is nonetheless allowing space here for a more generous evaluation of both the role of moral ideals in the course of history, and the personal flaws of those who espouse such ideals. One benefit of showing such generosity might lie in enabling us to cross the seeming chasm between liberal and conservative in present-day America. Even the terms themselves become problematized in Wallace's dialogue: as Glendenning tells X, when the latter dubs him a conservative, "'There are all kinds of conservatives depending on what it is they want to conserve'" (132).

For Wallace, the question of moral education had become all the more pressing because the 1960s had ushered in more than an increased social egalitarianism and a healthily skeptical attitude toward previously cherished values. While in *Infinite Jest* Wallace was concerned to ask how technological developments should alter our political commitments, in *The Pale King* it is the rise of the corporation that is front and center, placing historic ideas of citizenship under crushing pressure. Nichols, whose ideas become increasingly prominent in the final movement of the dialogue in §19, summarizes this strand when he remarks that "'[p]olitics is about consensus, and the advertising legacy of the Sixties is that consensus is repression'" (147). This is an argument Wallace's readers have been familiar with since "E Unibus Pluram," but the analysis offered here has deeper roots within American intellectual history, so that the Sixties no longer represent some kind of origin point for American irony, as that decade did in Wallace's celebrated essay. Writing retrospectively from a point in the early twenty-first century, and in keeping with swathes of emerging scholarship on the era of "neoliberal" capitalism, Wallace now places the key transitional moment to contemporary American society in and around 1980, as demonstrated by Glendenning's summary of Nichols's argument: "'I think Stuart's tracing the move from the production-model of American democracy to something more like a consumption-model, where corporate production depends on a team approach whereas being a customer is a solo venture. That we're turning into consuming citizens rather than producing citizens'" (146). Wallace did not live long enough to witness the full onset of the credit crisis and "the great recession," but the economic and sociological ideas underpinning Glendenning's summary certainly contain the ring of truth in a post-2008 social climate.

My other main observation concerning the debate in §19 is that although he is clearly engaging with the discourse of political ideas, Wallace, through Glendenning, displays a palpable discomfort with understanding the problem only in narrow terms: "'It's probably part of my naivete that I don't want to put the issue in political terms when it's probably irreducibly political'" (136). Similarly, for Stuart Nichols, "'it goes beyond politics, civics. [. . .] It's almost more a matter of metaphysics'" (142).[19] This is vintage Wallace, of course: as a writer at home in virtually every discourse imaginable, he understood the specific resonances of each one, and utilized the novel as what Bakhtin would call a heteroglossic space in which those discourses could productively collide. There is therefore no bottom line in Wallace's novels, no master discourse, whether logic, culture, politics, or history: there are instead a plurality of ways to approach the problem Wallace is addressing. Yet this is not relativism either, not even a respectable Rortian version of relativism in which new vocabularies create new problems to solve. Rather, Wallace is genuinely addressing a single question by thinking it through a plurality of languages, discourses, and dialogues. That question is the one that haunted him for so much of his career: what has gone wrong with America? And in *The Pale King*, more than in any previous work, he was attempting to ask an even more ambitious question: what can we do to make it better?

Novel ideas

In Bakhtin's account of Dostoevsky, the latter's originality as a novelist lies in the way "the idea really does become almost the hero of the work" (78). Yet to call Dostoevsky a novelist of ideas, or even a philosophical novelist, is simply a category error, according to Bakhtin: "For Dostoevsky, there are no ideas, no thoughts, no positions which belong to no one, which exist 'in themselves'" (31). That this latter quotation makes Dostoevsky sound like a candidate for Philip Rahv's critique of the experiential bias of the American novel perhaps demonstrates nothing so much as the uselessness of the category "novelist of ideas"; Rahv, after all, explicitly had in mind the Russian novel of the nineteenth century as a counterweight to the tradition of American realism embodied by Henry James. Nevertheless, when considering these questions Wallace presents us with a new and complex case; a deeply philosophical thinker, Wallace's ideas seem to exist both "in themselves" and in more embodied forms within both the dialogues his characters engage in and the fictional worlds they inhabit. These fictional worlds became more and more embedded with culture, politics, and history as Wallace's career as a novelist developed, so that ideas increasingly appear as part of a dialectical process, both radically situated within the work and somehow seeming to govern it. In "The Meaning of a Literary Idea" (1949), Lionel Trilling contended that "[t]he question of the relation which should properly obtain between what we call creative literature and what we call ideas is a matter of insistent importance for modern criticism" (*Liberal* 281). While this statement may have looked out of date in the many decades between the publication of Trilling's essay and the century's end, Wallace's novels bring critics and readers back to its active contemplation. And this is not only a literary matter: Wallace's way of dealing with ideas through dialogue, both within his individual novels and in the relationship between them, accounts for more than his untimely originality as a novelist. It also suggests his wider importance for our twenty-first-century world, a world that now, more than ever, requires some fresh thinking.

Notes

1   Rahv's position on American fiction is far from unusual. In the same year that "The Cult of Experience" was published, Lionel Trilling, in "Reality in America," defended Henry James as a novelist of ideas but still lamented the critical preference offered to Theodor Dreiser over James, a preference explained by American culture's "chronic belief that there exists an opposition between reality and mind and that one must enlist oneself in the party of reality" (*Liberal* 10). As late as 1981, in *Ideas and the Novel*, Trilling's fellow New York intellectual Mary McCarthy was still mourning the absence of ideas from the American novel, and criticizing writers under the sway of James for suppressing their instinct to build fiction around abstract concerns. Summarizing this critical line in a recent essay, Mark McGurl broadens its scope from American fiction to classic realist fiction more generally: "All of the ideas in realist fiction on the Jamesian model are made subservient to the experience of thinking them. For all the intelligence exerted in their articulation, they are never valuable or interesting in and of themselves."

2   For one example among many of the wider influence of Wallace's revisionist reading of postmodernism, see Gladstone and Worden's introduction to a recent issue of *Twentieth-Century Literature* on the theme of "Postmodernism, Then," where they open with an account of "the predictive or, perhaps, programmatic power" of "E Unibus Pluram" (291).

3   In focusing on Wallace's use of dialogue in what follows, I mostly ignore the role ideas play in the narrative and narrational aspects of his novels. Elsewhere in this volume, Toon Staes argues that Wallace's ideas about active reading are articulated through complex narrative omissions; Andrew Warren outlines how modes of narration are themselves treated as ideas to be explored in the novels; and Stephen J. Burn sketches Wallace's attempt to convert the narrative architecture of *The Pale King* into a "container of consciousness" modeled on new scientific conceptions of the mind and brain.

4   Burn has discussed the influence of Gaddis's dialogue on Wallace, most notably the way Wallace takes a minor variation in Gaddis's fiction—in which a line of ellipses draws attention to the nonverbal reaction of an interlocutor—and exploits it "to acknowledge and dramatize the role of the silent partner" in the literary process (Burn 31). Wittgenstein's profound influence on Wallace, identified by the writer himself in his interviews with McCaffery and Lipsky, has been the subject of a number of critical treatments, the fullest of which is found in Marshall Boswell's *Understanding David Foster Wallace*, discussed below.

5   While in his Dostoevsky book, Bakhtin is consistent in the terms he uses
     to discuss his conception of dialogue, across his broader career there are
     variations in terminology. For instance, Morson and Emerson find "at least
     three distinct senses" of the term "dialogue" in Bakhtin's work, with regard
     to only one of which the distinction between dialogic and monologic
     makes sense (130–1).

6   This basic structure, which recurs consistently throughout Wallace's novels
     and stories, lies at the heart of his search for what I have elsewhere called a
     "new sincerity" in his fiction (Kelly, "New Sincerity").

7   In a footnote to his Dostoevsky essay, Wallace commends Joseph
     Frank's critique of Bakhtin's tendency to "downplay FMD's ideological
     involvement with his own characters" (*CL* 269), but suggests that Frank
     overlooks the political constraints that Bakhtin faced in constructing his
     interpretation of Dostoevsky's works. In making this claim Wallace implies
     that Bakhtin's conceptions of "polyphony" and "dialogic imagination" are
     simply necessary ideological covers rather than genuine descriptions of
     Dostoevsky's artistic procedures. I would contend that, in following Frank
     on this point, Wallace misinterprets Bakhtin's claims about Dostoevsky,
     and assumes that "ideological involvement with [one's] characters" is the
     same thing as privileging one character's truth over another's. As I will
     demonstrate below, Wallace does not repudiate ideological involvement
     with his characters, yet he still presents genuine debates in which the
     flaws of both sides of the argument bring to light important truths about
     the discursive and historical context in which the debate takes place.
     Furthermore, it is not consistent on the one hand to hold dialogue as a
     goal and as a means of truth-seeking—as Wallace explicitly does, and as
     Bakhtin argues Dostoevsky does—and on the other hand to subscribe to
     a single truth of authorial intention existing independently of the dialogic
     process (unless that truth lies in the value ascribed to dialogue itself).
     Another way to make this point is to say that Frank's exhaustive readings
     of the meaning of Dostoevsky's novels (readings that Wallace praises)
     cannot hold truly definitive status if the dialogic process that Wallace
     values is to retain any of its redemptive status in the act of reading. See my
     reading of *Broom* below for further clarification of this point.

8   O'Donnell takes this generic designation from Northrop Frye, for
     whom the Menippean satire differs from the novel in its approach to
     characterization, "which is stylized rather than naturalistic, and presents
     people as mouthpieces of the ideas they represent" (qtd. 8). O'Donnell
     points out that *The Broom of the System* is equally invested, nevertheless,
     in "exploring the nature of personhood existentially and affectively" (8).
     From his earliest published work, therefore, Wallace's engagement with the
     complex demands of the novel of ideas is overt and manifest.

9   For an excellent treatment of the wider theoretical implications of
     Wallace's claim about diagnosis and cure, see Baskin.

10 Thus Boswell's explanations of the respective purposes in the novel of Gramma Lenore, of the Great Ohio Desert, of the Nabokovian/Updikean plotlines surrounding Rick Vigorous and Andy Lang, even of the violet color of Lenore's dress, are all very convincing, which makes for skillful literary criticism. Yet the very possibility of such telling explanations manages to contradict somewhat the idea that Wallace is trying to place open dialogue with the reader in the place of the elaborate authorial mastery he associates with the postmodern metafictionists. In his more recent treatment of *Broom*, O'Donnell implies that the place to look for the undermining of postmodern mastery may instead be in Wallace's "post-paranoid" disruption of the relation of part to whole (21). While the meaning of specific textual elements might be clear, O'Donnell argues, the reader must still intervene at the level of plot: "all of these stories can only be filled out and connected (or not) through extrapolations entirely dependent on the unpredictability, responsiveness, and individuality of the singular reader, Wallace's audience first and last" (14). See Staes's essay in this volume for more on this point.

11 It is worth noting that while he was composing *Broom*, Wallace was also writing a philosophy thesis on modal logic, now published as *Fate, Time and Language: An Essay on Free Will*.

12 See also Bradley Fest's reading of the novel's concluding line in the present volume. Rather than see *Broom* as successfully instantiating an open system, as both Boswell and O'Donnell do, Fest contends that the novel displays Wallace's understanding of "novelistic discourse as a kind of systemic irony, a mode of ordered breakdown, of never being able to have a letter arrive at its destination." This results in what might be termed undecidability without ambiguity, a situation that I would argue likewise fixes the reader's position and negates their agency as a dialogic partner for the text.

13 Connie Luther and David Hering ("Theorizing") have offered strong evidence of Wallace's developing engagement—in "Westward and the Course of Empire Takes Its Way" and *Infinite Jest*, respectively—with Jamesonian ideas of cultural postmodernism, ideas which culminated in Jameson's landmark *Postmodernism, or, The Cultural Logic of Late Capitalism* (1991). The work of these critics supports my suggestion that one aspect of Wallace's development as a writer was his willingness to address conceptual problems that remained unresolved in earlier work. In this volume, Marshall Boswell also notes problems with Wallace's approach to history in his early work. Writing of *Broom* and *Infinite Jest*, Boswell claims that "both novels achieve an almost ahistorical and, at times, even spectral quality that, whether intended by Wallace or not, sometimes obscures the historical contingency of their signature themes."

14 For a list of further parallels between *Infinite Jest* and *The Brothers Karamazov*, see Jacobs.

15 Not only that, but this monocultural specter—inextricable from a media context that Wallace elsewhere dubs "Total Noise" (*BFN* 301)—can in fact be understood as a direct consequence of the historical predominance of negative liberty, of the fragmentation of the public sphere that results from citizens following their own ends without thought for the wider health of the community. I am grateful to Allard den Dulk for drawing my attention to this point; den Dulk's essay in this volume examines a similar development on the individual level, through the frame of Kierkegaard's distinction between the aesthetic and ethical attitudes.

16 It is tempting to associate X in §19 with Shane Drinion, who is referred to as "Mr. X" in §46 of the novel (446). However, the characters of these two men seem entirely at odds with one another, which may indicate that the X in §19 was simply a placeholder for the name of a character as yet undecided by Wallace.

17 See, for instance, "Authority and American Usage" and "Host" in *Consider the Lobster*, and "Deciderization 2007—A Special Report" and "Just Asking" in *Both Flesh and Not*. See also Boswell's essay in this volume.

18 For a summary of the problems posed by Jefferson's "character" for the intellectual history of the early national period, see Hutchison 10.

19 For an analysis on Nichols's "existential tirade," as well as further connections between *The Pale King* and the ideas of neoliberalism, see Ralph Clare's essay in this volume.

2

Wallace and Empathy:
A Narrative Approach

Toon Staes

A question for Wallace readers to ponder: since we attribute feelings to others when we put ourselves in their shoes, is empathy but a projection of the self? Perhaps the novels that touch us most are novels that, in our reading of them, reflect our own states of mind. In her analysis of the "affect" of fiction, Eve Kosofsky Sedgwick suggests that the pleasure of novel-reading lies in the admiration she can muster up for both the work and its author, in particular for the latter's sensitivity to thoughts and emotions to which she herself somehow feels prone. "Except of course," she writes, "it's not 'them' I invest in this way, but their titles or their authors' names as valued, phantasmatic objects internal to myself" (627). Sedgwick touches upon an issue not many of us may want to admit, but is no less true for that: the special connection we feel with the novelists we love and praise exists only in our heads.

Judging by his writings, David Foster Wallace was quite sensitive to the dangers of reading a writer's personal life into his work. In a scathing review of Edwin Williamson's *Borges: A Life* (2004), which he panned for doing just that, Wallace held that fans of a writer are usually also "idealizers of that writer." Thus they tend to let their particular view of her or him influence their reading:

> Part of the appeal of the writer's work for these fans will be the distinctive stamp of that writer's personality, predilections, style, particular tics and obsessions—the sense that *these* stories were written by *this* author and could have been done by no other. And yet it often seems that the person we encounter in the literary biography could not possibly have written the works we admire. (*BFN* 285–6)[1]

Of course, as Wallace wrote in a footnote, throughout his career Borges played with the illusion that literature brings us closer to the person behind the text. I would add that Wallace did so too, and this showed from early on: "Once I'm done with the thing," he said to McCaffery in 1993, "I'm basically dead; it becomes simply language, and language lives not just in but *through* the reader" (*CW* 40). Yet for all the extratextual info that surrounds Wallace's aura today (the essays and interviews, the tragic suicide, the eulogies, the guru commencement speech), the question to ask is how our perception of the man interferes with our appreciation of the work.

Although the notion of the implied author may well be drawing heavy criticism in recent narrative theory, empirical research indicates that readers infer a representation of the writer while reading, merging the information they gather from the text with the knowledge they have about its author. This "dynamic author image," as Luc Herman and Bart Vervaeck have called it, originates "in a process of negotiation between reader, text, context, and the author's self-presentation" (12). Given his widely quoted views on literature, the average reader may already have a keen image of Wallace before touching the first page of his books. No matter how often a writer brandishes his opinions, however, it would be unwise to take these at face value: especially for novels as challenging as Wallace's, the possibility exists that we start reading things into them that are simply not there. The following pages address this problem by raising questions about the relationship between author, narrator, and text: how does Wallace present himself as a writer, how does that translate into his novels—with *Infinite Jest* and *The Pale King* as most interesting test cases—and which narrative strategies does he use to that end? As I clarify early on, Wallace's ideas on moral fiction were modeled on the so-called empathy-altruism hypothesis, the popular belief that readers learn to substitute "experiences of narrative empathy" for "shared feelings with real others" (Keen vii).[2]

The Victorian connection

Wallace's claims about the use of fiction are so well-known that they have become almost formulaic. It is an established fact in Wallace criticism that he—in his own words—sought to reinstate a "meaningful connection" between literature and the outside world (*SFT* 33), that he aspired to "aggravate this sense of entrapment and loneliness and death in people, to move people to countenance it" (*CW* 32), and that he wanted to write "morally passionate, passionately moral fiction" that was also "ingenious and radiantly human fiction" (*CL* 274). Early book-length studies see "E Unibus Pluram" as a stepping stone, comparable to the influence "The Literature of Exhaustion" had on the unfolding of John Barth's career

(Boswell 9). Yet the zeal with which critics have since latched on to the essay and the accompanying interview by Larry McCaffery has given Wallace's work an uncomfortable air of the holier-than-thou.[3] The question remains how, if at all, his novels reflect their author's moral(izing) impulse.

One possible answer could be that neither *Infinite Jest* nor *The Pale King* shies away from characters most people would rather ignore in real life. In an important study in which she traces the literary career of empathy, Suzanne Keen writes that one of the more appealing aspects of novel-reading is that novels provide "safe spaces" within which we can bond with both the oppressed and the oppressor, with both rulers and outcasts (131). *Infinite Jest* adds to that process of narrative bonding through its abundant use of internal focalization when it comes to addiction. We crawl inside the mind of marijuana addict Ken Erdedy as the narrator describes his paralyzing anxiety (17–27). We read Poor Tony Krause's withdrawal hallucinations as if they were real (299–306). Similarly, the nested narratives told by recovering addicts at Alcoholics Anonymous meetings are meant to make the listener "Identify" (345). In *The Pale King*, what makes the description of Toni Ware's youth so bleak is that events are only described from a third-person unobtrusive perspective. The narrator does not comment when Toni gets abused by one of her mother's lovers (63), nor when Toni prepares sandwiches with broken glass for a man who attacked her (58) or when she learns to cut a car's brake line "so the failure would be delayed until such time as the depth of the cut determined" (57).

A follow-up question, then, is whether such passages distinguish Wallace from his peers or predecessors. Are the castaways in his novels more radiantly human than, say, the guilt-stricken V-2 rocket engineer Franz Pökler in Thomas Pynchon's *Gravity's Rainbow* (1973), or than Ethel and Julius Rosenberg in Robert Coover's *The Public Burning* (1977)? To state the obvious, Wallace projected most of his arguments about moral fiction onto writers like Coover or Pynchon, canonical postmodernists who supposedly exchanged strong opinions for crippling self-awareness. His familiar take on postmodern metafiction was that it developed in the Sixties both as a radical attack against its "great theoretic nemesis, Realism," and as a critical, though inadequate, response to television and "the atomized mass of self-conscious watchers and appearers" it produced: "Metafiction simply called it as it saw itself seeing itself see it" (*SFT* 34). As smart a reader as Wallace was, that view was not without its weaker points.

The classic example of big-R Realism, George Eliot's *Middlemarch* (1872), proves that the Victorians, too, were obsessed with seeing and being seen. Character, as Eliot's narrator confidently asserts, unfolds in the gaze of the other: "we too can be seen and judged in the wholeness of our character" (762). In another of the book's many intrusions, the narrator compares storytelling to holding up the world to a scratched pier-glass: "It is demonstrable that the scratches are going everywhere impartially, and it is only your candle which produces the flattering illusion of a concentric arrangement, its light falling with an exclusive optical selection" (264). The narrative mirror is of course a central image in realist fiction. But that mirror, like consciousness ("reflection") itself, distorts the picture. In the renowned seventeenth chapter of Eliot's *Adam Bede* (1859), the narrator, posing as the author, pauses the story to explain that she aspires to give a faithful account of events as they have mirrored themselves in her mind: "The mirror is doubtless defective; the outlines will sometimes be disturbed; the reflection faint or confused; but I feel as much bound to tell you, as precisely as I can, what that reflection is" (161).

As neuroscientists have it, empathy, or other-directedness, is a form of mirroring. We differentiate between self and other, even ascribe thoughts and feelings to others, through the "mirror matching mechanisms" of the brain (Gallese 46). The ability to infer other people's mental states from their actions, familiar to narratologists through the work of Lisa Zunshine, is what cognitive theorists call Theory of Mind. For Zunshine, we read fiction to exercise our mind-reading ability (4). That argument would sound rather trite, were it not for Zunshine's overwhelming neurological evidence, because this is also the point novelists themselves have been making at least since George Eliot. The realists were the key figures in the transformation of novel reading from a "morally suspect waste of time" to "an activity cultivating the role-taking imagination" (Keen 38). Eliot was their most eloquent advocate for moral fiction, and subsequent pleas for the usefulness of literature mostly fall back on the idea she made famous: it teaches the reader to empathize. The first defense of novel reading on moral grounds, according to Keen (54), was Eliot's "The Natural History of German Life" (1856), the gist of which must sound familiar to Wallace readers:

> The greatest benefit we owe to the artist, whether painter, poet or novelist, is the extension of our sympathies. Appeals founded on generalizations and statistics require a sympathy ready-made, a moral sentiment already in activity; but a picture of human life such as a great artist can give, surprises even the trivial and the selfish into that attention to what is apart from themselves, which may be called the raw material of moral sentiment. ("Natural History" 270)

Good fiction, Eliot summarized, extends "our contact with our fellow-men beyond the bounds of our personal lot" ("Natural History" 271). Wallace made the same point to McCaffery: "I guess a big part of serious fiction's purpose is to give the reader, who like all of us is sort of marooned in her own skull, to give her imaginative access to other selves" (*CW* 21–2). The McCaffery interview appeared years before Wallace's most accredited fiction, to be sure, yet novelists who make empathy a specific goal also copy this agenda within their texts (Keen 121). Since the reader's empathy depends on identification, it comes as no surprise that Wallace embeds representations of compassion throughout his books.

A key factor in identifying with a narrative is immersion.[4] Successfully listening to an AA speaker in *Infinite Jest,* for instance, means "getting embarrassed for him, killing him by empathetically dying right there with him" (368). In *The Pale King*, Shane Drinion is so enthralled by a troubled colleague's story that he starts levitating, which he only does "when he is completely immersed" (485). Wallace had written on a note appended at the back of *The Pale King* by Michael Pietsch that their "ability to be immersed" makes the novel's main characters worth following (547), yet it remains unclear what we should make of this. In the context of moral fiction, Victorian writers of course championed immersive techniques. Modernists and postmodernists both recast the reader as a thinking collaborator, but a number of more conservative critics in the second half of the previous century still argued that the only novels worth reading were novels in which readers could immerse themselves. John Gardner, for example, maintained in *On Moral Fiction* (1979) that literature should uphold "an imaginary world so real and convincing that when we happen to be jerked out of it by a call from the kitchen or a knock at the door, we stare for an instant in befuddlement at the familiar room where we sat down, half an hour ago, with our book" (112–13).

Coincidence has it that Gardner, in one of his famous spats with William H. Gass, also insinuated to Larry McCaffery that "one can understand important human issues by writing novels," but that "most academically popular writers are completely uninterested" in these matters ("Gass and Gardner" 46–7). Wallace's pleas to McCaffery, although they came 15 years later, boiled down to much of the same.[5] If anything, however, complete immersion in *Infinite Jest* and *The Pale King* appears to be more dangerous than helpful. The eponymous film in *Infinite Jest* is so captivating that it poses a threat to society. The television show *M*A*S*H* so obsessed Hugh Steeply's father in the same novel that it ruined him: "The gradual immersion. The withdrawal from life" (640). Completely engrossed by tax returns, the IRS examiners in *The Pale King* display tics and twitches up to the point that they start seeing ghosts (314), and one of these is the ghost of a former examiner who died at his desk without being noticed until three days later because his colleagues were too immersed in their work (542). The difference between these passages and the passages that do point to empathetic identification, then, is that the latter require the active participation by the person who is doing the empathizing.

Narrative empathy, to paraphrase Keen, hinges primarily on the reader's willingness to engage intellectually and emotionally with the text (34). Whereas a recent study performed at the New School for Social Research suggests, for instance, that reading "literary" fiction leads to a better performance on empathy tests than reading popular fiction or nonfiction, the criterion for texts of the former category was that they engage readers "in a discourse that forces them to fill in gaps and search for meaning" (Kidd and Castano 377). The many underspecified actions and textual gaps in *Infinite Jest* indicate that it is up to the reader to reorganize the seemingly unrelated narrative strands into a meaningful whole. The Notes and Errata that make up the novel's final 96 pages further prove that she or he will have to put in a fair share of work to do so. *The Pale King* is an atypical case in this respect, since the organization of this posthumously edited novel entirely results from Michael Pietsch's work on the manuscripts. Yet here, too, we get hints that Wallace had a collaborative reader in mind. These include the representation of important plot info in anonymous dialogue scenes (130–49), in heavily edited interview transcripts (100–17), and in long digressive I-narratives (154–252) by a narrator later nicknamed "Irrelevant" (271). More strikingly, the book's frame narrative introduces a character-narrator named "David Wallace," who identifies himself as the author of *The Pale King*, "a nonfictional memoir" (73).

Infinite Jest, naturalization, and unnatural narration

If we want to understand *how* Wallace's novels could encourage the reader's empathy, we will have to look into the ways his narrators present events or in fact fail to do so. In what follows, I expand on the suggestion that *Infinite Jest* and *The Pale King* draw in the reader by singling out a number of narrative strategies that relate to the empathetic connection between reader and text. While *Infinite Jest* primarily shifts between an aesthetic of immersion and an aesthetic of interactivity, it also contains many passages that revert to so-called unnatural narration—consciousnesses bleeding into one another, multiply embedded narratives, and other examples that obscure the idea that narration is a form of communication involving a sender and a receiver (Alber et al. 115). A discussion of these passages will further lead to a consideration of the I-narrative in the "Author-here" sections of *The Pale King*, in which "David Wallace" explicitly elaborates on the "contract" between writer and reader (73).

I have argued above that reader's empathy depends on identification: we surrender our outsider position and place ourselves inside the narrative world when being immersed in a story. Nevertheless, through the many gaps and ambiguities that remain in the text, *Infinite Jest* does not unequivocally promote such recentering. To give two well-known examples, readers, try as they might, will never be able to prove, solely from textual evidence, if and how Avril Incandenza relates to the Québecois terrorists. Likewise, the opening scene in which Hal Incandenza makes such a miserable impression on the University of Arizona deans chronologically takes place after all other events in the novel, yet nowhere does the book reveal just how Hal came to be so isolated—whether that is because of his "abrupt and total" marijuana withdrawal (784), or because he swallowed the "incredibly potent" drug DMZ (170), or because of whatever took place after the Canadian wheelchair assassins did or did not succeed in taking over the Enfield Tennis Academy fundraiser (965). The several explanations that readers can come up with testify that they should take these indeterminacies as invitations to complete the story themselves.

Every reader who fills in the gaps in a text does so on the basis of her or his own knowledge, preferences, and experiences (Ryan, *Virtual Reality* 44). Central to this process is the fairly common idea that narration involves communication, generally speaking, as a transfer of information. The narrator provides the plot elements, and the reader processes them. *Infinite Jest* turns this assumption around, in that several crucial narrative events are deliberately left out. Gaps and indeterminacies have been a staple of reader-response theory ever since its initiation by Wolfgang Iser, Umberto Eco, and Jonathan Culler. In *Der Akt des Lesens* (1976), Iser equates all reading to gap-filling: "it is the gaps, the fundamental asymmetry between text and reader, that give rise to communication in the reading process." Missing information thus stimulates the reader "into filling the blanks with projections" (167–8). But whereas most texts rely on the reader's inferences to flesh out the contours of the storyworld—the setting of a particular scene, say, or the context of a conversation—gaps take center stage in *Infinite Jest*. Wallace said as much during an online chat session with some of his fans, quoted by D. T. Max: "an 'end' can be projected by the reader somewhere beyond the right frame. If no such convergence or projection occurred to you, then the book's failed for you" (321).[6]

In order to achieve a complete and satisfying interpretation of Wallace's tome, readers actually have to *produce* information. Jonathan Culler coined the term "naturalization" for the interpretive strategies readers use whenever they are confronted with inconsistencies and still try to restore a text's "communicative function" (134). Since *Infinite Jest* does not specify where Avril stands in connection to the Canadian separatists or why Hal can no longer express his emotions at the beginning of the novel, readers will have to naturalize these plot elements and come up with their own explanations. Naturalization is not necessarily the same as refamiliarizing the unfamiliar. Rather, as Monika Fludernik explains, it refers to reading strategies that explain the strange within a larger cognitive framework, and which thus allow readers to keep the bonds they have established with the text in place (*"Natural"* 12). To take just the simplest of illustrations, when we read about a wraith communicating to Gately in the hospital, we might adjust our mental representation of the storyworld of *Infinite Jest* to a world in which ghosts are nothing out of the ordinary. Conversely, since Gately refuses anything else than "non-narcotic painkillers" (818), we might naturalize the wraith as a hallucination caused by great pain. In the former case, we will likely attribute the bizarre happenings at E.T.A., such as Ortho Stice's "hovering" bed (943) or the reappearance of all sorts of equipment in the strangest places (632), to such a ghost. In the latter case, the new information in these passages will again force us to renegotiate our conception of what is and is not possible in the world of the novel.

Wallace's choice to place the chronologically most recent information at the start of the book seems a deliberate attempt to test his readers' naturalization skills. For one thing, this arrangement prompts them to read the remaining pages as a broad analepsis to events leading up to the beginning of the novel, the point where Hal fails to convince the Arizona deans that he is a human being with feelings and beliefs. Several references to this opening passage throughout *Infinite Jest* further amplify this prompt. The "incredibly potent DMZ" is synthesized from an "obscure mold that grows only on other molds" (170), which resonates with both Hal's interior-monologue-type explanation, "'Call it something I ate,'" and the story he subsequently tells about how he once swallowed a "really unpleasant-looking" mold as a child (10). Hal's thoughts of Canadian-born E.T.A. talent John R. Wayne "standing watch in a mask" as Hal and Don Gately dig up the head of Hal's father (16) are foreshadowed by Gately's fever dream of "digging some dead guy's head up" in a graveyard "with a very sad kid" (934). Of course such signs only hint at some ultimate explanation, and even these remain open to scrutiny.

By the same token, the novel's intricate chronology complicates the reader's ability to empathize with the protagonist of these opening pages. As cognitive narratologists have it, a key component of the reading process is the way both narrators and readers inhabit the minds of characters. If we try to understand what happens to Hal in *Infinite Jest*, for instance, we need to infer a global image of his personality from the local passages in which he plays a role. This is what Alan Palmer refers to as the "continuing-consciousness frame," a reader's construct which gathers all the isolated references to a character and molds them into a consciousness "that continues in the space between the various mentions of that character" (175–6). Fictional minds are incomplete by themselves, since every character appears only a number of times in a novel. We thus attribute a mind to characters based both on their actions, their opinions, and the way other characters perceive them, as well as on our ability to read other people's minds in reality. Hal remains something of a blank slate throughout the novel: he can manipulate others "well enough to satisfy everyone but himself that he's in there, inside his own hull, as a human being," but in fact "inside Hal there's pretty much nothing at all, he knows" (694). Hal's empty interior life resembles the snippet of interior monologue on the opening page: "I am in here" (3). Note, then, the similarities (surely not coincidental) with cognitive philosopher Daniel Dennett's allusion to the talking computer Hal 9000 from Stanley Kubrick's *2001: A Space Odyssey* (1968). As Dennett writes in *Consciousness Explained* (1991), not much is required for us to attribute fully fledged mental lives to other beings, be they human, animal, or machine: "Speaking—as Hal does—will serve about as well, in the absence of an expressive face, to secure the illusion that there is someone in there, that it is like something to be Hal" (432).

If we want to empathize with an actual "human" character rather than with a mere representation, Palmer summarizes, we construct an image of the character's mind that is coherent both on the novel's microstructural level and on its macrostructural level (181–3). The mysteries surrounding Hal Incandenza illustrate this principle quite well. The unresponsive and uncommunicative protagonist in the first few pages of *Infinite Jest* typifies Hal's own portrayal, in an essay he wrote for one of his E.T.A. classes, of the new hero in fiction as "the hero of non-action, the catatonic hero … divorced from all stimulus" (142). We might consequently view this specifically local passage as an accurate description of Hal's personality throughout *Infinite Jest*. Conversely, if we do so, we might let our interpretation of later passages, in which Hal for instance finds himself "paralyzed with absorption" when the game of Eschaton breaks into a fight (340) or in which he spends his time "lying perfectly still and staring at the ceiling" (900), be determined by our now global conception of Hal as a hero of nonaction.

Whatever image readers construct of him, Hal Incandenza remains a curious case of the continuing consciousness frame, mainly because of the diverging narrative perspectives in the passages that involve him. We get introduced to Hal as a first-person narrator who seems completely withdrawn in his own mind. The end of the opening passage features Hal's own projection of what will happen after he has been dragged to a hospital: he will be checked out and well-rested in time for "tomorrow's semi" of the WhataBurger tennis tournament, he will no doubt beat his opponent Dymphna while there, and he will "play either Stice or Polep in Sunday's final" (16). Whereas the reader has to speculate about what happens to Hal between the penultimate scene in which the E.T.A. players are just about to face the Canadian terrorists (964–71) and the interview scene, Hal provides his own speculative ending to *Infinite Jest* at the start of the novel. Furthermore, Hal's subjunctive mood surprisingly concludes with a question that some blue-collared hospital worker "will" inevitably ask him, related in free direct speech: "So yo man what's *your* story?" (16).

The latter question signals the point where the narrative goes back in time to events leading up to the first few pages. Should we then read the entire novel, including the plot lines revolving around Gately and the A.F.R., as Hal's story? Since, once again, there is no textual evidence to fully prove or disprove this theory, allow me to try some naturalization of my own. Apart from Hal Incandenza, the only first-person narrators with a clear identity in *Infinite Jest* either come up in nested narratives told by addicts or recovering addicts, such as Clenette (37–8) or "yrstruly" (128–35), or in book chapters, such as James O. Incandenza's account of how he became interested in annular systems (491–503, 1034 n208). These could very well be part of Hal's main narrative: James O. was his father after all, and Hal might have heard some of the addicts' stories after his first visit to Ennet House Drug and Alcohol Recovery House *(sic)* (785–7). But leaving aside the opening passage, Hal only appears as an I-narrator in the first half of the novel when he relates the "really unpleasant dream" that made him pick up a marijuana habit around the age of 15 (67–8). Toward the final pages of *Infinite Jest*, Hal, who has now given up smoking and has been feeling bad "for almost a week" (851), suddenly reemerges as first-person narrator after waking up from another bad dream (851–4). Between the two sections, we only learn about Hal's thoughts and actions from a seemingly omniscient third-person narrator.

These passages ultimately confront us with narrative elements that no longer can be naturalized, or at least, not unequivocally. What do we make of the bad dreams that link up Hal's narratives? Are they somehow related to Gately's dream of digging up James O. Incandenza's head—which Hal explicitly remembers in the novel's opening pages—and does that somehow suggest that the novel is partly a dream? While such questions cannot and perhaps should not be answered, some third-person narratives in *Infinite*

Jest can still be ascribed to a single narrating consciousness, possibly Hal's. As he brings up the anecdote of an unaffiliated junior tennis player whose suicide accidentally poisoned the boy's entire family, the otherwise objective narrator suddenly adds "plus I should mention the odd agonized gurgling-sounds" made by the dying family members (437). Referring to the sexual abuse that Matty Pemulis suffered as a child, the narrator wonders in a footnote: "Where was Mrs. Pemulis all this time . . . is what I'd want to know" (1052 n278).

Even so, readers would be hard-pressed to argue that the novel has but one, autonomous narrator. Representing Don Gately's experience of his first days at AA through simple thought report, the third-person narrator still comments that terms like "stone-faced chieftains" and "shamanistic fiat" (354) do not come from Gately himself (1026 n137). In a passage that explains the origins of Canadian terrorism, the narrator's word "whinged" (311) is actually an "Incandenza-family term" (1022 n111). Even more mystifying is the fact that Michael Pemulis at one point addresses the reader directly by dictating to Hal (1023–5 n123) the rules of a game we learn about in the third person (321–42), and we find out that the man who told the yrstruly episode might have been Randy Lenz when the third-person narrator of an unrelated passage calls him "yrstruly" out of the blue (562).

What we see here, then, are illustrations of what Brian Richardson has called "permeable" narration, the strange and unexplainable "intrusion of the voice of another within the narrator's consciousness." Permeable narrators go against most general conceptions of narrative as they violate the assumption that the presence of a narrator implies "an autonomous, individual consciousness" governing the text (95–6). Since it resists naturalization, this "unnatural" strategy continuously challenges a standard supposition about storytelling, "the model of narrative communication," namely the belief that the reader should be able—explicitly or implicitly—to identify the story's source (Alber et al. 124). I have argued above that distinct voices intrude the narration several times in *Infinite Jest*. In addition, it happens on multiple occasions that one character's consciousness inexplicably bleeds into another, as when Hal's graveyard memory in the opening pages reappears in Gately's dreams. The clearest indication of such a permeating consciousness would be the wraith's, even though the reader can never be quite sure if the wraith actually exists. For one, it only interacts with Gately in the hospital bed as the latter recovers from his extremely painful gunshot wound, and even Gately, the focalizer in these episodes, tries to naturalize it as a "dream" (830). Curiously, though, the wraith soon intrudes "Gately's personal mind" and starts projecting "in Gately's own brain voice" terms that Gately "knows for a fact he doesn't have any idea" what they mean—words like "PIROUETTE," "ANNULATE," and "POOR YORICK" (832).

To borrow Richardson's terms, *Infinite Jest* distorts the humanistic concept of the narrator "who is like a person" because there seems to be no discrete narrative voice that dominates the novel (102). What we get instead are fictional minds corrupted by the debris of others, in some cases even narrative fragments that lack a narrator or a narratee—such as censured letters between different characters (663–5), the technical specifications of an "InterLace Telentertainment" system (60), and, curiously, the transcript of "*Tennis and the Feral Prodigy*," a film "narrated by Hal Incandenza" (172). While *Infinite Jest* does have local narrators, attempts to understand or empathize with the novel's global narrative are ultimately centered around an absence in the text. The wraith is an especially problematic figure in this respect, since it acts out what most of the book's third-person narrators covertly do by taking over another character's brain voice.

In narratology, the problem of narrative voice is notoriously complex. Gérard Genette introduced the term to bridge all aspects that involve "the way in which the narrating itself is implicated in the narrative" (31), but whereas Genette took voice for granted even in texts that do not have an obvious speaker, Fludernik, in a lucid analysis of interpretive strategies, counters that the presence of narrative discourse is not always a reason to conclude "that somebody must be narrating the story" ("New Wine" 621–2). Doing so, she writes, merely perpetuates an illusion: we tend to project a real-life communicational framework onto prose texts, but since that framework breaks down in narratives without "a clear speaker function," our inclination to identify a "narrative voice" ultimately reflects our inclination to identify "the voice of the *author*" ("New Wine" 622). Although readers may not always be aware of that catch, Wallace surely was, as he explained to David Lipsky:

> I think with writing it's really feeling that, [the writers'] brain voice for a while becomes *your* brain voice. . . . That just, they feel intimate with you, in a way. Or that you'd be, not just that you'd be somebody that it'd be great to be friends with, but that they *are* your friend. . . . But it's also a delusion, and it's kind of an invasive one. (275)

It might be crucial, then, that the wraith in *Infinite Jest* is likely the spirit of James O. Incandenza, Hal's dead father and in many ways the absent element that ties together Hal, the AA, and the terrorists. The wraith was once an experimental filmmaker (835–6) and avid drinker (839) who had the terrifying feeling when alive that his son, "the one most like him," could not communicate with him (837). As a final resort he tried to "make something so bloody compelling it would reverse thrust on a young self's fall" into silence (839), a description which resonates heavily with *Infinite Jest*, James O. Incandenza's "final opus" (788), the lethally entertaining film so desired by the Canadian separatists, and the source for the title of Wallace's novel. Perhaps all this suggests that the wraith may well be the permeating consciousness that informs *Infinite Jest*. This, of course, remains to be seen.

The Pale King and the overdetermined text

The role of James O. Incandenza in Wallace's novel raises a number of questions about the concept of authorship. Is the death of the artist who made *Infinite Jest* in a book with the same title an evocation of Roland Barthes's "Death of the Author," and does that signal the "birth of the reader" (Barthes, "Death" 148) as the ultimate authority in Wallace's text? What, then, are we to make of the author's return as a ghost who speaks through the minds of other characters? Gately, for instance, wonders if the wraith is a visitation from his "personally confused understanding of God," who governs his thoughts as if it were "a higher power or something" (833).[7] I have suggested that *Infinite Jest* on several occasions distorts the idea that a narrator resembles a person, but consider this against Marie-Laure Ryan's assertion that "the style of impersonal narrators cannot be distinguished from the style of the author" (*Possible Worlds* 68). Does the author's presence account for the fact that in Wallace's novel the wraith "had no out-loud voice of its own, and had to use somebody's like internal brain-voice if it wanted to try to communicate something" (831)?

Obviously it would be overzealous to put the wraith on a par with the actual author, but it remains an interesting thought that the creator of *Infinite Jest* haunts the story and tries to communicate to other people by appropriating "brain-voices" that are not his own. In a sense, this description also applies to Wallace's posthumously edited novel *The Pale King*. Purely on the structural level, the publication of an unfinished novel entails that someone other than the author—in this case Little, Brown editor Michael Pietsch—has gathered the work in progress, drawn up an outline of the book, made corrections and even added new passages "in the spirit" of the deceased author (Richardson 118). While I am less concerned with the implied author as a theoretical concept, it is a striking fact that *The Pale King* itself introduces a narrator named "David Wallace" in an Author's Foreword that only appears as the ninth of a total of fifty chapters (66–85).

"Wallace" addresses the reader as "the real author" of *The Pale King*, "the living human holding the pencil, not some abstract narrative persona" (66). He insists that for legal and commercial reasons such a narrative persona does exist in the text, but his message here is that "[a]ll of this is true. This book is really true" (67). Of course, the fictional foreword is a familiar plot device, even though the fictional "Wallace" cleverly directs the reader to the paratextual information on the copyright page: the legal disclaimer which says that all events and characters in *The Pale King* are fictitious is supposedly "the only bona fide 'fiction'" in the book (68).

The suggestion to go and read the disclaimer poses somewhat of a snag. In most I-narratives, the only undisputable evidence that allows readers to decide whether what they are reading is autobiographical or fictional is the narrator's identity or non-identity with the author (Lanser 206). Since "David Foster Wallace" is also the name on the dust jacket, readers who do not know that the real author of *The Pale King* never worked for the Internal Revenue System can either take the narrator at his word or look for signs outside the text that disprove him. Yet although the disclaimer may be fictional, the generic indicator "An Unfinished Novel" on the book's title page unfortunately is not. Further paratextual indications that the I-narrator in the Author's Foreword is not the actual David Foster Wallace are the Editor's Note (v–x) and the Notes and Asides that Michael Pietsch culled from Wallace's manuscript (539–47), which even include the suggestion that "David Wallace disappears—becomes creature of the system" (546).[8] But then, all these examples are only in the book because *The Pale King* was left unfinished, and so the question remains how Wallace would have avoided these generic markers had he been able to finish the novel.

Whereas *Infinite Jest* blurs the idea of an autonomous narrator governing the text, *The Pale King* gives voice to its author—be it a fictional one or not. According to Susan Lanser, readers do not always separate the first-person voices within a text from the actual author's voice, "even when they 'know' that a speaking 'I' is fictional and 'ought' to be considered purely as such" (211). Lanser's argument hinges on the reader's inclination to "attach" a familiar identity to the narrating voice (208). Readers might be more emotionally involved in the story of someone they know (or someone they think they know), and it is arguably with such inclinations in mind that "Wallace" foregrounds himself as the author of *The Pale King*. That much is clear when he brings up "the unspoken contract between a book's author and its reader" (73). Labeling *The Pale King* a "nonfiction memoir, with additional elements of reconstructive journalism," "Wallace" emphasizes that "the subliminal contract for nonfiction is very different from the one for fiction" (73).

Philippe Lejeune's seminal theory of autobiography is the obvious inspiration here. In 1975, Lejeune defined life writing as "a contract of identity" between writer and reader, "sealed by the proper name" (19). According to the autobiographical contract, the author guarantees that the name on the cover of the book matches the identity of the person who witnessed the events within. Readers feel shocked and betrayed when it doesn't, as "Wallace" adds in the Author's Foreword: "The feelings of betrayal or infidelity that the reader suffers if it turns out that a piece of ostensible nonfiction has made-up stuff in it (as has been revealed in some recent literary scandals, e.g. Kosinski's *Painted Bird* or that infamous Carcaterra book) is because the terms of the nonfiction contract have been violated" (73 n9). These feelings of betrayal ostensibly stem from the belief that the reader has been empathizing with a narrative that is untrue, despite being told otherwise.[9]

Even when we do not consider how some characters negate the novel's reality effect—the levitating Shane Drinion, "fact psychic" Claude Sylvanshine (118)—most elements in the first-person frame narrative are entirely made up. New IRS employees do not receive a new social security number on their first day at work (66 n1). The real David Foster Wallace never got suspended from an "extremely expensive and highbrow" college for plagiarism (74). Yet this is obviously very specific information that not all readers can know about. Even if they do, some untrue plot elements might still be explained as the "willed incongruities" and literary embellishments that come with the memoir genre (72). "Wallace" comments that he started writing *The Pale King* as nonfiction because memoirs are way more profitable than novels, and he mentions as proof that "in 2003, the average author's advance for a memoir was almost 2.5 times that paid for a work of fiction" (81). As it happens, the controversy surrounding one of the bestselling memoirs of that same year, James Frey's *A Million Little Pieces*, sheds new light on the contract "Wallace" establishes in *The Pale King*.

A Million Little Pieces only became a real success when Oprah Winfrey picked it up for her Book Club in 2005, after which it topped the *New York Times* nonfiction bestseller list for weeks on end. Yet even if we believe "Wallace's" claim in *The Pale King* that he is writing the Author's Foreword "in the cultural present of 2005" (80), this does not suggest that he might somehow have Frey in mind: the vehement attacks against Frey's memoir did not start until the beginning of the next year, when it turned out that the author had embellished and even made up large chunks of the book. But more important to the present discussion than the actual memoir is the outcome of this revelation. The ensuing public outrage forced Frey to defend himself on several US talk shows. Oprah Winfrey withdrew her support for the book and openly accused its writer of "betrayal" during his embarrassing second appearance on her show, and Frey's publisher released an official statement offering refunds to buyers of *A Million Little Pieces* "following accusations the author exaggerated his story" (qtd. in Nielsen 286–7). A number of readers subsequently filed a lawsuit, which included the allegation that the "back cover classified the Book as 'memoir/literature'" (Nielsen 288).

It remains a curious fact that the accusations against Frey focused without exception on the generic classification of *A Million Little Pieces*, and disregarded the actual content of the book. In *The Pale King*, "Wallace" explains to his readers that the publisher's legal counsel has worked out that "you will regard features like shifting p.o.v.s, structural fragmentation" and other narrative devices as clear signals "that what was under way was fiction and should be processed accordingly" (72). Frey likewise maintained in an interview with Larry King that *A Million Little Pieces* features a true account of his recovery from drug and alcohol addiction, but that to represent certain events a memoir still has to resort to fictionalization: "One of the things I think is interesting is there are two hundred pages of recreated conversations in the book, but people haven't been questioning those" (Frey in Nielsen 290). In this sense, the shocked reactions to violations of the contract between writer and reader again boil down to standard conceptions of narrative communication. Classical narrative models state that in nonfiction the communication invariably takes place between author and reader, whereas in fiction a narrator addresses a narratee. Narratives in which author and narrator are hard to distinguish pose obvious difficulties for such models, which explains why Dorrit Cohn in *The Distinction of Fiction* (1990) simply refers to them as "indeterminate fictions" (34).

"Indeterminate fiction" seems an uncomfortable fit for texts that *are* defined by their author or narrator. Henrik Skov Nielsen has recently proposed the useful term "underdetermined text" for books that, like Frey's *A Million Little Pieces*, present themselves to the reader as neither fiction nor nonfiction, and which can therefore be read as both. Conversely, an "overdetermined text" presents itself "in some cases at different times, in others at the same time," as both fiction and nonfiction (284).[10] Underdetermined texts send no clear message to the reader as to how they should be read. Overdetermined texts send diverse or mutually exclusive messages. *The Pale King* would be a good example of such an overdetermined text: the title page names it an unfinished novel and many of its plot elements are evidently fictional, but at the same time the author is introduced inside the narrative, and he establishes a "contract" with the reader based on both his "veracity" and the reader's "understanding that any features or semions that might appear to undercut that veracity are in fact protective legal devices" (73). Overdetermined texts thus allow readers to put a familiar face on the narrative voice while they retain the distinction between author and narrator to keep readers from feeling betrayed. Scandals are more likely to occur with underdetermined texts, as Nielsen suggests, especially if they are first read as nonfiction and then as fiction (285).

Nielsen uses the concept of the underdetermined text to argue that fictionality is not necessarily a global quality, but rather that texts can be fictional or nonfictional at local sites as well (281–2). Whereas memoirs like *A Million Little Pieces* may be true-to-life in their global outline, the reconstructed dialogues in the book surely are not. For an overdetermined text like *The Pale King*, however, the novel's fictionality depends largely on interpretive strategies. Susan Lanser, for instance, contends that readers routinely "vacillate" and "oscillate" and even "double the speaking voice" of a narrative to connect the fictional 'I' with the actual author (207). In this view, we are likely to ascribe a novel's plot events purely to a fictional narrator, whereas we might link the text's "nonnarrative elements," such as the narrator's opinions on writing, on politics, etcetera, to the author as well as to the narrator (Lanser 216).[11] The Author's Foreword in *The Pale King* feeds into this interpretive process by playing around with the assumption that narrative involves direct communication.

"Wallace" arguably brings up the autobiographical contract to highlight the reader's inclination to empathize with a narrative, and it is indeed fascinating to think that here we have the actual voice of the author reaching out to us. In a similar vein, readers familiar with Wallace's repeated calls for passionately moral fiction might attribute the opinion expressed in *Infinite Jest* that "the lively arts of the millennial U.S.A. treat anhedonia and internal emptiness as hip and cool" (694), or the wraith's subsequent defense of "complete unfiguranted egalitarian . . . realism" (836), to David Foster Wallace himself. Compare this to Brian Richardson's revival of "the implied author" to explain why the ideas that novelists develop in critical essays sometimes return in their fiction: "In such cases, the narrator may be temporarily 'emptied' and his character dispensed with as the author speaks directly and sometimes incongruously through that character's mouth" (128–9). Perhaps we should believe that through the wraith and through "David Wallace," the actual author's voice haunts *Infinite Jest* and *The Pale King*. Or perhaps we should not. Appropriately, the wraith in the former novel has the final word: we "might as well stop trying to figure it out and just capitalize on its presence" (830).

Notes

1   A decade earlier, Wallace wrote in "Joseph Frank's *Dostoevsky*" (1996) that the "distinctive singular stamp of himself is one of the main reasons readers come to love an author." He then added that "critics' attempts to reduce it to questions of 'style' are almost universally lame" (*CL* 260). Let the reader be warned.

2   My reader-oriented approach forms something of a linked pair with Andrew Warren's essay in this collection. Whereas Warren describes four models with which *Infinite Jest* and *The Pale King* establish narrative relations, I extend my focus to the complex transaction between text and audience.

3   The following remark by Greg Carlisle, who has otherwise proven himself to be an astute Wallace reader, captures the idea: "I think a world in which Wallace is a household name would be a more mindful, passionate, and compassionate world. It's up to us now to continue the conversation he started" (20). Unless Carlisle refers to the rise in global literacy required for any novelist to become a household name, casting Wallace as a smart and considerate sage (an image the Wallace industry almost cynically promotes) strikes me as misleading. In the second edition of his guide to *Infinite Jest*, Stephen J. Burn identifies the need for critics to move beyond Wallace's own reading of his work (21). For a skillful analysis of the blind spots in "E Unibus Pluram" and the McCaffery interview, see Andersen.

4   According to Marie-Laure Ryan, fiction elicits real-life emotions only when it allows the reader to be completely immersed in the storyworld (*Narrative* 148–9). A recent empirical study by Bal and Veldkamp draws a parallel between readers' self-reported "emotional transportation" and their empathy skills (4).

5   Wallace said to McCaffery that he did not align himself with Gardner: "I'm not trying to line up behind Tolstoy or Gardner. I just think that fiction that isn't exploring what it means to be human today isn't good art" (*CW* 26). Naturally, Gardner thought the same, and many others with him. Long before Gardner, Lionel Trilling complained that contemporary writers lacked the spirit to address the "human will" (258). Before Trilling, Walter Benjamin wrote that the rapid distribution of information had removed the "fragile human" from storytelling (77). So often have critics decried a lack of humanism in fiction, in fact, that the argument has lost all meaning. Case in point: in James Wood's infamous review of Zadie Smith's *White Teeth* (2000), Wallace tops the list of novelists whose books "are not really alive, not fully human" (42).

6   Note that Iser's concept of gap-filling adds to the dialogic dimension of the book, central to Adam Kelly's essay in this volume. While I consider Kelly's argument a powerful reconsideration of the novel of ideas, I disagree with his remark (through O'Donnell) that the openness of Wallace's plots hints at some kind of "post-paranoid" poetics. The network of connections in

Infinite Jest rather left me asking the same question that adorns the poster on Michael Pemulis's bedroom wall: "YES, I'M PARANOID—BUT AM I PARANOID *ENOUGH*?" (1035). Reader's paranoia, the urge to connect the dots until meaning begins to emerge, is a default mechanism when it comes to texts that do not immediately cohere: "antiparanoia, where nothing is connected to anything," to borrow a famous line from Pynchon's *Gravity's Rainbow*, is simply "a condition not many of us can bear for long" (434). The importance of the gap in *Infinite Jest* shows the lingering influence of postmodernists such as Pynchon, who made the radically open text their trademark (see McHale on Bakhtin and postmodernism; 165–72). If, as Kelly suggests, there is indeed a hint of mastery or totality in postmodern fiction, that is only if the reader would have it so: "the impression of endless depth, of all-inclusive totality—in short, of openness—that we receive from every work of art is based on both the double nature of the communicative organization of the aesthetic form and the transactional nature of the process of comprehension" (Eco 39).

7 In their essay on the dynamic author image, Herman and Vervaeck compare the author's felt presence to that of a god: "No one has ever seen God, so no one really knows what she or he looks like" (12). Both Gately's words here and Wallace's words in the McCaffery interview have similar inflections: once a piece of prose has left the author's hands, Wallace told McCaffery, "[t]he reader becomes God, for all textual purposes" (*CW* 40).

8 There are obvious continuities between this plot riff and the death and ghostly resurgence of the "Auteur" in *Infinite Jest* (788). As I write elsewhere, the manuscripts and drafts of *The Pale King* at the Harry Ransom Center indicate that while Wallace did not conceive of the frame narrative in its autobiographical form until late 2006, he had been toying with related ideas as early as 1997 ("A Genesis").

9 Lejeune's contract theory also translates into Jonathan Franzen's status and contract models of fiction, which *The Pale King* alludes to in passing. Following his take on the literary contract, "Wallace" scoffs that like "so many other nerdy, disaffected young people," he once dreamed of becoming "an immortally great fiction writer à la Gaddis" (73). In an essay on William Gaddis, Franzen names two opposite ways in which literature relates to its audience: the status model of authors like Gaddis, which "invites a discourse of genius and art-historical importance," and the contract model to which both he and Wallace subscribe, a form of writing that aims "to sustain a sense of connectedness, to resist existential loneliness" (240). For all its attempts to demonstrate how Gaddis and his peers disregard the reader, however, Franzen's diatribe boils down to the rather weak point that status novels are difficult. Joseph Tabbi has since shown that Franzen must have lifted both status and contract from page 393 of Gaddis's *JR* (1975), proving that the books he rails against "aren't nearly so hard that readers will miss in them the source of ideas, arguments, and attitudes Franzen wants to pass off as his own" (406).

10 Nielsen's example of overdetermined fiction is Bret Easton Ellis's mock memoir *Lunar Park* (2005). Despite their authors' mutual dislike, *Lunar Park* and *The Pale King* have significant overlaps, from their fictional writer/narrator's recollections of their earliest writing days to their insistence that the fantastic events described within really happened.

11 Dorrit Cohn's analysis of the generic ambiguity of Marcel Proust's *Recherche* cycle (1913–27) corroborates that point: "A glance at any of the many volumes and essays that deal with the philosophical (psychological, aesthetic, sociological) discourse in the *Recherche* quickly reveals that—although their authors as a rule pay lip-service to the notion that it is a novel—its ideas are almost invariably attributed to Proust" (70).

3

Boredom, Irony, and Anxiety: Wallace and the Kierkegaardian View of the Self

Allard den Dulk

Boredom is one of the main themes of David Foster Wallace's posthumously published, unfinished novel *The Pale King* (2011). In the novel, Wallace suggests that boredom might in fact serve as a path to meaningful existence. For example, in the "Notes and Asides" at the end of the novel, he writes:

> It turns out that bliss [. . .] lies on the other side of crushing boredom. Pay attention to the most tedious thing you can find [. . .], and, in waves, a boredom like you've never known will wash over you [. . .]. Ride these out, and it's like stepping from black and white into color. Like water after days in the desert. Constant bliss in every atom. (546)

The subject of boredom connects *The Pale King* to what I consider to be the larger, philosophical dimension of Wallace's oeuvre, and especially of his magnum opus *Infinite Jest* (1996), namely: the challenges to becoming a coherent self and realizing a meaningful existence amid the fragmented plurality of the contemporary Western world. Or, as Wallace has expressed it himself, somewhat more generally: "Fiction's about what it is to be a fucking *human being*" (*CW* 26).

In its portrayal of human existence Wallace's work displays strong affinities to existentialist thought. Nevertheless, in the critical and scholarly interpretation of his fiction this illuminating philosophical perspective has been largely ignored.[1] The classic existentialist motif of the individual fleeing from fundamental existential questions plays an important role in Wallace's oeuvre. *Infinite Jest* describes a large host of characters who evade responsibility for their lives through irony and addiction, and end up in a state of depression. But the novel also portrays the possibility of changing one's way of life and finding meaning and becoming a human self, as in the case of the character Don Gately. *The Pale King* addresses this anxiety—that is, the "dread" one feels when confronted with existential responsibilities—through the subject of boredom, which is represented, above all, by the extreme tedium of the work of the employees of the Internal Revenue Service (IRS) who form the main focus of the novel. In *The Pale King*, Wallace portrays boredom as a state that one can either try to avoid or embrace. Perhaps surprisingly, the novel affirms the latter option as the possible route to a meaningful life.

The connection between these themes—boredom, anxiety, irony, and meaningful life—in *Infinite Jest* and *The Pale King* can best be understood in light of the philosophy of Danish existentialist thinker Søren Kierkegaard (1813–55). Wallace's works express a view of the self that is almost identical to that of Kierkegaard. The fundamental distinction in Kierkegaard's philosophy of self-becoming, between the aesthetic and the ethical life, applies to Wallace's existentially lost drug addicts and his heroic Alcoholics Anonymous supplicants and IRS agents, respectively. Kierkegaard's critique of irony plays an important role in the distinction between the aesthetic and ethical, and connects in many ways with Wallace's irony critique.[2] Similarly, Wallace's treatment of boredom and anxiety, as leading to meaning and happiness (a suggestion repeatedly stated but not much elucidated in *The Pale King*), resembles Kierkegaard's own in-depth analysis of these states. Therefore, using Kierkegaard's philosophy as a heuristic perspective will provide a clear analysis of the role of boredom and of related concepts in *Infinite Jest* and *The Pale King*, and thereby of the connections within Wallace's oeuvre.

The existentialist view of the self in Kierkegaard and Wallace

In Kierkegaard's view, an individual is not automatically a self but has to become one. A human being merely embodies the possibility of becoming a self. For Kierkegaard, there is no "true core" that an individual always already "is" or "has" and that underlies selfhood. *Becoming* a self is the *task* of human life (cf. *Either/Or* 2: 250–1). We can recognize this view throughout Wallace's writing.

First of all, it is important to acknowledge the difference between the existentialist and the "postmodernist" view of the self. Existentialist and postmodernist philosophies agree in their denial of a preexisting, unified self. Subsequently, a postmodernist thinker such as Michel Foucault would affirm that this fragmentation (or decentering) of the self should be honored, even celebrated.[3] However, a strange paradox underlies this argument: namely, the postmodernist celebration of the fragmented self is based on the assumptions that the individual is not whole and cannot be made whole without being selective and therefore "untruthful" to all the different things the individual is, and that such an untruthful unification is always imposed and dictated by outside forces. The self, in other words, is a fiction produced by cultural conventions. This whole picture reveals a romantic longing for the impossible authenticity of a fragmented, self-less "entity," free from forces that corrupt that "genuine" state of fragmented diversity (cf. Guignon 109, 113–19).

For Kierkegaard, the fact that the self is something "made" does not imply that it is a fiction, in the sense of an imperfect artificiality that corrupts the diversity of the individual. What exactly is it that is corrupted when there is no preexisting self? The postmodernist view turns freedom into a goal in itself. (We will see that this view of the self—which is also the view criticized in Wallace's work—strongly resembles the so-called aesthetic attitude that Kierkegaard critiques.) Conversely, Kierkegaard posits that the self is fragmented but should be made whole—this is the task of human life (*Concept of Anxiety* 155). For Kierkegaard, and existentialist philosophy in general, human existence is characterized by both "facticity" and "transcendence."[4] On the one hand, the individual finds himself in a factual situation, not of his own making. It is, in a sense, a product of coincidence—he is born in a certain country, to certain parents, brought up in a certain culture and community, etcetera. On the other hand, the individual is freedom, that is, he has the potential to place himself in relation to his accidental situation, and thereby "own" it instead of just being unwillingly determined by it. In addition to this, he can choose from new possibilities that lie before him, thereby reshaping his situation, becoming more than what was determined for him. In other words, he can transcend his facticity. This is what Kierkegaard means by "becoming a self": a human being has to take up his individual limitations and possibilities, and integrate them into a unified existence. If the individual does not take himself up in this way, he does not acquire a self; he is just an immediate, natural being—"a thing among the things." Such a human being does not "exist"; he just "is" (cf. Taels 96, 102).

Wallace formulates an almost identical view of the self in a talk he gave on Franz Kafka, who is also an important representative of the existentialist tradition (Bennett 236; Marino xv). Wallace remarks that in our present age it is a common mistake to think "that a self is something you just *have*." According to Wallace, we should realize the central insight of existentialism, "that the horrific struggle to establish a human self results in a self whose humanity is inseparable from that horrific struggle. That our endless and impossible journey toward home is in fact our home." Wallace also explicitly compares Kafka to Kierkegaard in this respect (*CL* 64–5). In this context Wallace's statement, "Although of course you end up becoming yourself"—which became the title of David Lipsky's 300-page "road trip" interview with Wallace—has a strong existentialist ring to it (Lipsky 52).

This view of the self underlies *Infinite Jest*'s description of its characters suffering from addiction as having no self, as being "empty" inside. In the novel, addiction is a metaphor for not taking up responsibility for one's life, and, as a result, suffering from "internal emptiness." Conversely, the novel describes Don Gately, in his process of recovery, as "returned to himself" (694–5, 860). In *The Pale King*, Lane Dean Jr's remark that he is "just broken and split off like all men" (42) expresses the same view, that the self is not based on some preexisting unity but rather something that is constantly torn between freedom and facticity and, therefore, has to be *made* whole. Additionally, in the chapter about the boy who wants to kiss every part of his body, the narrator remarks, "Every whole person has ambitions, objectives, initiatives, goals" (394).[5] A person becomes "whole," becomes a "self," by giving direction to her own situation through choices and taking on responsibilities.

Irony in the aesthetic and the ethical life-view

Kierkegaard further thematizes the problem of becoming a self in his distinction between the aesthetic and the ethical life-view. Both life-views are stages in the development of the individual. To be sure, Kierkegaard also describes a third stage that follows on the ethical, namely the religious life-view. However, when examining the matter at hand, this view is often combined with the ethical and referred to as the ethical-religious life-view. The fundamental separation in this analysis of self-becoming lies between the first two stages, in which Kierkegaard opposes the aesthete, who fails to become a self, to the ethicist, who does take up the task of self-becoming.

The crucial difference between these two stages lies in the use of irony. For Kierkegaard, irony is not just a verbal strategy, an indirect or ambiguous way of expressing oneself, but an *attitude toward existence*. In Kierkegaard's *Concluding Unscientific Postscript* we read: "Irony is an existence-qualification, and thus nothing is more ludicrous than regarding it as a style of speaking or an author's counting himself lucky to express himself ironically once in a while" (1: 503–4). According to Kierkegaard, irony initially fulfills an important role in the existence of the individual: "just as philosophy begins with doubt, so also a life that may be called human begins with irony" (*Concept of Irony* 6). Through irony, the individual frees himself from what Kierkegaard calls "immediacy," from what is "given"— the individual's upbringing, social background, culture, that is, his facticity. Kierkegaard values irony's initial, liberating potential. Through irony the individual obtains a negative freedom, a freedom-from. As such, irony constitutes an indispensable step toward freely choosing a personal interpretation of one's moral life, a positive freedom, or, a freedom-to.

However, irony cannot be the source of that "positivity," because it is pure negation. "In irony," Kierkegaard writes, "the subject is continually retreating, talking every phenomenon out of its reality in order to save itself— that is, in order to preserve itself in negative independence of everything" (*Concept of Irony* 257). Hence, irony, in its liberating potential, should be employed only temporarily. In his essay "E Unibus Pluram," Wallace, too, acknowledges that irony can initially be a valuable means of freeing oneself from what has become the standard, immediate way of seeing things that does not hold true anymore. But Wallace also notes, quoting Lewis Hyde, that "[i]rony has only emergency use. Carried over time, it is the voice of the trapped who have come to enjoy their cage." Wallace goes on to argue that irony "serves an almost exclusively negative function. It's critical and destructive, a ground-clearing. Surely this is the way our postmodern fathers saw it. But irony's singularly unuseful when it comes to constructing anything to replace the hypocrisies it debunks" (*SFT* 67).

Kierkegaard and Wallace agree that irony can initially have a liberating effect. However, Kierkegaard recognizes the danger of the ironist getting wrapped up in his ironic freedom, and turning irony into a permanent attitude. This is the defining characteristic of the aesthetic life-view. For Kierkegaard, the aesthete uses an endless "total negative irony"[6] to avoid all commitment, all responsibility, and to retain his negative freedom. It is to this aesthetic attitude of total negative irony that Kierkegaard is strongly opposed. Wallace's irony critique targets the same form of irony: an automated, total irony that is no longer a means to overthrow hypocritical, unquestioned truths, but rather an instrument of cynicism, that makes it incredibly difficult for individuals to realize a meaningful life.[7] The contemporary Western individual, confronted with endless possible ways of shaping his life and therefore with the feeling that he has to shape it into exactly what he wants it to be, can easily come to resemble Kierkegaard's aesthete, wanting to retain his freedom and bring his life into accord with his fantasy (cf. Dewey 191–2).[8] According to Wallace, this contemporary ironic attitude has become "poisonous," functioning as a "mechanism for avoiding some really thorny issues," resulting in "the contemporary mood of jaded weltschmerz, self-mocking materialism, blank indifference" and, as such, is the cause of "great despair and stasis in U.S. culture" (*CW* 46; Wiley; *SFT* 63, 49).

In the ironic-aesthetic life-view, all reality is "suspended," because the real is just an unnecessary limitation to the endless possibilities of the aesthete's own thinking, to the *ideality* that he can shape in his own mind. And as all distinctions and criteria have become invalid for the aesthete, the only arbiter that remains for him is pleasure. The aesthete wants to "aestheticize" his life, to make it exactly as it should be according to his own fantasy and desire; to this everything is secondary. The aesthete accepts no limitations, everything should be possible. In the end, the aesthetic life-view leads to despair. By neglecting reality, by not realizing a new, freely chosen relation to that reality, the self is also neglected. Worse, it is completely emptied out. And as we read in Kierkegaard's *Repetition*: "such a mistake is and remains a person's downfall" (137).

The resemblance between Kierkegaard's aesthete and the addicts portrayed in *Infinite Jest* is clear (cf. Boswell 138). In the novel, the aesthetic ironizing of values and actions leads to the point where for most of these addicts "the cliché 'I don't know who I am' unfortunately turns out to be more than a cliché" (204). The result of the addict's aesthetic attitude is the feeling of emptiness and despair that *Infinite Jest* describes as "anhedonia" or depression (a term that Kierkegaard uses as well): "a kind of emotional novocaine," "a hollowing out of stuff that used to have affective content" (692–3). To give an example, from the perspective of Hal Incandenza:

> It's of some interest that the lively arts of the millennial U.S.A. treat anhedonia and internal emptiness as hip and cool. . . . We are shown how to fashion masks of ennui and jaded irony at a young age . . . And then it's stuck there, the weary cynicism that saves us from gooey sentiment and unsophisticated naïveté. (693–4)

In *The Pale King* we can recognize the aesthetic life-view and its consequences in Chris Fogle's descriptions of his old life as a "wastoid," and when he considers "that I might be a real nihilist, that it wasn't always just a hip pose. That I drifted and quit because nothing meant anything, no one choice was really better" (223).

But perhaps the most striking instance of the aesthetic life in *The Pale King* is the case of the "tortured father" (405), because it contains such salient similarities to the so-called Seducer's Dairy, included in Kierkegaard's work *Either/Or*, vol. 1. The fictive author of this diary, who goes by the name of "Johannes the Seducer," represents the most extreme embodiment of the ironic-aesthetic life-view.[9] Both the father from *The Pale*

King and Kierkegaard's Johannes are "serial seducers": they constantly long for new women. The father has an aesthetic disgust with obligation and routine (he is described as becoming "nauseous," a typically existentialist term),[10] yet at the same time wants to retain all possibilities (all the women he started seeing) (405–7). Although the father is motivated by physical sexual desire, while Johannes seeks a mental gratification—he enjoys his own manipulation of each girl, stirring up her love to greater and greater heights—, both their lives are caught in a terrible frenzy without end. About Johannes we read: "he soon perceives that it is a circle from which he cannot find an exit" (*Either/Or* 1: 308). And, in the case of the father:

> Thus began the father's true cycle of torture, in which the number of women with whom he was secretly involved and to whom he had sexual obligations steadily expanded, and in which not one of the women could be let go or given cause to detach and break it off, even as each became less and less a source of anything more than a sort of dutiful tedium of energy and time and the will to forge on in the face of despair. (405–6)

The tragic fate of the aesthete raises the question: how can the individual liberate himself from the ironic-aesthetic attitude and realize a meaningful life? Kierkegaard's answer is deceptively simple: by choosing. In *Either/Or*, the ethicist affirms that "the ethical constitutes the choice" and that this choice is "the main concern in life, you can win yourself, gain yourself" (2: 169, 163). The aesthetic life is characterized by not-choosing; the aesthete wants to retain his negative freedom. To overcome the empty despair in which this life-view runs aground, the negative freedom established through irony should be followed, as mentioned above, by taking up the responsibility to give shape and meaning to one's life, thereby realizing a positive freedom. This is the choice that, for Kierkegaard, characterizes the ethical life-view.

Wallace states something very similar in an article on Dostoevsky, another cornerstone of existentialism (Marino xv): "Dostoevsky wrote fiction about the stuff that's really important. . . . His concern was always what it is to be a human being—that is, how to be an actual *person*, someone whose life is informed by values and principles" (*CL* 265). In an interview, Wallace adds that "some of the sadness" that seems to "[infuse] the culture right now has to do with this loss of a sense of purpose or organizing principles" that, according to Wallace, are needed to be an actual person (interview with Michael Silverblatt).

In *Infinite Jest*, the characters Remy Marathe and Hugh Steeply explicitly discuss—in terms very similar to Kierkegaard's—the importance of choice in self-becoming and in overcoming the emptiness of contemporary, aesthetic life. Marathe says that Americans talk about freedom without fully understanding what it implies:

> Your freedom is the freedom-*from*: no one tells your precious individual U.S.A. selves what they must do. It is this meaning only, this freedom from constraint and forced duress. . . . But what of the freedom-*to*? . . . How for the person to freely choose? . . . How is there freedom to choose if one does not learn how to choose? (320)

In *The Pale King*, the elevator discussion between several IRS employees similarly expresses the neglected bond between freedom and choice, between rights and responsibilities: "Americans are in a way crazy. We infantilize ourselves. We don't think of ourselves as citizens—parts of something larger to which we have profound responsibilities. We think of ourselves as citizens when it comes to our rights and privileges, but not our responsibilities" (130).

Choice is always an action in which the individual connects to reality, to the world. Choice always means taking responsibility for a certain commitment to the world. And it is through that choice, through that connection to reality, in consciousness transcending itself toward the world, that the self emerges.

This also implies that choice means paying attention; it means attending to something in the world. It is important to see the enormous difference between this "ethical" ability to pay attention and the aesthete's constant self-reflective absorption (as Chris Fogle remarks in *The Pale King*: "awareness is different from thinking") (190). The problem with the latter—and why it cannot possibly be called "attending to something"—is that it has no object, except for itself; the self-reflecting aesthete is solely interested in his own reflexive processes, absorbed by the endless associations produced by the ideality of his own mind. However, the aesthete ends up lost in his own "hyperreflexivity," or "*Analysis-Paralysis*" as it is called in *Infinite Jest* (203). We can recognize this dynamic in Hal Incandenza, whose self-reflection "gets too abstract and twined up to lead to anything"; it just leads to getting "lost in a paralytic thought-helix" (54, 335). We also see it in the second chapter of *Infinite Jest* where Ken Erdedy's thoughts, about whether or not to call his marijuana supplier, send his mind into a frenzied overdrive (26–7). In *The Pale King*, this "oblivion of indecision"—as Gregory Carlisle aptly labels it—is expressed in Lane Dean Jr's description of his "real vision of hell": "It was of two great and terrible armies within himself, . . . opposed and uncomprehending, for all human time. Two hearted, a hypocrite to yourself either way" (41). Another *The Pale King* character, Claude Sylvanshine, experiences a similar "paralysis," when considering the logistics of getting to his new place of work and apartment:

> the whole thing presented such a cyclone of logistical problems and complexities that Sylvanshine was forced to do some Thought Stopping . . . trying to merge his own awareness with the panoramic vista, . . . an oceanic impression so literally obliterating that Sylvanshine was cast or propelled back in on himself and felt again the edge of the shadow of the wing of Total Terror and Disqualification pass over him. (24)

In contrast to hyperreflexivity, paying attention means that consciousness is completely "in" the world, unaware of itself, fully attending to the object of attention. In *The Pale King*, Shane Drinion's ability to pay full attention and dispel self-consciousness is accompanied by levitation: "Drinion is actually levitating slightly, which is what happens when he is completely immersed; . . . Drinion himself [is] unaware of the levitating thing by definition, since it is only when his attention is completely on something else that the levitation happens" (485).

So, choosing to pay attention forms the transition to the ethical life-view. But how does this transition take place? In both Kierkegaard and Wallace's *Infinite Jest* and *The Pale King* the realization of the importance of attention is crucial. This realization in itself, when it is the full recognition of the failure of the aesthetic life-view and the necessity of ethical choice, is already the first choice, the first action, through which the individual leaves the aesthetic attitude behind. The ethicist B in Kierkegaard's *Either/Or* calls out to the aesthete A: "What, then, is there to do? I have only one answer: Despair, . . . not as a state in which you are to remain, but as an act that takes all the power and earnestness and concentration of the soul. . . . [A] person must truly will it; but when he truly wills it, he is truly beyond despair" (2: 208, 213). Despair means recognizing the need for change, and that means changing despair from a situation to a self-chosen action. With that choice the individual leaves despair behind.

In *The Pale King*, this insight seems to be the essence of the "visions" that both Chris Fogle and Lane Dean Jr experience. In the novel, both men experience a moment of insight into what they should do with their lives. While accidentally attending an Advanced Tax class, Fogle experiences his "calling" to join the IRS. He realizes:

> It had something to do with paying attention and the ability to choose what I paid attention to, and to be aware of that choice, the fact that it's

a choice. . . . If I wanted to matter—even just to myself—I would have
to be less free, by deciding to choose in some kind of definite way. Even
if it was nothing more than an act of will. (187, 223–4)[11]

The Pale King describes the run-up to exactly such an act of will on the
part of Lane Dean Jr, when he and his girlfriend Sheri have to decide what
to do with their unplanned pregnancy. Lane realizes that "[h]e was not a
hypocrite. . . . What if he is just afraid, if the truth is no more than this,
and if what to pray for is not even love but simple courage, to meet both
her eyes as she says it and trust his heart?" (42–3). This choice changes
everything: "for had he once said it, avowed that he did love her, loved
Sheri Fisher, then it would have all been transformed" (40). Kierkegaard
describes such moments as moments of "redemption," as the decisive choice
through which "*nothing new is added to the old, but the old has become new*"
(Eriksen 7–9).

Another way of saying that choice always implies attention, is that choice
always implies the present. Attending to something is an action "in" the
world. As already mentioned, the aesthete neglects the relation to reality
and, instead, is absorbed by the ideality of his thoughts; therefore, the
aesthete does not really have a present either. There is no moment in which
he connects to reality and his self becomes real. Choosing, on the other
hand, is always part of the present.

In *Infinite Jest*, the importance of choice, the present and the transition
to the ethical life-view comes to the fore in the description of Don Gately
"kicking" his addiction:

> [Gately] remembered Kicking the Bird for weeks on the floor of a
> Revere Holding cell. . . . He had to build a wall around each second just
> to make it. . . . A breath and a second, the pause and gather between
> each cramp. An endless Now stretching its gull-wings out on either side
> of his heartbeat. And he'd never before or since felt so excruciatingly
> alive. Living in the Present between pulses. (859–60)

The choice, the action, the ethical connection with the world in the
Kierkegaardian sense is something that repeats itself with each new present,
and is something that *has* to be repeated by the individual, if it is still to
qualify as a choice.

Boredom, anxiety, and meaningful life

This brings us to the subject of boredom, since repetition and prolonged attention entail the possibility of "getting bored." *The Pale King* suggests that enduring boredom leads to meaning and happiness, but hardly explicates how this works. This might be an instance of Wallace's well-known narrative strategy of "exformation"—not giving all the information needed to make sense of something and leaving it up to the reader to think about how this might work. This activity, attending to the "boring" subject of boredom (with the risk of becoming bored), might in itself be regarded as an example of boredom leading to meaning, or embodying a meaningful pursuit (paying attention to something difficult, not instantly gratifying).

First of all: what is boredom? Kierkegaard categorizes boredom as a mood (*Concept of Irony* 284–5). Lars Svendsen explains the difference between moods and emotions as follows: "Broadly speaking, we can say that an emotion normally has an intentional object, while a mood is objectless. Moods have more to do with the totality of all objects, i.e., the world as a whole" (110). To this "lack [of] determinate objects," William McDonald adds that moods are "states of mind which condition the individual's whole orientation to existence" (63).

What characterizes this mood of boredom? In *The Concept of Irony*, Kierkegaard calls boredom an "eternity devoid of content" (285). In *Either/Or*, the aesthete describes boredom as follows: "Boredom rests upon the nothing that interlaces existence; its dizziness is infinite, like that which comes from looking down into a bottomless abyss" (1: 291). This dizzying abyss is the confrontation with the endless possibility that is existence (Bigelow 258). In boredom, the individual experiences the implication of the transcendence, the freedom of his existence, namely: that there is no automatic, intrinsic meaning. In boredom, the world is *emptied* of meaning.

This absence of meaning connects boredom to anxiety, Kierkegaard's famous term for the individual's confrontation with nothingness. Kierkegaard distinguishes anxiety from fear, in that the latter is always directed at something specific, a (supposedly) concrete object, "while anxiety does not have a specific object—or, rather: the object of anxiety is nothing" (Grøn 5). When the individual is gripped by anxiety, he is placed in relation to himself. In anxiety, the individual experiences that he is not automatically a self but has to *become* one, precisely because a human being is not a thing, but a relation to himself, who can therefore determine himself through choice (Grøn 12).[12]

In an interview, Wallace again formulates a very similar, existentialist view. Even though he uses the term "fear" instead of "anxiety," it is clear that what he is referring to is connected to what Kierkegaard calls anxiety. Wallace says that "the fear is the basic condition, and there are all kinds of reasons for why we're so afraid," but "the job that we're here to do is to learn how to live in a way that we're not terrified all the time. And not in a position of using all kinds of different things, and using *people* to keep that kind of terror at bay" (Lipsky 292). The individual feels anxiety when confronted with existential responsibilities and therefore constantly tries to distract himself, fleeing from existential questions that have to be faced in order for a meaningful life to be attained.

This motif of the "anxious" flight from responsibility plays an important role in Wallace's work. In *Infinite Jest*, for example, Avril Incandenza, explains to her son Mario that "[t]here are, apparently, persons who are deeply afraid of their own emotions. . . . Dolores describes these persons as afraid of obliteration. . . . I am saying that such persons usually have a very fragile sense of themselves as persons. As existing at all." Avril adds: "This interpretation is 'existential,' Mario, which means vague and slightly flaky. But I think it may hold true in certain cases" (765).

In *The Pale King*, Lane Dean Jr experiences the dizzying vertigo of anxiety before committing himself to Sheri and their unborn child: "a terrible kind of blankness had commenced falling through him" (39). The feeling of "dread" experienced by another character, David Cusk, is both brought on by and causes his attacks of enormous "public" sweating (91, 94). Perhaps the notion of anxiety appears most explicitly in the case of Claude Sylvanshine, who, as mentioned above, feels the shadow of "Total Terror" pass over him (24). Part of the solipsistic illusion of the aesthetic life-view is that the individual thinks he is unique in this "anxious" suffering: "What if there was something essentially wrong with Claude Sylvanshine that wasn't wrong with other people? . . . What if he was simply born and destined to live in the shadow of Total Fear and Despair?" (14).

But what is the difference, then, between anxiety and boredom, since both are described as a confrontation with nothingness, with the fact that the individual's relation to the world does not have automatic meaning but is infinite in its possibilities? The difference lies in the fact that in anxiety the individual is firmly gripped by the insight into the endless possibility of his existence: he stares deeply into the abyss, unable to turn away. Boredom, on the other hand, "recoils from this abyss [of possibility], refus[ing] to recognize it" (Bigelow 258). Anxiety refers to a highly agitated state of being, while boredom is exactly the opposite: it is utter apathy. As Patrick Bigelow writes, "It is the despairing insistence that the nothing means nothing, since in the indifference of boredom, nothing matters, not even the nothing" (259–60).

This last remark points to the "double" nature of boredom. Boredom is the flight from the confrontation with nothingness, the attempt to negate the significance of this confrontation. But, in doing so, boredom becomes at the same time a constant, although passive, confirmation of this nothingness. This double nature of boredom is also expressed by the fact we use the term "boredom" to describe both the individual's basic, languid state of apathy, as well as the frenetic attempts that he might undertake, "out of boredom," to distract himself from that boredom.

Perhaps we could say, as the portrayal of contemporary Western life in Wallace's novels also appears to suggest, that in our time anxiety has been absorbed by boredom. Svendsen observes: "Boredom simply seems to be a more contemporary phenomenon than anxiety. We no longer suffer as much from anxiety, but all the more from boredom" (116). Whereas the insight into the groundless existence of man once caused deep, existential anxiety, in our time we have come to regard this insight as an insignificant platitude, a "cliché" that our aesthetic minds find hard to bear. Instead of experiencing anxiety, we regard ourselves as "just" bored, and no longer seem to hear the existential call of the nothingness underlying that boredom.

How is this analysis of boredom connected to the earlier discussion of the aesthetic and ethical life-view? Irony, by liberating the individual from immediacy, opens up the nothing and, thereby, the possible "call" of anxiety, to realize a positive freedom. But the total irony of the aesthete negates this possibility. In doing so, the aesthete ignores his relation to reality, ironizes himself into boredom, from which he tries to distract himself through fantasy and pleasure.

It is important to note that when, in Kierkegaard's *Either/Or*, we read the famous line, "Boredom is the root of all evil," it is the aesthete A who is speaking.[13] For the aesthete, who after all wants to brings his life into accord with ideal fantasy, boredom is the "[evil that] must be held off" at all cost, the worst enemy imaginable (1: 289). This is also what is meant by the passage from *Either/Or* that is quoted in *The Pale King*: "*Strange that boredom, in itself so staid and solid, should have such power to set in motion*" (385).[14] In *Either/Or*, this line comes directly after the aesthete's previous quotation; the passage goes on to read, "The effect that boredom brings about is absolutely magical, but this effect is one not of attraction but of repulsion" (1: 285). What is expressed in these lines is that the aesthete is permanently looking for ways to distract himself (which explains boredom's "power to set in motion"), because he is "repulsed" by even the idea of being bored.

However, again, we can immediately recognize the double nature of boredom. The aesthete's constant striving for distraction from the nothingness of boredom can only lead back to boredom. As Kierkegaard writes, "Boredom is the only continuity the ironist has" (*CI* 285). Karl Verstrynge phrases it as follows: "The aesthete's entire existence seems to be supported and threatened by boredom at the same time. . . . Possibilities may offer a counterweight to boredom, but the wilful aesthetic indecision is at the same time the ground for its infinite emptiness" (296–7; my translation). The aesthete is convinced that his life-view "assures him complete suspension . . . [so that he is] able to play shuttlecock with all existence." But in the end, the aesthete turns out to be bored, empty, and unhappy. The aesthete A says: "my eyes are surfeited and bored with everything, and yet I hunger" (*Either/ Or* 1: 295, 294, 25).

Infinite Jest portrays the same dynamic of seeking distraction from nothingness which leads to even deeper boredom, emptiness, and unhappiness. In the novel, the different addictions of almost all characters symbolize their deep need for distraction from potentially difficult, existential issues. *The Pale King* describes this "dread" of boredom as follows:

> Maybe dullness is associated with psychic pain because something that's dull or opaque fails to provide enough stimulation to distract people from some other, deeper type of pain that is always there, if only in an ambient low-level way, and which most of us spend nearly all our time and energy trying to distract ourselves from feeling, or at least feeling directly or with our full attention. . . . This terror of silence with nothing diverting to do. (85)

What can the ethical dimension of boredom be? The following line from *The Pale King* might point us in the right direction: "*boring* also meant something that drilled in and made a hole" (378). This reference to boredom as "drilling a hole" can be understood in two distinct ways: (1) boredom makes a hole, in the sense that it creates a hole inside of me, emptying me out (this refers to the effect of boredom in the aesthetic life); (2) that drilling, making a hole, has to do with what in other places in *The Pale King* is called "single-point concentration" (293), that is, attending to something and understanding, *penetrating* it. This second interpretation is the starting point of the ethical value of boredom.

Compare *The Pale King*'s formulation of boredom as "single-point concentration" to the description of the importance of attention in Wallace's short story "Brief Interviews with Hideous Men #20." The story tells of a woman who tries to prevent being murdered by a sexual psychopath through "self-forgetful," empathetic attention, by "focus[ing] her way into the sort of profound soul-connection that would make it difficult for the fellow to murder her" (*BI* 252; cf. Boswell 196; Smith 298). We are told to "envision" this focus as an "intense concentration further sharpened and intensified to a single sharp point, to envision a kind of needle of concentrated attention whose extreme thinness and fragility were also, of course, its capacity to penetrate" (*BI* 257). Here, single-point attention has an explicitly ethical dimension: it implies a commitment toward another person.

The Pale King also connects enduring boredom to the ability to pay prolonged attention, to "attend" and thus commit to something outside oneself. The work of the IRS employees who are the main focus of the novel, symbolizes this capacity. Their daily tasks—processing tax forms—are described as extremely tedious, as requiring an incredible capacity to stay focused on one's work, to be able to deal with boredom. They do their job, not because it is pleasurable, but to provide for their families and because in our society someone has to perform that task.

In Kierkegaard's *Either/Or*, the aesthete A gives the following advice: "[n] ever become involved in *marriage*," because "through marriage one falls into a very deadly continuity with custom," and "[n]ever take any *official post*. If one does that, one becomes just a plain John Anyman, a tiny little cog in the machine of the body politic" (1: 296–8). This advice is very understandable from the aesthetic point of view, which aims to bring life into accord with fantasy. It is interesting to note that, in *The Pale King*, Lane Dean Jr, as part of his redemption, does exactly the opposite. Taking responsibility for his existence instead of fleeing from it, Lane marries his pregnant girlfriend and enters into public service, taking on a monotonous job characterized by extreme boredom that he will have to learn to endure. With Kierkegaard in mind, we can say that Lane has to make these choices, if he is to realize a meaningful existence. Only through choice, as a commitment to the outside world and to others, will the individual be able to develop a self.

William McDonald formulates Kierkegaard's ethical evaluation of boredom as follows: "modern individuals are increasingly unaware that they even have the achievement of selfhood as a task. Yet the best hope for awakening awareness of this task lies in the suffering inherent in [boredom]" (63).[15] Enduring boredom means attending to the nothingness that underlies it, to the infinite abyss of possibility. Here, the necessity of ethical choice can announce itself. That is why Kierkegaard sometimes calls the choice a "leap," to express the anxiety with which the individual chooses, jumps into, the ethical life.

We can see similar imagery in *Infinite Jest*'s description of an addict's "Bottom," his absolute low point. The word "Bottom" isn't quite the right term, recovering drug addict Don Gately feels: "it's more like someplace very high and unsupported: you're on the edge of something tall and leaning way out forward . . ." (347). This is "the jumping-off place for just about every AA you meet," the starting point of their recovery (349). The choice to get clean is like a Kierkegaardian leap over a dizzying abyss. Enduring boredom means that the individual resists fleeing—for example through addiction—into ideality, ignoring reality and the self. The substitute lecturer in *The Pale King* uses the same imagery, of boredom related to the anxious leap, in the speech that inspires Chris Fogle to join the IRS, making clear that this leap toward a meaningful life means a *return to reality*: "you will hesitate, you will feel dread and doubt. This will be natural. . . . To begin, in that literally dreadful interval of looking down before the leap outward. . . . Gentleman, welcome to the world of reality" (227–9).

By enduring boredom, we resist fleeing in aesthetic distraction and, instead, *choose* to attend to something. Thereby, we commit ourselves to the world and start to take up our task of self-becoming. In this way boredom leads us back to meaningful, *real* existence.

The Pale King contains the following passage about why we tend to avoid the topic of boredom: "Maybe it's because the subject is, in and of itself, dull . . . [. . .] There may, though, I opine, be more to it . . . as in vastly more, right before us all, hidden by virtue of its size" (85). Compare this to what Kierkegaard writes in *The Concept of Irony*: "Because reflection was continually reflecting about reflection, . . . [p]hilosophy walked around like a man who is wearing his glasses and nevertheless is looking for his glasses"; to which Kierkegaard adds: "he is looking for something right in front of his nose, but he does not look right in front of his nose and therefore never finds it" (272).

This emphasis on the importance of what is right in front of our noses, is a central theme in Wallace's work (cf. *This Is Water*). Like existentialism, it is about the experience of concrete human existence. One of the most valuable things that Wallace's fiction can contribute to our philosophical understanding of the current age is that it points out the real world and urges us to pay attention to it, to commit to it, and thereby, to become ourselves.

Notes

1   An important exception being Marshall Boswell, who has noted the relevance of Kierkegaard's philosophy in relation to Wallace's writing in *Understanding David Foster Wallace* (137–40, 143–4).

2 In my correspondence with him, Wallace himself wrote: "I too believe that most of the problems of what might be called 'the tyranny of irony' in today's West can be explained almost perfectly in terms of Kierkegaard's distinction between the aesthetic and the ethical life" (Letter from David Foster Wallace to Allard den Dulk, dd. 20th of March 2006). Cf. Den Dulk, "Beyond Endless 'Aesthetic' Irony."

3 We can find this view, for example, in the work of Michel Foucault, when he speaks of the passing of "the privileged moment of *individualization*" in "What Is an Author?" (197–8, 210) and of the effacement of the subject as a sovereign self, "like a face drawn in sand at the edge of the sea," the famous last line from *The Order of Things* (422). Compare this latter formulation to the last line from *Infinite Jest*: "And when [Gately] came back to, he was flat on his back on the beach in the freezing sand, and it was raining out of a low sky, and the tide was way out" (981). In the chronology of the story, this marks the start of Don Gately's recovery from addiction, his "return to himself" (instead of his "self" being "washed away," the "tide" is in fact way out).

4 Kierkegaard himself uses the expression: the self as "gift" and "task" (*Concept of Irony* 276, 277; *Either/Or* 2: 275, 279, 197). However, as the significance of "facticity" and "transcendence" will be more evident to readers who are not specialized in Kierkegaard's philosophy, I have chosen to use the latter two terms.

5 Other descriptions of the boy invite comparisons to Hal and Mario Incandenza, from *Infinite Jest*. For example, the boy is described as "prayerful" (Mario is repeatedly described as praying) and "catatonic" (similar to Hal). Also, as a result of his stretching exercises, the "boy's smile, which appeared by now constant," which is said of Hal and Mario as well. These states or qualities are regarded by most characters around Hal and Mario (and also the boy, it seems) as an indication that something is "wrong" with them, while, in my opinion, both can actually be seen as in the process of becoming a self (*TPK* 397–8; *IJ* 590, 3, 314, 875).

6 Term adopted from Scholtens 21 (my translation).

7 For other analyses of Wallace's irony critique, see for example: Den Dulk, "Beyond Endless 'Aesthetic' Irony"; Goerlandt, "'Put the Book Down and Slowly Walk Away': Irony and David Foster Wallace's *Infinite Jest*"; Holland, "'The Art's Heart's Purpose': Braving the Narcissistic Loop of David Foster Wallace's *Infinite Jest*."

8 Take, for example, romantic relationships. The freedom for every individual to choose his or her own partner, on the basis of what a person likes and what makes her happy, is of course a good thing. But it can also take on hedonistic forms, where everything comes to revolve around the continuous satisfaction of that person's needs, around what makes her happy, to which the other simply has to comply. If not, the other person is pushed aside as "no longer useful." In such a relationship the person in question does not really "engage" herself with the other (cf. Giddens 87–91).

9   In his works, Kierkegaard makes regular use of different pseudonyms, fictional narrators and characters, which all embody and articulate certain philosophical positions.

10   Cf. Sartre, *Nausea*.

11   It is interesting to note that Fogle is nicknamed *"Irrelevant* Chris Fogle" (257), and that his IRS Video Interview is a long and winding personal story (§22).

12   Grøn, just like Wallace in *The Pale King*, gives the example of test anxiety: "The question is whether to call it anxiety, because we can say to ourselves 'Don't worry, it is just an exam. Fortunately life goes on.' In order for it to be anxiety, 'the test' we are put to must be more difficult to define or keep ourselves out of. The question becomes who we are. This is where Kierkegaard wants to take us: that the object of anxiety is 'nothing' does not mean anxiety does not involve a situation. On the contrary, in anxiety we relate to our situation, but in anxiety the situation manifests itself as indeterminate. Kierkegaard compares anxiety with dizziness" (6). In *The Pale King* we read about "the theory that America had some vested economic interest in keeping people over-stimulated and unused to silence and single-point concentration [. . .] that the real object of the crippling anxiety in 'test anxiety' might well be a fear of the tests' associated stillness, quiet, and lack of time for distraction" (293 n47); cf. "E Unibus Pluram."

13   For example, Svendsen, in his otherwise compelling *A Philosophy of Boredom*, fails to recognize this when he writes: "I think Kierkegaard exaggerated when he claimed that 'Boredom is the root of all evil'" (16).

14   Wallace uses an older translation of Kierkegaard's text—for a more recent translation, see the edition used throughout this article (1: 285).

15   Cf. Wallace's above-quoted remark that in our age it is a common mistake to think "that a self is something you just *have*" ("Some Remarks on Kafka's Funniness" in *CL* 64).

4

Modeling Community and Narrative in *Infinite Jest* and *The Pale King*

Andrew Warren

But how to make that? How—for a writer today, even a talented writer today—to get up the guts to even try? There are no formulas or guarantees. There are, however, models.

DFW, "Joseph Frank's Dostoyevsky" (CL 274)

He'd been studying for the CPA exam for three and a half years. It was like trying to build a model in a high wind. "The most important component in organizing a structure for effective study is:" something. What killed him were the story problems.

The Pale King (9)

In this essay I explore a number of narrative models as they appear in *The Pale King* and *Infinite Jest*. I look, that is, at places where those novels explicitly or implicitly model how narration works within the discourse of fiction. I limit myself to four: what I call the Contracted Realism Model and the Spontaneous Data Intrusion Model in *Pale King*; and the Jargony Argot Model and the Free Indirect Wraith Model in *Infinite Jest*. The list is by no means exhaustive, but each example points toward a different way of constructing community within a novel, what I argue is a central aesthetic and ethical tension in Wallace's oeuvre. The opening section of each novel ends with an allegory of both reading and narrative: "Read these" (*TPK* 4); "So yo then man what's *your* story?" (*IJ* 17). This modeling of narrative within narrative isn't mere deconstructive play or postmodern recursion, but instead gets at the heart of why Wallace writes fiction at all. Further, it is crucial that there exist several competing, overlapping, and perhaps incompatible models at work in any given novel; this blend of competition and incompletion prompts a continual negotiation among the communities posited or contested in the novels.

Model#1: Contracted realism in *The Pale King*

In a working note included at the end of *Pale King* we find what appears to be one of the novel's crucial organizing principles: "Central Deal: Realism, monotony" (*TPK* 546). And yet: "Drinion is actually levitating slightly, which is what happens when he is completely immersed; it's very slight, and no one can see that his bottom is floating slightly above the seat of his chair" (485). And yet: "The truth is that there are two actual, non-hallucinatory ghosts haunting Post 047's wiggle room" (315). And yet: "he, the infant . . . like any other GM, had cleared its throat in an expectant way in order to get my attention . . . and, gazing at me fiercely, said—yes, said, in a high and *l*-deficient but unmistakable voice—'Well?'" (393). Or: "An obscure but true piece of paranormal trivia: There is such a thing as a *fact psychic*" (118). And finally: "Harriet Candeleria turns a page. Anand Singh turns a page. Ed Shackleford turns a page. Two clocks, two ghosts, one square acre of hidden mirror. Ken Wax turns a page. Jay Landauer feels absently at his face. Every love story is a ghost story. Ryne Hobratschk turns a page. Matt Redgate turns a page . . ." (312, column 2).

Each of these moments challenges *The Pale King's* Central Deal, albeit in different ways. They also offer up models of reading and narration—again, in different ways. Those models, and their *raison d'être,* will be this article's guiding concern, but let's first cite the note more fully: "Central Deal: Realism, monotony. Plot a series of set-ups for stuff happening, but nothing actually happens." In a sense, the explanation for the breaking of the Central Deal is written within it. If nothing is going to happen in *The Pale King*, then there needs to be a series of small readerly compensations: a couple of ghosts; a man levitating; a fact psychic; a talking baby; lyricism.

Realism, which Wallace here equates with a kind of narrative monotony, is both the novel's Central Deal and a Bum Deal, a "set-up." Hence, perhaps, the novel's continually positing alternative models for reading and narrative. They are perks, benefits that a human author can offer a human reader, a negotiation which mirrors the novel's "Big issue . . . human examiners or machines" (545). It also reflects one of Wallace's most persistent, if obviously problematic (see Aubry 117–25), formulations of how literature works: "writing is an act of communication between one human being and another" (*SFT* 144); or, more famously, "fiction is about what it means to be a fucking *human* being" (*CW* 26). Indeed, it's no accident that the term, *human,* recurs no fewer than 20 times in that celebrated interview. What the "real author, the living human holding the pencil" (*TPK* 67) can offer in a fiction like *Pale King* is, in a word, *wiggle room,* "some slack or play in the rules and procedures" (116) of a novel. This contract—the Deal—with the reader, in which the writer tenders a meditation on boredom and attention in exchange for the reader's actual boredom and attention, is therefore asymmetrical from the start, and it is so even if the writer's own boredom exceeds the reader's by a thousandfold.[1] The asymmetry is peculiar for the fact that both the reader and the writer sometimes appear to be giving up more than they are receiving, and this happens because the transaction is necessarily mediated through a vast, seemingly immovable economic and legal apparatus. It's the one discussed in the first "Author Here" section: "right here before us, hidden by virtue of its size" (85). Perhaps another name for the apparatus is "Reality" (or in the Kenyon Speech, "Water"), and any narrative which aims to render the readerly contract transparent must remain attentive to that arbitrating third party.

This is perhaps the most obviously foregrounded model for narration that runs through the novel: The Contracted Realism Model. It's a mode of storytelling that resonates with the novel's overtly political concerns, particularly the rise of the Neo-Liberal myth of the autonomous individual's right to choose: to pay taxes and participate in civic life; to join a particular community, such as a church or the IRS; to purchase or read a novel. Realism per se is perennially difficult to pin down, but in its classical form we might say that it is a mode of representation particularly attendant to the causes and minutiae involved in day-to-day human life. But, of course, no actual realist believes that they could ever produce in art an isomorphic correspondence with reality. Reality as such is simply too large and complex to fit within any given representational form. Take the case of "GS-9 fact psychic Claude Sylvanshine" (121), *fact psychic*, an example to which we will return in the Sudden Data Intrusion Model of Narration. He "tastes a Hostess cupcake. Knows where it was made; knows who ran the machine that sprayed a light coating of chocolate frosting on top; knows that person's weight, shoe size, bowling average, American Legion career batting average; he knows the dimensions of the room that person is in right now. Overwhelming" (121). The web of causation involved in any particular human event is simply too vast and tangled to represent in full and a process of selection and arrangement becomes necessary. Literary realism is therefore self-consciously structured by a delimited (and delimiting) set of codes and conventions about which the reader is, or should be, aware.

At its core, Contracted Realism, as I am calling it, aims to faithfully render reality's fine print legible; to, as it were, enlarge it. That task includes not only directing our attention to the vast interdependence of the contemporary United States's modes of production and distribution (its economies, legal codes, social and political values, and so on), but also pointing to the tacit contract between novel and reader. In the history of the novel that self-conscious discussion of the readerly contract is nothing new; with the "Bill of Fare" in *Tom Jones* (1749), for example, Fielding early on recognizes the novel as a genre ensnared in (ostensibly liberal) commercial and contractual discourses (Fielding 31–4). Such recursion in *Pale King* would be, in Mark McGurl's terms, "perfectly routine" (48); that is, simply a depiction of what it means to create and consume art within the context of a system, even if *Pale King* tells us new things about the systems that surround and create us. Contracted Realism is therefore both a mode of constructing communities (between reader and author, reader and other readers, &c) and of rendering the workings of already-present communities explicit (say, AA or the IRS). It is, in other words, a *model*[2] of community, a topic I discuss at much greater length below.

Consider, in this context, the speech that converts Chris Fogle to the IRS:

> To retain care and scrupulosity about each detail from within the teeming wormball of data and rule and exception and contingency which constitutes real-world accounting—this is heroism. . . . Routine, repetition, tedium, monotony, ephemeracy, inconsequence, abstraction, disorder, boredom, angst, ennui—these are the true hero's enemies, and make no mistake, they are fearsome indeed. For they are real. (231)

The emphasis on the "real," "real-world," and "detail" clues us in to the fact that the speech is in a sense allegorical of one of the novel's central goals. At the same time, however, Contracted Realism is keenly aware that "routine, repetition, monotony, ephemeracy, inconsequence" make for a poor story. This tension over classical realism is registered again in §9's collection of authors: "My specific dream was of becoming an immortally great fiction writer, à la Gaddis or Anderson, Balzac or Perec, &c" (73). Bold experimentalism (Perec, Gaddis) is here ballasted by French and American paragons of realism (Balzac, Anderson). And vice versa.

Hence the novel's aforementioned "compensations": the ghosts; the talking infant; the lyricism; the levitation. I do not believe, however, that these literary compensations are the same thing as mere "entertainment," that charged word in Wallace's oeuvre. Rather, they arise from Contracted Realism's alternate goal of faithfully representing the lived experience of human reality. This includes the notes' stated fact that "bliss—a second-by-second joy at the gift of being alive, conscious—lies on the other side of crushing, crushing boredom" (546). Levitation and lyricism are perhaps indirect techniques or analogies for conveying that human "bliss," a way of putting some space between oneself and the earth. Just as *Pale King* every so often attempts to communicate the incommunicable expanse of external reality, it also is tasked with communicating a boundless internal reality, what in "Good Old Neon" is described as "the millions and trillions of thoughts, memories, juxtapositions—even crazy ones like this, you're thinking—that flash through your head and disappear" (*OB* 178). Such apparent incommunicability would seem to limit the intensity or fullness of the communities we can forge at the same time that it ties us to a more inexplicable one—those who are similarly constrained. It's a central tension in Wallace's oeuvre which, I argue, often expresses itself at the level of narrative technique.

Community organizing and model#2: Jargony Argot in *Infinite Jest*

Central to my thinking about Wallace's narrative models has been Hillis Miller's work on the relation between literature and speech acts, particularly as they bear upon how novels seem to form peculiar kinds of communities. In his own thinking Miller draws primarily on Jean-Luc Nancy's *La communauté désoeuvrée* (*The Inoperative Community*, perhaps better translated as *The Unworked Community*), and his case study—a puzzling one—is Henry James's *The Awkward Age* (1902). Miller initially justifies his linking of literature and community via an appeal to J. L. Austin, positing that "the felicity of speech acts depends upon the existence of a viable community" (*On Literature* 84). But what's a speech act? In Miller's succinct phrasing, speech acts are examples of language that *act* rather than *describe*; they are performative rather than constative utterances (*Speech* 2-3). In the context of community speech acts—such as the buying or selling of property, the signing or breaking of contracts, getting married or divorced—are only possible because of more or less agreed upon sets of rules or codes. In Austin that set of codes and rules cannot be defined by any singular individual, but must be created by a community of language speakers. Meaning is therefore rooted in actual social usage, an assumption Wallace explicitly acknowledges in "Authority and American Usage": "But as Wittgenstein's *Philosophical Investigations* proved in the 1950s, words actually have the meanings they do because of certain rules and verification tests that are imposed on us from outside our own subjectivities, viz., by the community in which we have to get along and communicate with other people" (*CL* 87). Put perhaps another way, meaning is derived not so much from a singular as from a democratic authority (see *CL* 122-4);

speech acts work (or don't work) not because *I* say so, but because *they*—the community—say so.

Community, of course, is a necessarily vaguer concept than nation or even state, and yet Miller sharply distinguishes between two, albeit interdependent, notions of it. In the first conceptualization of community, whose origins overlap with those of the Neoliberal Mythos in *Pale King*, individuals are

> pre-existing subjectivities. These subjectivities have bound themselves together with other subjectivities for the common good. Their mode of communication with one another can be called "intersubjectivity." . . . Literature within such a community is the imitation, or reflection, or representation of community. It is the construction of cunningly verisimilar miniature models of community. *Bleak House* allows you to carry the whole of Dickens's London in your pocket. Literature is to be valued for its correspondence to a community already there, for its constative value, not for any performance function it might have in constituting communities. (88)

While a near-future, genre-defying novel like *Infinite Jest* poses some obvious and immediate problems for this view (which Miller is obviously depicting as naïve or uncritical), it's remarkable how much it can explain, albeit incompletely. Although you can't carry *Infinite Jest* (or *Bleak House?*) in your pocket, it does fairly describe *fin de siècle* American life, at least as it is or has been experienced. Many, for instance, take Hal's addiction to solitude as a description of what they themselves are feeling; and I for one can't drive along the Charles in Boston without mentally—or, if someone's in the car, loudly and fearfully—calling it "The Storrow 500."

Of course, these two examples are not merely constative; they are also performative, they accomplish something. Let's take a potentially on-the-mark description of Hal's loneliness, say: "Forget so-called peer pressure. It's more like peer-*hunger*. No? We enter a spiritual puberty where we snap to the fact that the great transcendent horror is loneliness, excluded encagement in the self. Once we've hit this age, we will now give or take anything, wear any mask, to fit, be part-of, not be Alone, we young" (695). This lyric description is formally offset from the paragraphs surrounding it by the inclusive "We . . . we young." Suddenly it is not merely Hal or Kate Gompert who's craving Unalone-ness, but us, and the narrative voice, and—we are compelled to postulate—David Foster Wallace (see, e.g., Wallace's interview with Laura Miller in *CW* 62). It's a sort of "community activism" that, in 1997, Wallace tried with palpable urgency to explain to David Lipsky:

> there's a certain set of magical stuff that fiction can do for us. There's maybe thirteen things, of which who even knows which ones we can talk about. But one of them has to do with the sense of, the sense of capturing, capturing what the world feels like to us, in the sort of way that I think that a reader can tell "Another sensibility like mine exists." Something else feels this way to someone else. So that the reader feels less lonely. (Lipsky 38)

In a deep sense the "We . . . we young" is redundant; the work of fiction always already assumes a performative aspect and even a simple third-person description of the loneliness would, or would hope to, have the same effect. When we hit the seemingly objective "one of the really American things about Hal, probably, is the way he despises what it is he's really lonely for" several sentences later we are meant to be drawn in by the same logic as the "we." One part of being not just "American," but "human" as Wallace uses the word, is being susceptible to being drawn in to such communities.

Such failed or felicitous attempts at community building are rife in Wallace's fiction. In *The Pale King* consider, for example, Lane Dean Jr's inability to make small talk during his 15-minute break at the IRS (126); or the description of the character David Wallace in high school not being "part of any one particular clique but [hanging] out on the fringes of several different groups" (337); or the second of the novel's "2 Broad arcs": "Being individual vs. being part of larger things—paying taxes, being 'lone gun' in IRS vs. team player" (545). This recursive back-and-forth between *The Pale King*'s explicit thematic (individual vs larger collective) and its self-conscious narrative forms is more than metafictional "titty-pinching." Rather, it's a consequence of a larger trend in Wallace's work that assumes that communities are built and dismantled by shared language. Similarly, it's far from random that in *Infinite Jest*'s most extended description of loneliness and isolation Wallace models his narrative form—"We . . . we young"—on his content.

All of this is fairly close to how Miller describes the second conceptualization of community: *la communauté désoeuvrée*. Recall that the more typical model of community is one composed of an aggregate of preexisting subjectivities who have freely chosen to unite. In the second formulation—the "unworked" community—there are not pre-given subjectivities, but what Nancy calls *singularities*. As Miller puts it: "In place of individuals with self-enclosed subjectivities, Nancy puts singularities that are aboriginally *partagés*, shared, sheared, open to an abyssal outside. Singularities are extroverted, exposed to other singularities at the limit point where everything vanishes. Language in such a community becomes literature, writing, not sacred myth. Literature is the expression of the unworking of community" (Miller, *Literature* 93). This connection or sharing among the singularities is aboriginal; it happens to them "from the beginning, by way of their shared mortality" (91). This second kind of community is therefore parasitic upon the first. It is in this sense that it is an "unworked" one; or rather, it is continually engaged in "unworking" the first kind of community, reminding the individuals within that community of their mortal limits at the same time that it works to bind them together through that shared mortality.

While we are on the topic of mortality, it's perhaps fair to return to The Storrow 500, which is nothing if not a reminder of mortal limits; indeed, it is a brief example of what I'm calling the Jargony Argot Model of Narration. For the characters in the novel, "The Storrow 500" is not merely descriptive of a harrowing thoroughfare; put in circulation, the phrase also works to unite them. An endnote explains that it is "local argot for Storrow Drive, which runs along the Charles from the Back Bay out to Alewife, with multiple lanes and Escherian signs and On- and Off-ramps within car-lengths of each other and no speed limit and sudden forks and the overall driving experience so forehead-drenching it's in the metro Police Union's contract they don't have to go anywhere near it" (*IJ* 1034 n202). It is both a threat to one's life and something that signals the more general breakdown of community that is, in a sense, the novel's central theme. People speeding along in their cars, typically alone, outside the rule of law, risking their lives to maintain social or personal obligations: to get home or to work on time; to keep up with the rest of the traffic; or, in Gately's case, to secure some time away from his duties at Ennet House—that is, to cordon off some me-time. Cutting between Boston and Cambridge the highway, as it is described in the novel, is both a temporary danger that individuals are pressed to endure and a persistent low-level threat humming in the novel's background. In a sense "The Storrow 500" names not the highway itself but that fear and circumambient hum.

The Storrow 500—the phrase and the thing itself—is not alone in the novel as a reminder of the limits of mortality and of any given community; two far more prominently featured limits are The Great Concavity / Convexity and the *Infinite Jest* tape itself. Those two cases perhaps represent something like external and internal limits of the general state of emergency at play in Y.D.A.U. Boston: caught between the environmental threat of annular waste on one horizon and of one's own impulse to repetitive pleasure on the other, internal horizon. The communities that form in the novel—such as A.A., or E.T.A., or the A.F.R.—are forced to hover between these two limits of and threats to life.

Interestingly, when we first hear about The Storrow 500 it is described in terms of both a cartridge and a distant horizon. Orin, in his room at BU, is compulsively watching looped video of himself punting footballs when we learn that "a cartridge revolving at a digital diskette's 450 rpm sounds a bit like a distant vacuum cleaner. Late-night car-noises and sirens drifted in through the bars from as far away as the Storrow 500" (298). The Storrow 500 is both distant (to the north, like the Concavity) and close (its sound is juxtaposed with the cartridge in the room, which itself sounds like a distant vacuum). It is also, tellingly, a source of the sirens that press through the window's bars. The sirens, the barred windows, The Storrow 500, the looped video, Orin's budding pathologies all register different pitches of the threat that pervades the novel. In this first instance The Storrow 500 is slipped innocuously into the free indirect discourse, and we have to guess at both the joke and referent; unexplained, it is shuffled into the scene's dull, ominous catalogue. It's not until Gately's weekly errand outing several hundred pages later that we are given a full description of what it is: "Basically the Storrow 500 is an urban express route that runs along the bright-blue Chuck all the way along Cambridge's spine" (478). Oddly enough, the novel redundantly defines the term twice there—once in the body of the text and also in a footnote—despite leaving it unexplained in Orin's narrative.

The reader is thus slowly drawn into the novel's language community. We are first given a clue as to how the term is used, and then a direct explanation of it, and then it is silently put back into use in the novel's dialogue and narrative. It's a tactic employed across many of the novel's "local argots." By the time The Storrow 500 is invoked for the last time the reader has become part of that community:

> Mario's gaze keeps going from Avril to the window behind her . . . right to the north over lots of different lights is the red rotating tip of the WYYY transmitter, its spin's ring of red reflected in the visible Charles River, the Charles tumid with rain and snowmelt, illumined in patches by headlights on Memorial and the Storrow 500, the river unwinding, swollen and humped, its top a mosaic of oil rainbows and dead branches, gulls asleep or brooding, bobbing, head under wing. (768–9)

The lyric pan across the evening comes at the end of the section where Mario asks Avril whether she is sad, a question he has been holding back for a good chunk of the novel. Her answer performs a typically Moms-like maneuver that shifts the burden of emotion back onto her children: "Mario Love-o, are *you* sad? Are you trying to determine whether I've been sensing that you *yourself* are sad? . . . Though of course the sun would leave my sky if I couldn't assume you'd simply come and tell me you were sad" (768–9). The narrative then zooms out to Mario view of the sunless landscape, out across the hill and down to the river illuminated by the headlights from The Storrow 500. Again, the phrase is lumped into a horizontic collection of low-level risk and isolation punctuated by the description of the brooding birds, "head under wing," simultaneously together and alone. Ugly as it is, The Storrow 500 has become available to the novel's lyric register, which so often acts as a transition between scenes. As in Nancy and Miller, the phrase—and mortal limits more generally—"unworks" pre-given communities (such as family) at the same time that it works to bind together other, more fragile communities.

This slipping between narrative registers is what I am calling the Jargony Argot Model of Narrative. Paul Giles has pointed out that one of Wallace's uncanny strengths is his ability to absorb jargons and discourses—say, business-speak or academese—and then demonstrate what sorts of human beings are formed by / within those discourses (Giles 335). Here, I am interested in what happens when Wallace is actively inventing those systems of discourses. Local argot—for example, *the squeak, eating cheese, interface, eliminating one's own map, howling fantods,* or in *Pale King, shoe squeezing, wiggling, titty pinching*—which starts out as a way of modeling community within the novel, becomes a tactic for organizing community outside of the novel. The horizons of the characters' communities and isolation come to be shared first by the novel's narrative voice and then, via a complex movement, by the reader. Put slightly differently, what first appears to be *constative* language eventually turns *performative*. One could trace, for example, a more involved evolution of *the squeak*, which comes to enter just about every register in the novel—from victims hearing *the squeak* of the Wheelchair Assassins, to Steeply's pregnant description of the American dream of a "squeak-free porch swing" (423), to Day's essay on the origins of the term *the squeak*, to the painful sequence in which James O. Incandenza and his father try to locate the source of a bed's squeak (491–503). Although there are, of course, "innocent" *squeaks* in the novel, one could track a similar movement of the term between narrative registers: from constative to performative, from description within the novel to literary technique. In *The Pale King* phrases like *wiggling* or *wiggle room* begin as local IRS argot and later come to signal a complex negotiation between writer and reader; reading and writing themselves become kinds of *wiggling.* Perhaps the greatest example of this movement between registers, however, is the phrase *Infinite Jest* itself. Over the course of the novel it moves from naming a film or set of films to naming the novel itself and the "work" of the novel, its literary task. *Jest*, after all, comes from the Latin, *gerere*, "to do;" the novel becomes a gesture, a perpetual performance.

Model#3: Spontaneous data intrusion in *The Pale King*

It is perhaps now fair to say that Wallace himself, more than anyone else, has structured the critical reception of his work. If Joyce's critics had Eliot's "*Ulysses*, Order and Myth" (1923) and Gilbert's *Ulysses: A Critical Study* (1930), then Wallace's have had, well, Wallace. Or more specifically, we have 1990s "E Unibus Pluram," some editorial work and reviews, and about a hundred hours of interviews aggregated across a few websites. (For the moment we'll leave aside the perhaps more vexed matter of the meta-commentary *within* the fiction, which is the meat in this essay's sandwich.) The nonfiction has provided fairly reliable footholds for those scaling *Infinite Jest* for the first time: "fiction is about what it means to be a fucking *human being*"; "make no mistake: irony tyrannizes us" (*SFT* 67); "I wanted to do something sad" (*CW* 58); *etcetera*.

As a critic—or more like a reader—the problem, as it's beginning to fall out, is that Wallace's commentary doesn't always add up to a coherent picture, either in itself or in relation to the fiction. This is a good thing—a good thing that's weirdly anticipated in a lot of his actual commentary about fiction. Consider, for example, these two seemingly contradictory comparisons of fiction and nonfiction:

1. I do not know why the comparative ease and pleasure of writing nonfiction always confirms my intuition that fiction is really What I'm Supposed to Do, . . . but it does, and now I'm back here flogging away (in all senses of the word) and feeding my own wastebasket. (Max, *Every Love Story* 260)
2. Writing-wise, fiction is scarier, but nonfiction is harder—because nonfiction's based in reality, and today's felt reality is overwhelmingly, circuit-blowingly huge and complex. Whereas fiction comes out of nothing. Actually, so wait: the truth is that both genres are scary; both feel like they're executed on tightropes, over abysses—it's the abysses that are different. Fiction's abyss is silence, nada. Whereas nonfiction's abyss is Total Noise, the seething static of every particular thing and experience, and one's total freedom of infinite choice about what to

choose to attend to and represent and connect, and how, and why, etc. (*BFN* 302)[3]

The obvious contradiction here involves the alleged ease or difficulty of writing fiction and nonfiction. What interests me, however, is what these statements—each made in the middle of composing his post-*Jest* "Larger Thing"—bring to bear on *Pale King*.

Let's take a closer look at the aforementioned definition of a *fact psychic*, keeping in mind Wallace's description of nonfiction's abyss of Total Noise:

> An obscure but true piece of paranormal trivia: There is such a thing as a *fact psychic*. Sometimes in the literature also known as a data mystic, and the syndrome itself as *RFI* (= *Random-Fact Intuition*). These subjects' sudden flashes of insight or awareness are structurally similar to but usually far more tedious and quotidian than the dramatically relevant foreknowledge we normally conceive as ESP or precognition ... They come out of nowhere, are inconvenient and discomfiting like all psychic irruptions. It's just that they're ephemeral, useless, undramatic, distracting. What Cointreau tasted like to someone with a mild head cold on the esplanade of Vienna's state opera house on 2 October 1874 ... The exact (not estimated) height of Mount Erebus, though not what or where Mount Erebus is. (*TPK* 118–19)

And so on. Claude Sylvanshine—a somewhat too obvious play on Claude Shannon, a founder of Information Theory—is afflicted by this disorder: "One reason [his] gaze is always so intent and discomfiting is that he's trying to filter out all sorts of psychically intuited and intrusive facts" (119).

Sylvanshine's curse is an uncanny juxtaposition of fiction's "silence, nada" ("they come out of nowhere"[118]) and nonfiction's awareness of the "seething static of every particular thing and experience." The difference, of course, is that "Claude Sylvanshine can't help it" (120); it is imposed on him from the outside. I would like to propose, however, that in the figure of Sylvanshine we come upon a third model of narration: the Spontaneous Data Intrusion Model. In it we are given a character—and, allegorically, an author or narrative voice—exposed to a pure, threatening Outside without order or meaning. Any fact, any utterance, any connection between characters is possible. §15's narrative voice collects examples of random facts as easily as Sylvanshine himself does, and then does something Sylvanshine cannot: it sorts them into a neatly narrated explication of what it means to be a fact psychic. It is fairly easy to connect the model to Wallace's quips about the difficulty of writing *Pale King*; that, for instance, he'd have to write "a 5,000 page manuscript and then winnow it down by 90%, the very idea of which makes something in me wither and get really interested in my cuticle, or the angle of the light outside" (Max, *Every Love Story* 289). How the model works in the texture of the novel's sentences, however, is far from straightforward.

As with the local argots in *Infinite Jest*, the SDIs first come to us unannounced in *Pale King*, as Sylvanshine is on a plane: "Men who cannot bear to wait or stand still forced to stand still all together and wait, men with calfskin Day-Timers and Franklin Quest Time Management certificates . . . trying to cover the monthly nut, fish thrashing in the nets of their own obligations. Two eventual suicides on this plane, one forever classed as an accident" (18). This last sentence turns out, in light of our eventual knowledge of Sylvanshine's SDI syndrome, to be a tricky piece of narratology. The sentence's closing clause, which contradicts the official record, tips us off to the fact that we are hearing an objective truth, perhaps one obtained via an act of narrative omniscience. We might even fear that one of those suicides is Sylvanshine himself. To the first-time reader the sentence is omniscient third person; to the rereader the sentence is free indirect style—free indirect style whose origins bizarrely mirror a kind of omniscient narration.

But let us think more carefully about a first reading of the chapter, which should appear to move between seemingly omniscient third-person narration and free indirect style. Take, for example:

> The interstate highway below disappeared and then sometimes reappeared at a spot Sylvanshine had to squash his cheek right up against the plastic inner window to see, then as the rain recommenced and he could tell they were beginning descent it reappeared in the window's center, light traffic crawling with a futile pointless pathos you could never sense on the ground. What if it felt this slow to actually drive as it looked from this perspective? It would be like trying to run underwater. The whole ball game was perspective, filtering, the choice of perception's objects. (15)

A first reader would pick up on the fact that the passage is written, more or less, in free indirect style: Sylvanshine thinks the traffic looks futile and pointless; *he* asks the question about traffic feeling slow, and he gives the answer ("it would be like trying to run underwater"); he thinks about what we presume to be Dr Lehrl's advice: "perspective, filtering, the choice of perception's objects." These very human-seeming thoughts are also peculiarly juxtaposed with free indirect data—for example, "Direct material price variance" (15)—that intrudes on the narrative. We know that this seemingly inhuman language is indeed free and indirect because on the plane Sylvanshine is studying to be a CPA. We should note, too, that the SDIs are not wholly "inhuman" pieces of data, but relate to humanly defined concepts, attributes, places; all of the data is, potentially, interesting to someone.[4] Perhaps the most inhuman aspect of the SDIs is simply their bare existence.

A rereader wouldn't have to rethink the above passage in terms of the SDIs, but there are a number of jarring, metafictional maneuvers at play in it. The question about how it feels to drive as slowly as it appears from an airplane, for example, is answered in §24, the second "Author Here" section. "David Wallace" begins with a note that "the next salient feature of that day [of his arrival at the IRS] is that traffic along the city's circumambient Self-Storage Parkway was totally horrible," and then proceeds to spend fourteen pages describing that horror in bureaucratic detail (267–81). In Dr Lehrl's schema it is a matter of perspective, specifically narrative perspective, and the failure to properly filter out irrelevant facts. The chapter should strike one as an exercise in self-parody, though perhaps in a different register from the already discussed "Author's Foreword." It is hard, for example, to imagine §9's David Wallace writing something like "I think you deserve better [reader], and that you're intelligent enough to understand and maybe even applaud when a memoirist has the integrity to admit that he's not some kind of eidetic freak" (257 n3). This note, which comes early in §24 and is followed by an exhaustive description of every inch of Self-Storage Parkway, pushes the episode squarely into parody.[5]

The point about perspective and filtering information in narrative, however, is a serious one. Consider the following introduction to Sylvanshine with that in mind:

> When Sylvanshine studied for the exam now the worst thing was that studying any one thing would set off a storm in his head about all the other things he hadn't studied and felt he was still weak on, making it almost impossible to concentrate, causing him to fall further behind. He'd been studying for the CPA exam for three and a half years. It was like trying to build a model in a high wind. "The most important component in organizing a structure for effective study is:" something. What killed him were the story problems. (9)

Wallace himself famously took high-level accounting courses in the late 1990s; and Michael Pietsch, his longtime editor, has spoken of a car ride where Wallace compared writing *The Pale King* to "trying to carry a sheet of plywood in a windstorm" (Max, "The Unfinished," 58), a sentiment not unlike Sylvanshine's analogy of "build[ing] a model in a high wind."

Anecdotes aside, we are still left with the passage's anxiety over "organizing structure" and "story problems." These are obvious points of concern for someone afflicted by SDIs, and have larger purchase on the way narration is modeled in the novel. Of course, the SDIs aren't the only narrative model in *The Pale King*; but what Sylvanshine's intrusions register is the worry of being alone at work, the horror at "one's total freedom of infinite choice about what to choose to attend to and represent and connect, and how, and why, etc." Fiction's "silence, nada" is quietly replaced by this excess of potential information once a work becomes a work in progress. One becomes alone in a new way.[6]

This excess, again, is Sylvanshine's (and perhaps the novel's) basic problem. Recall, for example, the incommunicable web of causation that "overwhelms" Sylvanshine as he bites into a Hostess cupcake: its origin; the factory worker's weight, bowling average, and so on (121). If the Contracted Realism Model is tasked with sorting through that mass of data—that is, negotiating with the reader so she continues to read—then we might say that the Sudden Data Intrusion Model is continually compelled to run us up against the data mass's implicit infinitude. Contracted Realism continually negotiates the terms of communion / communication / community with the reader; Sudden Data Intrusions interrupt those negotiations. They "unwork" it, in Nancy's terms, by threatening us with what Thomas Nagel would call a "view from nowhere," that is, a view that lacks any particular human perspective.

Tellingly, the SDIs come to Sylvanshine with "constant headaches. The data sometimes visual and queerly backlit, as by an infinitely bright light an infinite distance away" (121). Light rays from such a source would—theoretically—appear as parallel and would therefore not be localizable at any one point (Hecht 161); it would lack, quite literally, a determinate point of view even if Sylvanshine himself naturally has one. The SDIs signal a certain horror implicit in something like third-person omniscient narration or a "God's-eye" point of view. On the plane Sylvanshine is intruded upon by this: "*Yaw* was *way* in a mirror, it occurred for no reason" (14). What's spelled out in this optical play is, of course, *Yahweh* (God), and it does not occur "for no reason." It heralds or holds out hope for something like an organizing, negotiating principle at work behind the text.

Model#4: The Free Indirect Wraith in *Infinite Jest*

Perhaps a pre-cursor to the Spontaneous Data Intrusion Model, both for its emphasis on perspective and its sudden intrusions of language, is what I'm calling the Free Indirect Wraith model. I draw the idea from the extended scene in *Infinite Jest* (827–45) involving Don Gately and James Incandenza's wraith, who introduces his predicament thus:

> The wraith could empathize totally, it said. The wraith said Even a garden-variety wraith could move at the speed of quanta and be anywhere anytime and hear in symphonic toto the thoughts of animate men, but it couldn't ordinarily affect anybody or anything solid, and it could never speak right to anybody, a wraith had no out-loud voice of its own, and had to use somebody's like internal brain-voice if it wanted to try to communicate something, which was why thoughts and insights that were coming from some wraith always just sound like your own thoughts, from inside your own head, if a wraith's trying to interface with you. The wraith says By way of illustration consider phenomena like intuition or inspiration or hunches, or when someone for instance says "a little voice inside" was telling them such-and-such on an intuitive basis. (831)

Hence the wraith's choice of Gately, currently in the hospital after being shot in the shoulder: like the levitating and hyper-focused Drinion, Gately currently has the time to hear the wraith out.

The wraith, further, knows the community-building power of empathy, a technique both he (i.e. James Incandenza) and Gately learned in AA: "Boston AA, with its emphasis on the Group, is intensely social" (362). Its meetings, particularly "The White Flaggers," are rooted in a regular sharing of bottoming-out stories and shared performative language not unlike that described in the Jargony Argot Model. So, for example, "Empathy, in Boston AA, is called Identification" (345); and, "Only in Boston AA can you hear a fifty-year-old immigrant wax lyrical about his first solid bowel movement in adult life" (351). When you hear that story you Identify with the speaker and, as a community, you also Identify the more pervasive and general threat under which you live: addiction, mortality. The paragraphs in those episodes alternate between relating the speakers' verbatim testimony and Gately's own free-indirect reception of those stories. The narrative voice weaves the speaker's words, Gately's thoughts and the more general mood of the Group into a kind of choral refrain, a call and response.

In the episode with Gately and the wraith it is sometimes difficult to untangle Gately's thoughts from either the narrative voice and the wraith's linguistic intrusions. This is typical of how free indirect style works. Take, for instance, Hugh Kenner's rightly celebrated example of the so-called Uncle Charles Principle, from Joyce's "The Dead": "Lily, the caretaker's daughter, was literally run off her feet" (Kenner, *Joyce's* 15). As Kenner points out, in that context the word "literally" must come from Lily's vocabulary because, used in that way, it doesn't make grammatical sense. The narrative dips into her consciousness and standing reservoir of language and draws out "literally." But where the narrative voice ends and Lily's begins, or vice versa, is impossible to tell: we might guess that the explanatory "caretaker's daughter" belongs solely to the third-person omniscient voice, but what about "run off her feet"? The difficulty here is similar to that of sorting out the wraith's voice from one's own, since a wraith has to "use somebody's like internal brain-voice if it wanted to try to communicate something." The "like," here, is of course Gately's own version of Lily's "literally"—but the rest? This blending or entangling of voice is, perhaps, one of those 13 magical things Wallace thinks fiction can do.

There are, nevertheless, a few clear instances where we can quantifiably track the wraith's intrusions into Gately's mind and the text. In the starkest instance we hear that the wraith "holds one knee to its sunken chest and starts doing what Gately would know were pirouettes if he'd ever once been exposed to ballet, pirouetting faster and faster" (832). At this point the word *pirouette* appears to belong to the narrative voice, an intuition reinforced when almost immediately: "into Gately's personal mind, in Gately's own brain-voice but with roaring and unwilled force, comes the term PIROUETTE, in caps, which term Gately knows for a fact he doesn't have any idea what it means and no reason to be thinking it with roaring force, so the sensation is not only creepy but somehow violating, a sort of lexical rape" (832). "Lexical rape," of course, is no more in Gately's wordbank than "pirouette," but the basic idea of it is raised in high school classes across the country every day: characters wouldn't talk like that; that's just the author talking. In a writer like Jane Austen, where there is clear narrative framing and a relative uniformity in spoken language, we can explain—to the students' satisfaction or not—why that is so. In a work like *Infinite Jest*, where we so often have to rely on the vagaries of voice simply to identify who is saying or doing what, the matter is obviously more urgent. The scene with the wraith is, indeed, something of an interrogation of the ethics involved in narrating a character's—or, more strongly, someone else's—experience.[7]

After PIROUETTE, the rate of lexical intrusion dramatically accelerates as the wraith begins communicating at something closer to his natural pace (which seems to be roughly a few thousand times faster than regular, human time):

> Other terms and words Gately knows he doesn't know from a divot in the
> sod now come crashing through his head with the same ghastly intrusive

force, e.g. ACCIAC-CATURA and ALEMBIC, LATRODECTUS MACTANS and NEUTRAL DENSITY POINT, CHIAROSCURO and PROPRIOCEPTION and TESTUDO and ANNULATE and BRICOLAGE and CATALEPT and GERRYMANDER and SCOPOPHILIA and LAERTES — and all of a sudden it occurs to Gately the aforethought EXTRUDING, STRIGIL and LEXICAL themselves— and LORDOSIS and IMPOST and SINISTRAL and MENISCUS and CHRONAXY and POOR YORICK and LUCULUS and CERISE MONTCLAIR and then DE SICA NEO-REAL CRANE DOLLY and CIRCUMAMBIENTFOUNDDRAMALEVIRAT- EMARRIAGE and then more lexical terms and words speeding up to chipmunkish and then HELIATED and then all the way up to a sound like a mosquito on speed, and Gately tries to clutch both his temples with one hand and scream, but nothing comes out. (832)

The terms are, of course, straight from James Incandenza's private stash. But it also turns out that the wraith had been inhabiting and translating Gately's brain-voice even before the intrusion of the terms "in caps": "the aforethought EXTRUDING, STRIGIL and LEXICAL themselves" had slipped in unannounced, in lower case. And so—in this episode, maybe even the novel more generally—we are left with the following puzzle: what exactly is the relationship between Gately's thoughts, the wraith's communiqués, and the printed word? The problem of capitalization extends beyond the words in all caps to instances like: "The wraith says Just to give Gately an idea, he, the wraith, in order to appear as visible and interface with him, Gately, he, the wraith, has been sitting, still as a root, in the chair by Gately's bedside for the wraith-equivalent of three weeks, which Gately can't even imagine" (836). The marked break between "The wraith says" and what the wraith reportedly says is supremely puzzling, due in part to the almost parodic play of pronouns. In some sense the clarifications denote the blurring of identity between Gately and the wraith, and yet we are still left wondering what exactly the wraith "says" to / through Gately.

Deeper into the conversation we at least learn *why* the wraith is interfacing with Gately at all: to communicate, in some way and at some time, perhaps indirectly, with Hal. The wraith, for example, relates that "he [the wraith] spent the whole sober last ninety days of his animate life working tirelessly to contrive a medium via which he and the muted son could simply converse . . . A way to say I AM SO VERY, VERY SORRY and have it *heard*" (838–9). That medium is undeniably *Infinite Jest* (the cartridge), a sustained—if vexed—allegory for *Infinite Jest* (the novel). The problem, however, is that if the wraith's fear is not being heard by a mute interlocutor whom he loves, Hal nevertheless ends up utterly unable to communicate with anyone (save, not unproblematically, for those reading his story).[8] So the question stands: to what degree do Hal and James communicate in the novel? Perhaps no straight answer can be given, but a place to begin looking is with James's peculiarly worded plan. "To contrive a medium" should be understood in two ways: 1) as both inventing a form (such as a filming technique, or a kind of novel) to effect a plan; 2) and also of finding or waking or disturbing or stirring up (Latin, *turbare*) someone who could communicate for you (as in the occult sense of *medium*). Gately—who is found / disturbed / woken up by the wraith and eventually meets "the muted son," as we know from Hal's initial monologue (17)— becomes a medium in this second sense.

After the original encounter with the wraith we come across a fairly odd scene involving Don Gately admiring an attractive nurse: "And then when she reaches way up to unscrew a bolt in some kind of steelish plate on the wall over the empty bed the like hemline of her uniform retreats up north so that the white stockings' rich violinish curves at the top of the insides of her legs in the white LISLE are visible in backlit silhouette, and an EMBRASURE of sad windowlight shines through her legs" (919). Given the narrative and typological technique from the first encounter, LISLE (a kind of lacy fabric) and EMBRASURE (a beveled window, as in a castle) are straight from the wraith. On the next page we get the free indirect statement that, w/r/t the nurse and MD's relationship, "It'd be CIRCUMAMBIENT sexual tension, would be the ghostword" (920). *Would* it be the ghostword, or *is* it the ghostword? That is, is Gately recalling it or is the wraith slipping it into his brain-voice? A perhaps more unsettling observation involves Gately's careful attention to light throughout the scene, as though he were absorbing not merely the wraith's vocabularies but also his sensibilities; Incandenza had been, after all, an optical physicist and filmmaker. Indeed, the word LISLE points to an uncanny scatter of likely referents: the nurse's skirt; Lyle, Himself's friend who apparently possesses wraith-like abilities (933); and also L'Islet Province, where Hal, Gately, and John Wayne presumably dig up Himself's interred head (17, 907). The wraith, the mover of furniture, at times comes to blend with what Hugh Kenner has dubbed the Arranger, an inhuman voice which allows "details . . . to find their way on to the page without regard for the consciousness of anyone present." The Arranger would, like Hal, test at "Whatever's Beyond Eidetic": it "enjoys a seemingly total recall for exact forms of words used hundreds of pages earlier, a recall which implies not an operation of memory but an access such as ours to a printed book, in which pages can be turned to and fro" (Kenner, *Ulysses* 64–5).

Somewhere beyond the right frame

What does the Free Indirect Wraith Model bring to bear on the relationship between narrative and community that this essay has been drawing out? An answer might be found in the wraith's description of one of his reasons for making films: to depict "real life's real egalitarian babble of figurantless crowds, of the animate world's real agora, the babble of crowds every member of which was the central and articulate protagonist of his own entertainment" (835-6). This "radical realism" (836), as Tom LeClair has argued, is obviously allegorical for the novel's own project of giving voice to "figurants"—background characters—who would otherwise merely be attendant upon the protagonists' foreground (LeClair 36). It's an attempt to reorganize politics through formal technique and its ultimate source of tension is what Alex Woloch has called *the character-system*: "how the discrete representation of any specific individual is intertwined with the narrative's continual apportioning of attention to different characters who jostle for limited space within the same fictional universe" (Woloch 13). I do not think, however, that Incandenza (or, by analogy, Wallace) wants to obliterate that tension: the intertwining of characters' lives, their jostling for position in *character-space*. It is, in fact, what Himself's camera records: "the unfiltered babble of the peripheral crowd" (836) and, of equal importance, the viewer's struggle to arrange it into a narrative whole. Returning to the novel, we might say that its characters therefore struggle not merely against one another but, more generally, against its narrative structure even as that structure struggles to encompass them. A charged example might involve the—violent and perhaps overwrought—convergence of minor characters (Poor Tony, Ruth van Cleve, Kate Gompert, Lenz, Matty Pemulis, &c) that prefigures and models the unrecorded convergence of Hal and Gately. It is, in short, a model of narration that perpetually works to create and undo community. In Nancy's words, the "practice of sharing voices and of an articulation according to which there is no singularity but that exposed in common, and no community but that offered to the limit of singularities ... community, in its infinite resistance to everything that would bring it to completion" (Nancy 80-1).

Wallace's narrative models—Contracted Realism, Jargony Argot, SDIs, the Free Indirect Wraith—should also stand in perpetual tension with one another, and with other possible models. Alone, overlapping, or in concert they can never "complete" *Infinite Jest* or *Pale King*. It would be similarly naïve to explain the models' existence via a simple appeal to the harmonizing virtues of "community." The communities in Wallace's fictions are not all good, and nearly every one of them exists only in relation to the threat of vast, compounded catastrophe: addiction, collapsing ecologies, death, loneliness, unchecked mechanization, eliminating one's own map. *Pale King* and *Infinite Jest* aren't themselves communities; they are gestures to community, and to its limits.

Notes

1 We see this in, say, the first "Author Here" section: "I am reasonably sure that I am the only living American who's actually read all these archives all the way through. I'm not sure I can explain how I did it" (*TPK* 84 n25).

2 Perhaps the closest thing I have in mind to Wallace's narrative modeling is systems theory's emphasis on systems' tendency to model themselves in order to better control their operations; Luhmann calls this modeling "planning," among other things, and notes that "no system can provide itself with a complete self description" (470). Planning or modeling thus introduces even more complexity into a system. Hence, perhaps, the fact that Wallace's novels contain *several* competing and overlapping models of community and narration. A work like *Infinite Jest* is, in turn, itself a model of a much larger "Novel System" or "Art System."

3 Thanks to Adam Kelly for calling my attention to this passage.

4 Sylvanshine does not seem, for example, to intuit data about distant galaxies or microorganisms crawling along the Marianas Trench. The exact height of Mount Erebus, it turns out, might be connected to Sylvanshine on account of the mountain's being the site of a plane crash in 1977.

5 Relatedly, see Wallace's 2005 note to Franzen: "Karen is killing herself rehabbing the house. I sit in the garage with the AC blasting and work very poorly and haltingly and with (some days) great reluctance and ambivalence and pain. I am tired of myself, it seems: tired of my thoughts, associations, syntax, various verbal habits that have gone from discovery to technique to tic. . . . It's a dark time, workwise, and yet a very light and lovely time in all other respects" (Max, *Every Love Story* 281).

6 An analogy might be Derrida's discussion of "the invention of the other." In Hillis Miller's reading, Derrida claims that "a literary work is not the 'invention' in the sense of making up, fabricating, but in the more archaic meaning of finding, coming upon. What the writer invents, in the sense of finding or discovering it, is defined by Derrida as the absolutely 'other'" (*On Literature* 79). The SDI Model is the simultaneous horror at the thought that the invention is *wholly* other or wholly solipsistic.

7 In this context Marshall Boswell correctly reads the wraith as a particular inflection of Wallace's narrative voice (Boswell 170). Toon Staes's chapter in this volume also smartly discusses this section (*PAGES*).

8 Drawing on Nicholas Royle's work, Jonathan Culler has spoken of telepathy as a workable model for explaining narration's uncanniness (196). Perhaps

apropos here is a) the Madame Psychosis / metempsychosis pun that Wallace (perhaps) borrows from *Ulysses*, and b) Wallace's note scrawled on the first page of an early draft of *Infinite Jest*: "DMZ is ultimate phenomenal speed—halluce—believe you have radically sped up, whole world slow, ESP, no speech—Death[.] See Wraith & Gately" (Moore). Madame Psychosis is both Joelle's radio character, and a street name for DMZ. Perhaps a case can be made that a plane of telepathic communication exists in the novel for those who are dead (J.O.I.), on DMZ (the Army convict; Lyle? Hal?), speechlessly white-knuckling (Gately 812? Hal?), "sitting in fully awakened contemplation of one's own death" (Lyle 898?), or watching *Infinite Jest* (Mrs Lopate 818 and 825? Lenz 828 and 845?). Such a plane might be said to eerily transect that of readers reading *Infinite Jest*.

Part Two

The Novels

The Broom of the System (1987)
Westward the Course of Empire Takes Its Way (1989)
Infinite Jest (1996)
The Pale King (2011)

5

"Then Out of the Rubble": David Foster Wallace's Early Fiction

Bradley J. Fest

Our life has no end in just the way in which our visual field has no limits.
Ludwig Wittgenstein, *Tractatus Logico-Philosophicus*

Pursued to the end, an ironic temper can dissolve everything, in an infinite chain of solvents. It is not irony but the desire to understand irony that brings such a chain to a stop.
Paul de Man, "The Concept of Irony"

In the emerging field of David Foster Wallace studies, nothing has been more widely cited in terms of understanding Wallace's literary project than two texts that appeared in the 1993 issue of *The Review of Contemporary Fiction*. "E Unibus Pluram: Television and US Fiction" and a lengthy interview with Larry McCaffery have been significant landmarks for critics of his work in much the same way that T. S. Eliot's "Tradition and the Individual Talent" (1919) or Henry James's "The Art of Fiction" (1884) were for critics of those writers. Following Wallace's argument in "E Unibus Pluram," that the "postmodern irony" of such writers like Thomas Pynchon and Don DeLillo had infected US culture at all levels, and especially the medium of television, much of the conversation regarding his fiction has revolved around irony and his sense of being a latecomer in relation to his postmodern forebears.[1] Criticism approaching his work through the lens of "E Unibus Pluram" has been so prevalent that, one might be permitted to suggest, a "standard" reading of his fiction has emerged. Much of this criticism has been quite impressive, and the recent groundswell of work being done on Wallace since his untimely death in 2008 is in the process of forging new paths for understanding his contribution to American letters.[2] But there has been a notable lack of attention paid to one of Wallace's more important self-critical moments in the interview with McCaffery, specifically when he discusses his early novella, "Westward the Course of Empire Takes

Its Way," that appeared in the collection *Girl with Curious Hair* (1989): "My idea in 'Westward' was to do with metafiction what Moore's poetry or like DeLillo's *Libra* had done with other mediated myths. I wanted to get the Armageddon-explosion, the goal metafiction's always been about, I wanted to get it over with, and then out of the rubble reaffirm the idea of art being a living transaction between humans" (*CW* 41).

In a similar manner to how "Westward" explicitly targets John Barth's much anthologized short story "Lost in the Funhouse" (1968), the target of Wallace's comments to McCaffery were what Barth once called, in his own manifesto-like essay "The Literature of Exhaustion" (1967), the "apocalyptic ambience" surrounding the postmodern novel:

> If enough writers and critics *feel* apocalyptical about [the novel], their feeling becomes a considerable cultural fact, like the *feeling* that Western civilization, or the world, is going to end rather soon. If you took a bunch of people out into the desert and the world didn't end, you'd come home shamefaced, I imagine; but the persistence of an art form doesn't invalidate work created in the comparable apocalyptic ambience. (*The Friday Book* 72)

Referring at once to the persistence of eschatological discourse despite the failure of the prophesied apocalypse ever to arrive (a phenomenon whose historical features Norman Cohn traced in *The Pursuit of the Millennium* [1957]) and the claims about the novel's death, Barth arrives at a stunning insight. If one imagines the disaster often enough, here implicating literature in the work of imagination that brings the disaster about, it becomes a *considerable cultural fact*. Wallace's first novel, *The Broom of the System* (1987), and "Westward" resist the imminence of this considerable cultural fact, attempting to find ways *not* to bring apocalypse, either projectively or literally into the world.

In beginning to define his own literary project, Wallace was explicitly aware that he inhabited the untimely position of a Nietzschean latecomer in relation to literary postmodernism, a position that caused him to read American metafiction of the 1960s–80s as a literature obsessed with its own end. In contrast to someone like, say, DeLillo—who ended *White Noise* (1985) with a group of suburban Americans perched on the edge of a "computerized nuclear pulse," an "ambient roar, in the plain and heartless fact of their decline" (325, 326)—Wallace had arrived at the end-of-the-world-party after it was already over (though everyone was still standing around holding their drinks, wondering if they should go home). His comments to McCaffery reveal an exhaustion with exhaustion that often manifests itself through eschatological anxiety and resistance in *Broom* and "Westward." Consequently, for an emerging field of study, it is striking that one of the most fundamental aspects of *any* narrative, what Frank Kermode once called narrative's "sense of an ending," has yet to receive significant attention, especially considering how prevalent apocalyptic formations are in Wallace's work.

In this essay I will begin the work of rectifying this critical omission by analyzing Wallace's sense of an ending in *The Broom of the System* and "Westward the Course of Empire Takes Its Way." In order to work through his exhaustion with exhaustion, Wallace systematically develops, explores, and then out of the rubble "gets over" various aspects of American metafiction's "Armageddon-explosion" in each text, thereby preparing a narratological ground for the emergence of *Infinite Jest* (1996). I argue that *Broom* constructs this ground through its exploration of two eschatological poles: Lenore Beadsman Sr and Norman Bombardini, or rather, Ludwig Wittgenstein—whose importance for *Broom* has already been noted at considerable length by Marshall Boswell and others—and Jacques Derrida, whose influence on Wallace's work still remains largely unexplored.[3] Having thus emerged from his first novel with a theoretical sense of language capable of negotiating crises of textuality and communication networks, Wallace was then able to coherently confront the historical archive of "apocalyptic ambience," or rather, literary postmodernism. Drawing upon Paul de Man's "The Rhetoric of Temporality" (1969) and "The Concept of Irony" (1996)—a critic Wallace read carefully, but an influence that is only beginning to receive attention—I reconsider Wallace's relationship with irony in "Westward" through an apocalyptic lens. Though this essay admittedly retreads some of the ground familiar to Wallace's critics (Wittgenstein, irony, postmodernism, etc.), to explicate the centrality of eschatology in his early work, such a reconsideration provides a framework for the necessary task of reconfiguring the dominant reading of Wallace's irony. Furthermore, explicating Wallace's anti-eschatological project in his early fiction further serves to emphasize his engagement with the waning of a larger coherent national narrative. "Westward" presents a culture that was about to lose its Other with the dissolution of the Soviet Union and see the grand narrative of Mutually Assured Destruction begin to fade. Lacking a coherent reference point outside of its own, the US culture "Westward" interrogates is turned in on itself, parasitically consuming not only its own cultural products, but its waste and detritus as well. Wallace's insight in "Westward" consequently involves his perception of the reifying shackles of apocalyptic discourse and rhetoric, literary and otherwise, and the desperate need for US culture to articulate an alternative to the postmodern apocalyptic imagination.

Gardening the machine

The Broom of the System stages a complex exploration between Ludwig Wittgenstein and Jacques Derrida, and asks what it means to write a novel in the wake of poststructuralism.[4] This interaction plays out between two other theoretical constructs that are thinly veiled as characters, Lenore Sr and Norman Bombardini. These four poles form a semiotic square, describing strict asymptotic limits on the narrative's world. The novel's inability to end, as a text that could never be fully communicated to another, is demonstrated and dramatized in terms of thinking through Lenore Sr and Norman Bombardini's stated goals to their uttermost conclusions. As such, the form of the novel itself imposes a seemingly obvious paradox: A novel where text *is the world* cannot end and yet the novel you are holding *ends* (it has a last page). Among the wealth of other effects this theoretical novel narrates,[5] Wallace—in what I think should be read as a rather successful youthful exercise—asks some very basic questions about novelistic discourse at the beginning of his career, and most notably how our inability to communicate with one another could have quite disastrous, if often humorous consequences.

The novel begins with a systemic inability to communicate. The protagonist, Lenore Beadsman Jr, a telephone operator for the publishing company Frequent & Vigorous, experiences a repetitive technological problem: Telephone calls do not arrive at their intended destination and conditions somewhere in the Bombardini Building are to blame. Near the end of the novel a repairman reveals to Lenore that, because a sub-basement communications tunnel was somehow being kept at a steady 98.6°, the "'subpar service is due to your lines . . . bleeding calls into each other'"; the tunnel has "'kind of decided it's a real freakin' human being or something'" (*BOS* 457). At the center of this problem, Lenore knows, is her great-grandmother, Lenore Beadsman Sr, a former student of Ludwig Wittgenstein, whose inability to regulate her body-temperature demands that her environment be maintained at a steady 98.6°. Lenore Sr's absence throughout *Broom*, from her mysterious disappearance from a nursing home, to the manifestation of that absence as material disruption in the means of communication, is of immense structural importance throughout the novel. She is a liminal horizon the novel repetitively posits that serves to question the very possibility for *any* communication within the system of novelistic discourse, thereby dramatizing the inescapably ironic aspects of any narrative.

After disappearing, Lenore Sr left behind "her notebooks, yellow and crispy, old, and her copy of the *Investigations*, and a small piece of fuzzy white paper. . . . On the white back of the label something was doodled. There was nothing else in the drawer. Which is to say there was no *green* book in the drawer" (40, emphasis mine). Lenore Sr is quite clearly a fairly blunt construct, a character that initially appears as a stand-in for Wittgenstein. And she has taken with her the *green notebook*. As so much of Wittgenstein's work was unpublished in his lifetime, the presence/absence of this green notebook, as opposed to a blue or brown notebook, implies that there is further work he did beyond the posthumously published *The Blue and Brown Books* (1958) and *The Philosophical Investigations* (1953), and that Lenore Sr has privileged access to this work. Lenore Sr "has, from what little I can gather, convinced Lenore [Jr] that she is in possession of some words of tremendous power. No, really. Not things, or concepts. Words. The woman is apparently obsessed with words. . . . Words and a book and a belief that the world is words and Lenore's conviction that her own intimate personal world is only of, neither by nor for, her. Something is not right. She is in pain" (73). There is a hidden revelatory truth in this statement, particularly given that Lenore Sr never actually *says* anything in the novel. Lenore Jr's pain results primarily from her fear that she is nothing but words, a fictional construct, a text, a character in a novel. The irony that she indeed *is*, would be her (though not our) revelation.

For the Wallace of *Broom*, Wittgenstein's thinking in *The Philosophical Investigations* has unintended apocalyptic implications: namely, the horrors of complete solipsism.[6] Wallace clearly understands Wittgenstein's emphasis on the social *context* of language: for any meaning to be achieved by language, there must be at least two speakers, a self and other that are attempting to communicate. But the novel continually interrogates this formulation by asking, if we are in many ways constructed by language, what happens when language is no longer possible because there is no one to converse with, when there is only one lonely mind operating without social or discursive context? How is one anything except a *name*? Wittgenstein's answer deserves lengthy quotation:

> "What the names in language signify might be indestructible; for it must be possible to describe the state of affairs in which everything destructible is destroyed. And this description will contain words; and what corresponds to these cannot then be destroyed, or otherwise the words would have no meaning." I must not saw off the branch on which I am sitting.
>
>   One might, of course, object at once that this description would have to except itself from the destruction.—But what corresponds to the separate words of the description and so cannot be destroyed if

it is true, is what gives words their meaning—is that without which they would have no meaning.—In a sense, however, this man is surely what corresponds to his name. But he is destructible, and his name does not lose its meaning when the bearer is destroyed.—An example of something corresponding to the name, and without which it would have no meaning, is a paradigm that is used in connexion with the name in the language game. (*Investigations* 27ᵉ, 55)

Seemingly, Wittgenstein's formulation of the indestructibility of the name, of a word's ability to designate something that can be communicated, even in the absence or destruction of the signified, protects language against complete destruction and ensures one's ability to speak, even in the aftermath of the disaster. The problem with this for Wallace is that Wittgenstein's response to a possible refutation of the immanence of meaning does not go far enough in terms of pursuing the eschatological and solipsistic limits that would upset the language game. Namely, what if that world only exists as *text* without any of the linguistic context necessary for the language game? What if there is no one to speak with? If we are *just* words?

In an early review essay of David Markson's novel, *Wittgenstein's Mistress* (1988), Wallace tellingly acknowledges these questions:

the novel succeeds in doing what few philosophers glean . . . : the consequences, for persons, of the *practice* of *theory*; the difference, say, between espousing "solipsism" as a metaphysical "position" & waking up one fine morning after a personal loss to find your grief apocalyptic, literally millennial, leaving you the last and only living thing on earth, with only your head, now, for not only company but environment & world, an inclined beach sliding toward a dreadful sea. (*BFN* 78)

Wallace's assessment of Markson clearly expresses his apocalyptic reading of Wittgenstein. Lenore Sr functions, both in terms of being a character in the novel and a stand-in for Wittgenstein, as a foil, a limit within which the world of the text must always operate, a boundary necessary for any language game to be played, while simultaneously being a danger to the very act of communication itself in that she represents what happens when everything is a text. She is the ground upon which the language game depends, while simultaneously a material disruption within the system that makes communication impossible. The indestructibility of the name and the world for Lenore Sr is only possible if there is another participant in the language game. But Lenore Sr, for whom everything is language and who is only a name, saws off the branch upon which novelistic discourse must rest if it is not to slide toward a dreadful sea.

Wallace's decision to end the novel by erasing the word "*word*" complexly contends with the narrative liminality that Lenore Sr represents. In *Broom's* final line, Rick Vigorous says, "'You can trust me. . . . I'm a man of my'" (467). By omitting the final "word" here, Wallace blatantly calls attention to the textuality of the novel. We *know* the final word in this sentence is "word." Something in language has given us to understand that the entire novel is attempting to communicate a simple "word." We also know, however, that the final word of the novel could have perhaps been anything (say, "rutabaga" or Wittgenstein's famous philosophical grunt). Consequently, we can never know if whatever the novel is attempting to communicate actually comes across. This, in many ways, is a kind of inversion of Pynchon's final line of *The Crying of Lot 49* (1966), though it maintains Pynchon's refusal to provide any narrative revelation. Rather than fulfilling the language game of narrative closure promised by the title, by the name, and by the category of "novel," Wallace refuses to acknowledge that even a "word" has a stable meaning and that a "word" can fulfill the rules of the language game. The system of novelistic discourse prevents the communication of even a simple word, even while it depends upon its reader to provide the meaning for the absent or destroyed word. As such, Wallace is blatantly calling attention to the fact that not even a single word can escape ironic slippage in narrative discourse. There is, however, another reading of this moment that to my knowledge no one has yet suggested. This reading represents the other teleological limit of the text: Norman Bombardini's "eating to infinite largeness."

Early in the novel Norman Bombardini decides to incorporate the entire universe into himself by literally attempting to eat everything. He realizes, after both a disastrous divorce and an upsetting experience with Weight Watchers, that "Weight Watchers holds as a descriptive axiom the transparently true fact that for each of us the universe is deeply and sharply and completely divided into for example in my case, me, on one side, and everything else, on the other. This for each of us exhaustively defines the whole universe. . . . Self and Other" (90). Holding to this, it follows that Weight Watchers, in attempting to decrease one's weight, is *ipso facto* suggesting that there must be as much other and as little self as possible. Bombardini has taken the opposite approach:

> We each ought to desire our own universe to be as *full* as possible, that the Great Horror consists in an empty, rattling personal universe, one where one finds oneself with Self, on one hand, and vast empty lonely

spaces before Others begin to enter the picture at all, on the other. . . .
Rather than diminishing Self to entice Other to fill our universe, we
may also of course obviously choose to fill the universe with *Self.* . . .
Yes. I plan to grow to infinite size. (90–1)

What has not been suggested about the novel, however, is that Bombardini
actually accomplishes his goal, that he did in fact apocalyptically become
the universe, that he pursues solipsism to such an extent that he becomes
the world of the text.

There is evidence to support such a reading. At the climax of the narrative,
Bombardini, now quite massive indeed, is throwing his entire weight against
his own building. The narrative proper pretty much ends here, with a final
dénouement where Rick Vigorous provides the subsequent story. Other
than the final scene with Vigorous, we don't encounter any of the characters
again, and he, it could be said, is merely there to "speak" the last unuttered
"word." Nor do we really get an account of what Bombardini's ultimate fate
might be. Wallace, even this early in his career, is here committing himself
to a kind of aesthetic anti-eschatology, anticipating how he will frequently
omit the most crucial points of narrative information in his fiction, and
frequently eschewing any "ending," leaving events and how one might
read those events ambiguous and open to interpretation. The irresolution
of Bombardini's eschatologically narcissistic fate should then strike one
as significant (in the same way that the absence of the word "word" is
significant). In short, the absence of the final "word" of the novel implies
the possibility that Bombardini swallowed the world right before Vigorous
could complete the final sentence of the novel.

As stated earlier, Bombardini defines a semiotic relationship to Lenore Sr,
a teleological limit that, if not exactly reached, structures the novel at its
most basic level. The novel is everywhere concerned with the problems
of communication, especially how they manifest in the aporia between
self and other. What Bombardini's project makes clear is not simply a
fairly obvious critique of the American consumer, but that an eschaton
can be reached through *accumulation.* Lenore Sr, paradoxically enough,
embodies what might be called the *threat* of language, the reifying threat
toward the subject when the self is seen as possibly nothing more than a
linguistic construction. This threat, if not clearly destructive, empties the
subject of presence, and potentially even body, all the while withholding
that one transcendent revelatory *word* the green book might contain. On
the one hand, being consumed into Bombardini's "Project Total Yang" is
completely destructive, it erases the other while unifying the world into
"self." Bombardini's apocalypse, however, is also a limit that cannot be

achieved or transgressed. For, if the final "word" of the novel has been erased, then there is always something that resists the all-absorptive quality of "eating to infinite largeness." The word is not written down so it cannot be consumed. It is known *only* outside the novel (with all the appropriate Biblical implications). Infinite accumulation—apocalypse through absorption—is ultimately impossible for the very same reason counting to infinity is impossible. And on Lenore Sr's side, language might be eminently destructible, but there is always some name left behind.

It is no accident this name is in fact "Lenore." Lenore Jr is, in one sense, always already Lenore Sr, but as Lenore Sr is always absent, she is also most definitely *not* Lenore Sr. Rather, she functions as a kind of textual void whose role is to resist the novel's own necessary formal narrative reification, just as the novel resists reification by refusing to complete itself on its last "word." Unlike Pynchon's Oedipa Maas, Lenore does not ask, "*Shall I project a world?*" (*Crying of Lot 49* 82), but rather, "Am I the world's projection, an emergent signal from the background noise and texts?" One of the central problems in Lenore's world is that she is in charge of directing communication to the appropriate people, but the wrong connections are being made within the network. She cannot read the incoming and outgoing language. And this is not because there is something inherent in language that breaks down, but rather the system through which these codes are transmitted is flawed. Wallace consequently understands novelistic discourse as a kind of systemic irony, a mode of ordered breakdown, of never being able to have a letter arrive at its destination because of a gross ordering of the atmosphere to 98.6° and its disruption of technological communication.

By projecting Lenore futuristically into the year 1990 in Cleveland, Ohio, Wallace forces the text to inhabit a landscape further marked by ordered, systemic, material breakdown through his invention of the Great Ohio Desert, or G.O.D. In 1972 the governor of Ohio declared, "'Guys, the state is getting soft. . . . People are getting complacent. They're forgetting the way this state was historically hewn out of wilderness. There's no more hewing. . . . We need a wasteland . . . a desert. A point of savage reference for the good people of Ohio. A place to fear and love. A blasted region. . . . An Other for Ohio's Self'" (54). A tourist destination, a great blasted landscape with black sand, results from the governor's perception of this need. Lenore must inhabit, traverse, and commune with this desert space. To reverse Leo Marx's famous formulation, it is her garden in the machine, or rather, her wasteland in the machine.[7] Ohio is a thoroughly developed, machinic landscape wherein a network of human relationships has totally replaced any "wilderness" (to the point that one suburban development is "in the shape of a profile of Jayne Mansfield" [45]). Consequently, rather than commune with nature in some protected wilderness area, Ohioans go to a manufactured post-apocalyptic wasteland—ordered like a garden, built and maintained, but ultimately more savage than the landscape that was there in the first place. Within the logic of *Broom*, something like the G.O.D. must exist; its emergence from the surrounding suburban noise is necessitated by the very chaos of the communication systems that keep failing. The desert is a kind of ordered deconstruction, a breakdown necessitated by the ubiquitous (though failed) connectivity of a projected future. Rather than intrude upon the pastoral, the pastoral is hewn from the machine, not giving the illusion of some restored, idyllic past, but projecting a post-apocalyptic present instead.

The G.O.D., and specifically Lenore Jr's experience there, functions as an object of narrative resolution and synthesis. It is assembled and accumulated while always already being a space of ordered destruction. Lenore's experience of the desert allows her to complete the novel she inhabits as she subsequently finds an appropriate male love interest, moves away from the influence of her family, and escapes the parasitic Vigorous once and for all. The desert is a textual space that materializes the narrative's limits represented by Bombardini and Lenore Sr, and there she escapes both representation and observation, transforming from an object to a subject and leaving the narrative behind, vanishing from its pages. Wallace ends *Broom* and begins his literary project from a space that rigorously questions and problematizes liminality while still achieving affective narrative cohesion, even offering a relatively happy ending.

Many, including Wallace himself, have perceived *Broom* as a failure, a piece of juvenilia too self-aware and anxious to succeed in its literary project. And though some have contended otherwise, it should not surprise us that *Broom* might in fact be a failure.[8] *Broom* continually declines to aesthetically harmonize its various structural elements in favor of theoretically exploring what it means to be constructing such elements in the first place. In the words of Theodor Adorno: "What is qualitatively new in recent art may be that in an allergic reaction it wants to eliminate harmonizations even in their negated form, truly the negation of negation with its own fatality" (Adorno 159). If narrative textuality is a thing to be deconstructed, an object whose inability to transgress its eschatological limits structures the object itself, then Wallace's failure results from his attempts to negate the object's own destruction and fatality, to negate this negation. In beginning his career from a formally anti-eschatological stance, having already exhausted ends at his "origin," he questions the structure of narrative itself.

The "failure" of *Broom*, if it can indeed be located, is always already inscribed into Wallace's first attempt at a novel, for, as has here been enacted up until this point, the novel's other philosophical guide-post had already exploded the textual foundations upon which Wallace might have stood. He was acutely aware of this fact. If Lenore Sr is absent, a phantom, a name without material signification, a name that cannot be destroyed even if it ceases corresponding to a living breathing being, then we must understand this absence to also "signify" another unnamed specter: Jacques Derrida.

Wallace firmly felt, from the very beginning of his career, the critical importance that revolutions in theory and philosophy had to have on any of the fiction composed in theory's wake. He firmly believed at the time of *Broom*'s composition that it was impossible to contend with his literary forebears without also contending with the theoretical landscape of the era.[9] In other words, to compose a novel like *Broom*, obsessively concerned with its structure as it is, Wallace took the lessons of Derrida quite seriously, and perhaps especially, in terms of *Broom*'s broad questions, Derrida's famous critique of structuralism:

> And again on the basis of what we call the center (and which, because it can be either inside or outside, can also indifferently be called the origin or the end, *archē* or *telos*), repetitions, substitutions, transformations, and permutations are always *taken* from a history of meaning [*sens*]— that is, in a word, a history—whose origin may always be reawakened or whose end may always be anticipated in the form of presence. This is why one perhaps could say that the movement of any archaeology, like that of any eschatology, is an accomplice of this reduction of the structurality of structure and always attempts to conceive of structure on the basis of a full presence which is beyond play. (*Writing and Difference* 279, brackets in original)

To parse this in terms of the novel, we would do well to again refer to Norman Bombardini, and especially his own phantom-like nature at the end of *Broom*. In Bombardini's world of total-self, there cannot be a center, for a center would imply that there is some subject who is Norman Bombardini in the first place. In addition, such a universe would have no coherent "*archē*" or "*telos*," no origin or end. It would be a narrative-textual space that could never be an accomplice of eschatology, for it would be a kind of "universe without organs," a vast physical region with no distinction between one thing and another. If there is an anxiety in Wallace, the figure of Bombardini signals a problematic obsessively pursued on his part: that language and textuality prevent, before one even starts, the possibility of fashioning coherent meaning in something that had to first pursue the question of the "structurality of structure"—that is, the self-awareness of fashioning an aesthetic object. In *Broom*, Wallace discloses the failure inherent in any structural project attempting to refashion some solid ontological ground upon which to proceed in the wake of poststructuralism. Ultimately, *Broom*'s "failure" allows him to acknowledge that structural aporias— namely those of any eschatologies whatsoever—could not be resolved in a form obsessed by those very aporias; a novel cannot work through the structural aporias of the novel. Acknowledging this allowed him to then turn toward the historical, material archive of American fiction, an archive he represented by the "presence" of John Barth in "Westward the Course of Empire Takes its Way."

The threat of the text, ironic apocalypse

One of the most persistent fears Wallace's work revolves around is the suspicion that there may be something actually quite *dangerous* about literature, both in terms of its composition and its contemplation. Somewhere within the dialogic interaction between text and reader, and between author and writing, Wallace saw contemporary American literature following a potentially catastrophic path of recursivity and self-conscious irony despite the exhaustive and commendable lengths postmodern metafiction had pursued to complicate these dialogic relationships and to strip them of any pretense of transparency or authenticity. A US culture so often criticized as narcissistic and historically ignorant, as apocalyptically self-absorbed with the reproduction of itself, seemed to him acutely susceptible to the dangers of postmodern self-consciousness, of texts spiraling into total solipsism.

For Wallace, the threat of the text resides not in literature's possibilities for destruction, in either the material dissolution of the text nor in some sort of "lessening" of the reading subject, but rather in the vicious and infinitely recursive loop of contemporary US metafiction. The result of this loop is text dangerously *accumulating*. The danger of literature, for Wallace, is that metafictional recursivity has the potential to result in a kind of apocalyptically solipsistic fugue-state, a wholly self-absorbed text which threatens to absorb the cocreator of that text as well, ultimately threatening the possibility of any subjectivity when confronted with a text. This formally recursive loop, this infinite possibility for the dangerous accumulation of text, is evident in Wallace's early novella, "Westward the Course of Empire Takes Its Way," as it is with the Entertainment in *Infinite Jest*.

"Westward" quite unabashedly takes John Barth's 1967 story, "Lost in the Funhouse," as a model, reference, and polemical object. "Westward," rather than answering Barth's question, "For whom is the funhouse fun?"

(*Lost in the Funhouse* 72) asks a different one. Drew-Lynn Eberhardt, or
D. L.—self-proclaimed "postmodernist," student of Dr Ambrose (who
is clearly meant to be Barth himself), and recently married wife of Mark
Nechtr (the protagonist)—early in the novella scrawled the following
limerick on the chalkboard of an MFA creative writing classroom before
Ambrose arrived to conduct class:

> For lovers, the Funhouse is fun.
> For phonies, the Funhouse is love.
> But *for whom*, the proles grouse,
> Is the Funhouse a house?
> Who lives there, when push comes to shove? (*GCH* 239)

D. L. is clearly meant to be read parodically within the space of the novella,
oftentimes functioning as Wallace's own superego, sublimating his fears
about the act of composing "postmodern" fiction. So when she writes the
above "critique" of Ambrose's (Barth's) story "Lost in the Funhouse," Wallace
is simultaneously writing a critique of "Funhouse" (as well as "Westward"
itself), while acknowledging that critique as fundamentally shallow, the
result of a theoretical "fad," and yet somehow no less serious in terms of its
central question: "for whom is the Funhouse a house?" In other words, who
lives there, who are we asking to inhabit this metafictional terrain? Asking
who the text is *built* for acknowledges that indeed no one may be able to
feel comfortable within such a space; it cannot actually function as a *home*
at all. The text only serves to continually upset its reader, to be an object
whose goal is the production of the uncanny and a sense of homelessness (or
unheimlich). Consequently, as something built, the novella threatens what
it is built *for*.[10]

    As most critics have argued, "Westward" strives to overcome the
dangers of solipsistic recursivity with a kind of hyper-meta-irony, an
irony turned in on itself to the point of sincerity.[11] The question that drives
"Westward"—for whom is the Funhouse a *house*, who can actually *dwell* in
the story itself? —forces us, however, to reconsider Wallace's relationship
with irony. For it is crucial to understand that Wallace was implicitly aware
of the hopelessness of "transcending" irony, of going somehow beyond
Barth and other postmodern ironists, especially in his early work. His
famous "prediction" or desire for a new sincerity was nothing more than
a kind of hopeful non-transgressible limit imposed by the very historicity
of irony itself. The house is built. If there is no one to inhabit it, unlivable
as the postmodern condition might make it, there is no way to further
critique the house of metafiction without participating in the very mode

it suggests. Perhaps more clearly than any US writer of his generation, Wallace understood that textual *accumulation* in all forms—commentary, influence, theoretical complexity, critical engagement, reading *itself*—was a *danger*, a *threat*, precisely through the continual ironic treatment of there not only being no world "outside the text," but any world *in* the text, any house where we could live in the text itself.

In these terms, Paul de Man's essays "On the Rhetoric of Temporality" and "The Concept of Irony" are especially pertinent to Wallace's understanding and utilization of irony, not least because they afford us an insight into Wallace's conception and mobilization of de Manian deconstruction within his own work.[12] For de Man, when discussing irony, one is faced immediately with the problem of defining the term, for "in the case of irony, one cannot so easily take refuge in the need for a historical de-mystification of the term. . . . [O]ne has to start out from the structure of the trope itself, taking one's cue from the texts that are de-mystified and, to a large extent, themselves ironical" (*Blindness and Insight* 211).[13] In "Westward" Wallace saw the problem with irony and his own relationship to the development of literary irony in historical terms, and with the full awareness of how the very way he was approaching irony depended upon that history. Even though he is tangentially engaging US imperialism within the text of "Westward," its title forces us to pause in terms of the *directionality* of the novella's structure and its historical relationship to postmodern literature. Quite clearly he is suggesting that there is a deep and conflicted relationship between, say, Barth's project and the "project" of Empire. This relationship, to oversimplify it, is that postmodern metafiction capitulates to the homogenizing banality imposed by "the course of Empire." Metafiction follows this course rather than attempting to subvert it. The destructive capacity housed in literature's accumulation has itself been *absorbed* into the greater historical problem postmodern irony had sought to highlight. In other words, "[t]he target of [these texts'] irony is very often the claim to speak about humans as if they were facts of history. It is a historical fact that irony becomes increasingly conscious of itself in the course of demonstrating the impossibility of our being historical. In speaking of irony we are dealing not with the history of an error but with a problem that exists within the self" (de Man 211). For Wallace, this "problem that exists within the self" becomes literature's apocalyptic site, an ahistorical space without the possibility for coherent communication with the other.

Wallace felt that postmodern irony had backfired, its intended targets merely absorbed into capitalism's dominant aesthetic regime: advertising. In D. L.'s terms, metafiction could neither house the "proles" (proletariat), "lovers," nor "phonies," for its very operation had become one of control rather than providing a space for dwelling. But what would replace it? Wallace does perceive one specific answer coming from the culture at large, and consequently the *direction* "Westward" takes is toward the filming of a commercial so grandiose it not only borders on the apocalyptic, but attempts to achieve *revelation*. Wallace reimagines the Funhouse as a McDonald's-run night club whose grand opening will coincide with the filming of a reunion of everyone who has ever been in a McDonald's commercial before. The brains behind this operation, J. D. Steelritter—quite literally Barth commercialized—imagines the results in quite lurid and apocalyptic terms:

> And that, as they say, will be that. No one will ever leave the rose farm's Reunion. The revelation of What They Want will be on them; and, in that revelation of Desire, they will Possess. They will all Pay the Price—without persuasion. . . . Life, the truth, will be its own commercial. Advertising will have finally arrived at the death that's been its object all along. And, in Death, it will of course become Life. The last commercial. Popular culture, the US of A.'s great lalated lullaby. . . . Their wishes will, yes, come true. Fact will be fiction will be fact. Ambrose and his academic heirs will rule, without rules. *Meatfiction*. (310)

In US culture, Wallace perceives that subjective desire *itself* has become a completely manipulable object. No longer is labor, one's time and bodily energy, the object of capital's violence toward the subject, but the very process of desire—in Steelritter's vision of desire being synonymous with living—becomes merely an object of capital emptied of any "real" or "true" subjective content. Consequently, "Westward" contends with the disturbing fact that intellectual labor and the *avant garde*—that is, postmodern American metafiction—was not only complicit with the culture industry's reification of the subject, but through popular culture's appropriation of postmodern irony, it may have had a large hand in producing the very conditions that made this reification possible.

We should not be surprised that the limits of irony, both in terms of advertising and in terms of contemporary fiction, in other words, between "high" and "low" culture, are apocalyptic in the fullest sense of the term (as a revelation). Having learned the lessons of Roland Barthes's "The Death of the Author" (1967), Wallace understood how naïve it was to hold out for authenticity. Rather than evoking the all-too familiar claims of the "death of the novel," or the "end of literature" (etc.), Wallace's position in "Westward," in a kind of Arnoldian-reverse, is a critic working in an artists' time (despite writing fiction, of course), someone for whom the aesthetic landscape is *too* full, too aware of itself as full, and this landscape revels in that fact to the point of destruction. This is the logic of Steelritter's McDonald's commercial to end all commercials. Consumer desire, taken to its ironic limit, achieves a kind of advertising-aesthetic-stasis. There ceases to be any lag-time between the instantiation of desire and its object-fulfillment. Any discord will be resolved with the cultural unity created by total solipsistic desire. Wallace's great fear throughout "Westward" might simply be that his *own* fiction is contributing to such assemblages.

With this in mind, de Man is again useful for understanding Wallace:

> The moment the innocence or authenticity of our sense of being in the world is put into question, a far from harmless process gets underway. It may start as a casual bit of play with a stray loose end of the fabric, but before long the entire texture of the self is unraveled and comes apart. The whole process happens at unsettling speed. Irony possesses an inherent tendency to gain momentum and not stop until it has run its full course; from the small and apparently innocuous exposure of a small self-deception it soon reaches the dimensions of the absolute. (*Blindness and Insight* 215)

"Westward" takes us in the direction of the absolute as a kind of total-unraveling, a subject so turned in on herself as to vanish entirely. In refusing to actually reach Collision, Illinois, the site of the commercial, nor to end "Westward" properly in any sense at all, but rather to begin another narrative about the problems inherent in constructing a narrative, Wallace simultaneously acknowledges the impossible task of forging a direction toward something else, away from the course of Empire, while holding out a hope that perhaps *directionality itself*, or rather eschatology, can be overturned.

One of the ways this occurs is through a "casual bit of play." As noted above, in "Westward" Wallace "wanted to get the Armageddon-explosion, the goal metafiction's always been about . . . over with." To do so, however, he had to account for the fact that many of the modes of getting it "over with" had already acknowledged the fact of metafiction's eschatological thrust with a fair amount of absurdity and irony. Consequently, he presents this fact fairly early on through the character of Dr Ambrose: "Speaking of speaking about shit: Dr. Ambrose . . . could at this point profitably engage in some wordplay around and about the similarities, phonological and etymological, between the words *scatology* and *eschatology*. Smooth allusions to Homeric horses pooping death-dealing Ithacans, Luther's excremental vision, Swift's incontinent Yahoos" (256, emphases in original). Dr Ambrose's, or rather John Barth's *possible* (though unstated) ironic observation about the similarities between the words "scatology" and "eschatology" within the space of "Westward" are revealing with regard to Wallace's anti-eschatological project in two ways.

First, he *begins* from acknowledging that much of the veil-lifting of ironically treating the apocalypse has already been accomplished by postmodern metafiction. Significantly though, this accomplishment is posed as something Dr Ambrose *could* do if he so chose, but has not. Ambrose's potential wordplay occurs to Mark Nechtr while, "basically they're just standing around, as people will . . . tired, with that so-near-and-yet type of tension, a sense of somewhere definite they must be at by a definite time, but no clear consensus on how to get there. Since they're late. As Dr. Ambrose might venture to observe, they're figuratively *unsure about where to go from here*" (257, emphases in original). What should be understood, and perhaps Wallace could be said to be slightly heavy-handed here, is that his *own* relationship to eschatology is not only problematic, but slightly confused. Barth did *not* complete metafiction's "Armageddon-explosion"-type goal, though Wallace plays with the idea that he *could have* by ironically treating the theme of the end of the world as nothing more than the study of, or obsession with, excrement, a theme that has been digested and excreted since the beginning of Western literature. The surrounding situation accompanying Mark's musing about the possibility of what Ambrose *would* say also displays this confusion. (And it is important that there is a character in the novel who is constipated.) They are in the midst of traveling, having just disembarked from a plane at the Central Illinois Airport, and, having missed the shuttles transporting people to Collision for the commercial, have no means of going further toward their destination; they are "*unsure about where to go from here*." In other words, Wallace is perfectly aware of four things: 1) postmodern metafiction as a project has not been completed even though it "could" reach its goal through the imaginative extrapolation of an eschatological direction (which is undesirable and potentially dangerous); 2) literature with any pretention of being "after" postmodernism, because of that, is unsure where to go; 3) anyone attempting to "go anywhere" is in the difficult position of being a latecomer; and 4) a writer standing at this terminus is ultimately *exhausted*, an exhaustion produced by being a latecomer, as well as an exhaustion with teleological constructions themselves.

Second, the "full course" of this casual bit of play is expressed near the end of the novella in fairly succinct terms as the teleological limit of advertising's ability to turn anxiety into desire, and ultimately anxiety *par excellence*—one's fear of death—into a desire *for* death. It is nothing new that the end of the world as revelatory fulfillment, as a sublimation of the anxieties associated with inevitable subjective death is often presented as something to be *desired*, a goal toward which to strive. Wallace's irony transforms this apocalyptic desire into, not merely a cultural *telos*, but the goal of advertising itself. If postmodern advertising, as he is so aware, works first and foremost through the creation of anxieties that produce consumer desire to relieve those anxieties, then the "course of Empire," or rather, the pursuit of capital/advertising's goal must be the production of a desire for death.

Steelritter understands that the course of advertising has produced a strange aporia. On the one hand, advertising has had to constantly reinvent itself, to constantly confront the fact that its strategies for producing consumer desire through control and conditioning are only temporary solutions. Campaigns that were once effective are now "tired image[s]. Hackneyed jingle[s]. . . . Conditioning has obsolescence built right in" (340). On the other hand, the more effective, aesthetically complex, and subtle the advertising, the more it becomes indistinguishable from the very televisual entertainment it accompanies, and consequently the desire to actually "leave the couch" and buy the advertised product becomes more difficult through sheer inertia and enjoyment of the entertaining advertisement. "Your adman's basic challenge: how to get folks' fannies out of chairs; how to turn millennial boredom around, get things back on track, back toward the finish line?" (340). Steelritter's solution to the adman's problem is to manufacture a mass-desire for death, which he views as the one great universal fear, and which he imagines will make "the whole huge historical Judeo-Christian campaign . . . spin in reverse, from inside" (341). Steelritter hopes to turn scatology into eschatology, to leverage the ultimate form of cultural detritus, waste, and excrement—advertising—into a form that produces a desire for death, a love of death. For if the huge historical Judeo-Christian campaign's goal is love of the neighbor or the other, a desire for death is total solipsistic love, a love of that which is in the individual more-than-herself, something *no one* can ever access or confront but the self: death. (And it should be clear here that this solipsistic desire is in-and-of-itself impossible to achieve, for the subject cannot access her death—i.e., death cannot be *experienced*.) In this fashion, the historical formation of apocalyptic fear and desire, though clearly always an allegory for subjective death, is transformed, even if only slightly.

If metafiction's goal has always been an "Armageddon-explosion," then for Wallace this goal is ultimately not external, not an eschatology of the world, but of the subject. This desire for death is threatening because it is produced by and within the apparatus of postmodernism *par excellence*, the "~~text itself~~," and the object of this threat is the solipsistically absorbed self confronting that text (whether it is advertising or metafiction). Furthermore, this desire for death, for the ultimate end, is produced by a system with an onanistic *telos*. Capitalism does not have any aim except to endlessly reproduce itself, to create more capital. Wallace's conception of the postmodern condition is significant in that he sees capitalism performing this reification by mobilizing narrative's most basic feature: that it ends, that it is inherently eschatological. For any lines of flight to be available from this dominating logic, literary fiction, if it in any way hopes to go forward and present alternative possibilities, needs to divest itself of just such apocalypticism.

In these two ways—postmodernism's self-awareness of always already treating the apocalypse ironically, and its complicity with the culture industry's destruction of subjectivity by producing a desire for death, for the subject's reification produced *by* and *within* that subject—Wallace's project in "Westward the Course of Empire Takes Its Way" should be understood less as transcending irony, but rather, following Paul de Man reading Schlegel's "irony of irony" or meta-irony, as understanding that there is no *end* to irony whatsoever:

> The act of irony, as we know [*sic*] understand it, reveals the existence of a temporality that is definitely not organic, in that it relates to its source only in terms of distance and difference and allows for no end, for no totality. Irony divides the flow of temporal experience into a past that is pure mystification and a future that remains harassed forever by a relapse with the inauthentic. It can know this inauthenticity but can never overcome it. It can only restate and repeat it on an increasingly conscious level, but it remains endlessly caught in the impossibility of making this knowledge applicable to the empirical world. It dissolves in the narrowing spiral of a linguistic sign that becomes more and more remote from its meaning, and it can find no escape from this spiral. (*Blindness and Insight* 222)

By mobilizing de Man's theory of irony, I have tried to emphasize that irony by its very nature is totalizing and destabilizing—one is simply *never* saying what one means. Once we acknowledge Wallace's own familiarity with de Man, it becomes fair to say that we should not take Wallace entirely at his word in "E Unibus Pluram." The dominant mode of understanding Wallace's relationship to irony up until this point has been to read him as meta-ironic, or else to read his work as a valiant effort to leave irony behind toward what

Adam Kelly calls a "new sincerity." Though there are advantages to reading Wallace in either vein, I believe that "Westward"'s fictional project should instead be read as, if not as accomplishing, then at least pointing toward a relationship to irony that is anti-eschatological, that acknowledges irony's fundamental "temporality that is not organic," and that it "allows for no end, for no totality." In other words, Wallace's mode of getting metafiction's Armageddon-explosion "over with," is based on an acknowledgment that not only can there *not* be such an explosion, but that the whole aesthetic approach that privileges such an eschatology is not only problematic, but threatening. "Westward" ultimately opens up and points toward how such an aesthetic project might be conceived. This project's fruition can everywhere be seen in *Infinite Jest*, a work that not only confronts the more "real" apocalyptic limits in the United States and the world—nuclear war, environmental disaster, the catastrophe(s) of capitalism, the tyranny of networked-being—but is everywhere engaged in proposing alternatives to the reifying dominance of apocalyptic discourse.

Notes

1　For instance, see Marshall Boswell's influential study of Wallace, *Understanding David Foster Wallace* (2003). For a discussion of irony in Wallace's work see Jon Baskin, Iannis Goerlandt, Timothy Jacobs, and Lee Konstantinou (2012). Robert L. McLaughlin also claims that Wallace allows us "the opportunity to consider what we can call, for lack of a better term, post-postmodernism and its potential" (55). And A. O. Scott claims that the postmodernism has caused in Wallace's writing a "panic of influence." For a discussion of Wallace and sincerity, see Adam Kelly (2010b).

2　For a thorough assessment of the emerging field of Wallace Studies, see Kelly (2010a).

3　In David Lipsky's book-length interview with Wallace, conducted after the publication of *Infinite Jest*, Wallace emphasized that he considered *Broom* "a conversation between Wittgenstein and Derrida" (Lipsky 35).

4　For a discussion of Wallace, poststructuralism, and humanism in contemporary US fiction, see Mary K. Holland.

5　See Kelly's discussion in this volume of *Broom of the System* as a novel of ideas.

6　In an early article on *The Broom of the System* Lance Olsen claims that Wallace and Wittgenstein share a "termite consciousness" (201).

7　For a further exploration of Wallace's fictional landscapes and his relationship to Marx, see Graham Foster.

8 Clare Hayes-Brady, for instance, thinks that "that *The Broom of the System* deserves to be considered not as the juvenilia of a potentially talented author, but as the self-assured declaration of an artistic and philosophical project that would give rise not just to an impressive career, but also to a rebirth of American fiction" (36).

9 In an early essay on the state of fiction within the academy, published shortly after *Broom*, Wallace emphasized the familiarity a contemporary novelist must have with the major theoretical and philosophical achievements of twentieth-century thinkers (with overtly self-conscious name dropping): "The climate for the 'next' generation of American writers—should we decide to inhale rather than die—is aswirl with what seems like long-overdue appreciation for the weird achievements of such aliens as Husserl, Heidegger, Bakhtin, Lacan, Barthes, Poulet, Gadamer, de Man. The demise of Structuralism has changed a world's outlook on language, art, and literary discourse; and the contemporary artists can simply no longer afford to regard the work of critics or theorists or philosophers—no matter how stratospheric—as divorced from their own concerns. . . . Language's promotion from mirror to eye, from *organikos* to organic, is yesterday's news (except in those two lonely outposts, TV and the Creative Classroom) as the tide of Post-Structuralism, Marxism, Feminism, Freudianism, Deconstruction, Semiotics, Hermeneutics, and attendant –isms and –ics moves through the ('Straight') US academy and into the consciousness of the conscious American adult" (see "Fictional Futures and the Conspicuously Young" in *BFN* 63–4).

10 The same could be said about how Mark Z. Danielewski constructs his "house" in the remarkable novel, *House of Leaves* (2000).

11 Boswell, McLaughlin, and Scott all treat this issue in "Westward" to varying degrees.

12 For instance, see Wallace's review of H. L. Hix's *Morte d'Author: An Autopsy* in "Greatly Exaggerated," where he shows a more-than-passing familiarity with the history of the intellectual formation of deconstruction: "Hix's discussion isn't comprehensive, quite: Heidegger and Hegel are scarcely mentioned, Husserl (a major influence of Derrida) is absent, as are such important contemporary figures in the debate as Stanley Cavell . . . *Paul de Man*, Edward Said, Gayatri Spivak" (*SFT* 141, emphasis mine). By calling attention to absent thinkers in Hix's text, Wallace is also slyly demonstrating his own wide reading in the subject. Recall also that de Man was one of those "aliens" Wallace referred to in his "Fictional Futures" essay.

13 De Man also confronts this problem of definition in "The Concept of Irony."

6

Representing Entertainment in *Infinite Jest*

Philip Sayers

The word "entertainment," in this essay, is used in three different senses. The first is perhaps the most obvious: entertainment as a part of popular culture, including but not limited to movies and television. Wallace uses the second sense of the word in *Infinite Jest*, prefixed by an indefinite article or made plural—"an entertainment" or "entertainments"—to refer to specific movies or television shows: characters in the novel spend a great deal of time watching "entertainments." Finally, the third sense of the word is usually capitalized, and preceded by the definite article: "the Entertainment" (*Infinite Jest* 90) refers to a specific, fictional film, directed by one of the novel's characters, James O. Incandenza. This film provides what Wallace refers to (using, not untypically, a term taken from the realm of cinema[1]) as the novel's "*MacGuffin*" (Lipsky 157). "The Entertainment" is, however, "not just a *MacGuffin*" (157). It is a film apparently so compelling—so entertaining—that anyone who catches as much as a glimpse of it becomes utterly entranced, unable to engage in any activity other than watching the film, over and over, until death. As such, it is also "kind of a metaphorical device" (157), through which Wallace explores both of the other senses of the word: the entertainments within the novel, and entertainment in contemporary US culture.

The first half of this essay, then, provides an overview of Wallace's representation of entertainment in general and of the Entertainment, and suggests that, for him, both film and the novel can (despite the specificities of their respective media) fulfill similar goals. In the second half, I look at *Infinite Jest*'s representations of specific entertainments: I argue that Wallace's use of ekphrasis (the verbal description of the visual) and filmic language make *Infinite Jest* a semiotically hybrid project, in which novel and film are shown to be fundamentally intertwined.

In his short 1975 essay "Upon Leaving the Movie Theater," Roland Barthes writes about the cinema in a manner strikingly reminiscent of the Entertainment in *Infinite Jest*. He compares the movie-going experience to hypnosis, and he describes the spectator as glued by the nose to the screen, "riveted to the representation" (3). Essay and novel are both concerned with the question of how to "loosen the glue's grip" (3), and both present film as conducive of sleep: Barthes writes of "spectators slip[ping] into their seat as they slip into a bed, coat and feet on the seat in front of them" (2). This description is echoed in the way Wallace describes the viewing habits of the Canadian/ Saudi medical attaché who becomes the Entertainment's first victim. For him, watching a selection of entertainment cartridges is a method of relaxation after a long and stressful day of dealing with the maxillofacial yeast of the Saudi Minister of Home Entertainment: "at the day's end, he needs unwinding in the very worst way" (*Infinite Jest* 34). "Worst," here, presumably means most effective, but the choice of word implies that the attaché's methods of relaxation are bad for him. Indeed they are. After Wallace explicitly compares entertainment with drugs and alcohol ("the medical attaché partakes of neither kif nor distilled spirits" [34]), the soon-to-be-victim settles down to watch the lethal Entertainment. His usual routine is to eat dinner "before the viewer in his special electronic recliner," which, when his entertainments have had their soporific effect, tilts backwards so that he "is permitted to ease effortlessly from unwound spectation into a fully relaxed night's sleep, still right there in the recumbent recliner" (34).

The torpor-inducing effect of the Entertainment is far more potent than that of the attaché's usual selection of cartridges, but, for Barthes and for Wallace, even normal entertainment (as opposed to *the* Entertainment) brings about sleep. Entertainment, for Wallace, lies on one side of a "continuum," at the other side of which is art (Lipsky 80): whereas entertainment's "chief job is to make you so riveted by it that you can't tear your eyes away, so the advertisers can advertise" (Lipsky 79) and "gives you a certain kind of pleasure that I would argue is fairly *passive*" (80), art "requires you to *work*" (174). Wallace portrays entertainment in terms that recall Barthes's descriptions of his visits to the cinema, and Wallace's own essay on David Lynch: "a commercial movie doesn't try to wake people up but rather to make their sleep so comfortable and their dreams so pleasant that they will fork over money to experience it" (*Supposedly Fun Thing* 170).

He also frequently compares it to candy—"Real pleasurable, but it didn't have any calories in it" (Lipsky 79)—in that both are "treats that are basically fine and fun in small amounts but bad for us in large amounts and *really* bad for us if consumed in the massive regular amounts reserved for nutritive staples" (*Supposedly Fun Thing* 37). This analogy has slightly different implications than Wallace's other favorite point of comparison, drugs and alcohol, in that candy is something associated with childhood.

Childhood can, for Wallace, be a time of "total, entranced, uncritical absorption into this fantasy world of TV" (Lipsky 149). For Barthes, drawing on Lacan, childhood is characterized not only by rapt spectation but also by narcissistic (mis)identification: "I glue my nose, to the point of disjointing it, on the mirror of the screen, to the imaginary other with which I identify myself narcissistically (reportedly, the spectators who insist on sitting closest to the screen are children and cinephiles)" (3).

Here Barthes draws an analogy between the relationship of the spectator to the image onscreen and the relationship of the infant to his reflection in the mirror, as explained by Lacan through his concept of the *stade du miroir* (an analogy earlier made explicit: "I am locked in on the image as though I were caught in the famous dual relationship which establishes the imaginary" [3]). This would figure the spectator not so much as a child but as an infant: although Lacan later expanded the idea to the status of general structural relationship of human life, the *stade du miroir* was, in his seminal 1949 paper "The Mirror Stage as Formative of the Function of the I as Revealed in Psychoanalytic Experience," a phase that took place in an infant aged between 6 and 18 months (Lacan 75–6). In *Infinite Jest*, as mentioned above, it is narcissistic identification with an infant that seems to provide one of the keys to the power of the Entertainment: as Joelle says, "I don't think there's much doubt the lens [used to film the Entertainment] was supposed to reproduce an infantile visual field. That's what you could feel was driving the scene" (940). James Incandenza, appearing postmortem to Don Gately, confirms that the viewer (or at least one viewer in particular) is meant to identify with the infant, sharing his or her emotional, as well as optical, point of view: the film is described as a "magically entertaining toy to dangle at the infant still somewhere alive" in Hal (839). Again, we see a degree of ambivalence in Wallace's writing: infancy and childhood represent narcissistic susceptibility to the fatal Entertainment, yet they also represent something of humanity, "since to be human . . . is probably to be unavoidably sentimental and naïve and goo-prone and generally pathetic, is to be in some basic interior way forever infantile" (695). These pejorative words come from the cold and mechanical Hal; the novel seems to suggest to the reader that Hal is right about what it means to be human, but perhaps wrong to believe that this is necessarily a bad thing (certainly the infantile internal self is preferable to "the hip empty mask, anhedonia" [695]).

Whereas entertainment (epitomized by *the* Entertainment—which is "what entertainment ultimately leads to" [Lipsky 79]) gives a passive pleasure that Wallace associates with substances and infancy (bringing these threads together, Hugh/Helen Steeply, the American agent attempting to track down, in female disguise, the Entertainment, describes one victim as resembling "some drug-addicted newborn" [507]), art on the other hand is active and engaging. Wallace in the David Lynch essay: "An art film's point is usually more intellectual or aesthetic [than that of a commercial movie], and you usually have to do some interpretive work to get it" (*SFT* 170). The same is true of other forms of art, including, most significantly, literature. Certainly *Infinite Jest* requires some interpretive work, as well as the plain old effort involved in devoting oneself to finishing a book that concludes at page 1079, after close to 100 pages of notes and errata—not to mention reading it, as Wallace hopes, twice. He states in a radio interview:

> The really hard and really scary thing was trying to make it fun enough so somebody would want to [read it twice], and also—and how to have it be fun without have it be reductive or pandering or get co-opted by the very principles of commercialism and, you know, "like me, like me, like me" that . . . the book is partly about. (Interview with Michael Silverblatt)

Wallace here explains the double bind in which he finds himself, stuck between a rock (entertainment, "commercialism") and a hard place (art, demanding too much of the reader without sufficient reward). Some kind of balance must be achieved: as Wallace tells Lipsky, "we're not equipped to work all the time. And there's times when, for instance for me, commercial fiction or television is perfectly appropriate" (174). Both film and literature are subject to the entertainment/art continuum, and excess in either direction can be dangerous. In *Infinite Jest*, when, in the 1998 of the novel's alternate future, America is faced with a lack of new television to watch, "domestic-crime rates, as well as out-and-out suicides, topped out at figures that cast a serious pall over the penultimate year of the millennium" (415). Once again, then, we have ambivalence; speaking about *Infinite Jest*, Wallace exclaims: "God, if the book comes off as some kind of indictment of entertainment, then it fails" (Lipsky 80–1).

Although, as I have mentioned, both literature and film are subject to his entertainment/art continuum, Wallace is clearly aware of important differences, not only between literature and filmed entertainment (TV or movies), but also between filmed entertainment and other forms of art:

> But I think what we need is seriously engaged art, that can teach again that we're smart. And that there's stuff that TV and movies—although they're great at certain things—cannot give us. But that have to create the motivations for us to want to do the extra work, you know, to get

these other kinds of art. And I think you can see it in the visual arts, I
think you can see it in music . . . (Lipsky 71)

Wallace's point is that this "seriously engaged art" will, as long as it is
sufficiently engag*ing* to keep the reader's attention, teach us not only that
"we're smart" (unlike TV, which teaches "the insidious . . . meta-lesson
that you're dumb" [Lipsky 71]), but also that filmed entertainment has
different properties than those of other media. It would therefore also
suggest that the "seriously engaged art" would not itself be in the form of
movies or television. Wallace's tentative manifesto comes in the context of
a discussion of the relationship between books and television, and Lipsky
focuses on the differences between TV and the novel, but Wallace, through
his comparison with the visual arts and music, suggests that "seriously
engaged art" may not be the exclusive domain of literature. Given Wallace's
tendency to distinguish between (commercial) "movies" and (art) "film,"
however, it seems possible that the "stuff that TV and movies . . . cannot
give us"—such as, for example, the lesson "that we're smart"—might just as
conceivably be given to us by an art film as by an avant-garde novel.

My interpretation so far has tended to emphasize that which is shared
between film and literature more than that which distinguishes them,
arguing like W. J. T. Mitchell in his essay "Ekphrasis and the Other" that,
in many ways, there is "no essential difference between texts and images"
(*Picture Theory* 160). Both can serve the function either of entertainment or
of art. Wallace's argument here does however concede that there are certain
things that certain media "cannot give us." Similarly, Mitchell continues:
"there are important differences between visual and verbal media at the
level of sign- types, forms, materials of representation, and institutional
traditions" (161). This would allow one to make an argument in favor of the
idea of medium specificity, an idea for which Lipsky a little earlier voices his
support: "the best thing is to show what TV can't, to use the ways books are
better than TV" (71).

The medium specificity thesis is defined by Noël Carroll as the "idea . . .
that each art form, in virtue of its medium, has its own exclusive domain of
development" (5). Those who subscribe to it tend to "believe that the proper
direction of their art form will be involved in the isolation and definition of
the quidity [sic] of the . . . medium" (6)—that is, more or less what Lipsky
suggests. It is, however, important to note that Lipsky's proposal as to what
the novelist should do rests on a characterization of the novel that defines
it against television, and in so doing posits a relationship of rivalry between
the two media. Wallace is more circumspect, with regard both to the nature
of the relationship between TV and novel ("We sit around and bitch about

how TV has ruined the audience for reading—when really all it's done is given us the really precious gift of making our job harder" [Lipsky 71]) and to the question of medium specificity in general:

> For me a fair amount of aesthetic experience is—is erotic. And I think a certain amount of it has to do with this weird kind of intimacy with the person who made it.

No other medium gives that to you?

> Yeah—although you feel a kind of weird intimacy with actors in drama, although it's a bit different. *That's* more I think an enabling of the fantasy that you are them, or getting you to desire them as a body or something. It's interesting: I've never read really good essays about the different kinds of seduction in different kinds of art. (Lipsky 72)

The beginnings of such a "really good essay" might be found in the work of Roland Barthes, who, as well as writing about the reader's erotic relationship with the text, characterizes the basis of the hypnotic power of film in "Upon Leaving the Movie Theater" as "a distance . . . not an intellectual one . . . [but] an amorous distance" (4). The quotation above also connects with Barthes's essay in Wallace's description of the intimacy of filmic spectation: both the "fantasy that you are them" and the "getting you to desire them as a body" are straight out of Lacan, or perhaps more accurately, not *straight* out of Lacan, but from Lacan via those film theorists, from Christian Metz ("film is like the mirror" [45]) to Barthes himself, who have adapted Lacan's ideas and applied them to film. Wallace suggests that these forms of narcissistic misidentification (*méconnaissance*) and desire are more appropriate to the moving image (and perhaps theatre also, given his use of the word "drama") than to literature. He also implies, however, that the effect of these reactions—a "kind of weird intimacy"—is essentially the same as the intimate effect engendered by other types of aesthetic experience: it is just the means that are different. This would suggest a convergent model for the different media, wherein the differences "at the level of sign-types, forms, materials of representation, and institutional traditions" (Mitchell, *Picture Theory* 161) do not give rise to diverging goals (as in the medium specificity thesis) but rather to different techniques for the achievement of a similar set of goals, a "kind of weird intimacy" numbering among them.

A further goal that certain films and certain novels may, for Wallace, have in common is to reverse the sleep-inducing effect of entertainment: "if the writer does his job right, what he basically does is remind the reader of how smart the reader is. Is to *wake the reader up* to stuff the reader's been aware of all the time" (Lipsky 41, my italics). Similarly, he writes elsewhere that the essential aim of art film is "to '*wake the audience up*' or render us more 'conscious'" (*SFT* 169, my italics). In this respect, the endeavors of Wallace's ideal novelist and of the art-film director bear a great deal of resemblance to the project of ideological critique. Barthes, when considering the problem of how to achieve separation from the filmic image, considers ideological critique a possible solution: "going [to the cinema] armed with the discourse of counter-ideology" (4) may wake us from the cinematic dream, or even prevent us from falling asleep in the first place. As well as using Lacanian ideas to draw an analogy between the movie-going experience and the *stade du miroir*, Barthes uses quasi-Althusserian terminology to compare the "filmgoer" to the "historical subject" and, correspondingly, the cinema to "ideological discourse." Althusser, who himself draws on Lacan's idea of "the *function of misrecognition*" (80) to explain the process of ideological interpellation and recognition, aims, through the process of ideological critique, to achieve "*knowledge* of the mechanism of this recognition" (Althusser 47). This knowledge can potentially help one to achieve some kind of separation from the sleep-inducing (metaphorically speaking) ideological discourse.

Wallace too (not to mention many of his characters in *Infinite Jest*) seeks knowledge of the mechanism of the Entertainment. As we have seen, he does so via analogy and comparison: with sleep, candy, infancy, literature, and ideology. He also does so via the technique of ekphrasis, and it is this that the second half of the essay will explore.

Establishing a definition of ekphrasis is a notoriously difficult task; as Ryan Welsh writes, "Few pieces of media jargon have as long a history or as considerable an evolution" (n.p.). Today, the primary sense of the term might best be expressed by James Heffernan's definition: "verbal representation of a visual representation" (3). A narrower definition might specify the "verbal representation" as poetry and the "visual representation" as a painting, sculpture, or comparable *objet d'art* (as in the ur-example, Homer's description of the shield of Achilles). A broader definition, such as those of Siglind Bruhn or Claus Clüver, might open up both categories— the object and its representation— regarding as necessary only the process of "transmedialization" (Bruhn 51). This would include transfers such as music to poetry, painting to song, dance to sculpture or—most importantly for our purposes—film to novel, as well as the reverse of all of these. For this essay, however, I propose to use Clüver's definition: "Ekphrasis is the verbal representation of a real or fictitious text composed in a non-verbal sign system" (26). As he points out, this conception of ekphrasis, as well as allowing for the verbal representation of nonvisual works such as music (while limiting the target medium to the verbal), "makes explicit the fact that these non-verbal texts may exist only in their verbalization" (26). This is particularly relevant to *Infinite Jest*, wherein the films described by Wallace for the most part exist only as fictional, verbal entities (at least at the time of the novel's writing).

There is relatively little writing about ekphrasis that focuses specifically on filmic ekphrasis (i.e. the verbal description of films, as opposed to the description of visual representations in film, which is one of the foci of Laura M. Sager Eidt's 2008 book *Writing and Filming the Painting*). As François Jost points out, "scholars tend to reflect more on the transformation of written texts into images than on the converse transformation" (71). Two of the most important recent essays on the subject refer to the ekphrasis of film in passing. Mitchell writes: "I have not mentioned the verbal representation of other kinds of visual representation such as . . . movies . . . each of which carries its own peculiar sort of textuality into the heart of the visual image" (*Picture Theory* 181). Similarly, Clüver mentions briefly some of the

> peculiar instances of the ancient and common practice of inserting ekphrastic passages into various kinds of narrative, of assigning verbally represented real or fictitious sculptures or sonatas and also dances and *films (as in Manuel Puig's* Kiss of the Spider Woman*)* a whole range of functions in epics, novels or short stories. (31, my italics)

Infinite Jest is certainly one such instance, and the verbally represented films therein certainly, as discussed in the previous section, serve a whole range of functions. This section focuses on one specific function of the way in which Wallace verbally represents films: namely, how the act of ekphrasis questions the relationship between film and novel.

A conventional ekphrasis of the Entertainment is in some sense impossible (at least within the novel's diegetic world), for, as Remy Marathe (a member of separationist Québécois terrorist cell who seeks the Entertainment) asks, "Who can know what is on them [cartridges containing the Entertainment]? Who can study the Entertainment while detached?" (*Infinite Jest* 489).[2] Watching the cartridge renders the viewer incapable of speaking for any purposes other than to beg for more viewings, and therefore certainly incapable of the process of transmedialization. We know as much because the US government has lost "several U.S.O. test-subjects, volunteers from the federal and military penal systems . . . in attempts to produce a description of the cartridge's contents"; one volunteer managed a brief ekphrasis of the opening moments, before his "mental and spiritual energies abruptly declined to a point where even near- lethal voltages through the electrodes couldn't divert his attention from the Entertainment" (549).

The ekphrasis of the Entertainment that the US government seeks would be a "safe" form of the cartridge, one that presumably would not have its hypnotic effects. This difference in power between original representation (the Entertainment) and its re-representation (the ekphrasis) is a more pronounced version of the common belief that films are capable of provoking far more intense reactions in their audiences than written words are in theirs. Bruce Morrissette quotes an article written in the 1950s by Walter Pitkin of Columbia University, which claimed that "movies are '10 to 100 times more effective per unit of time' than printed matter," or even, elsewhere in the article, "1,000,000,000 times more effective than the printed" (26). Such a figure would cast no small doubt over the worth of the work of those writers engaged in the ekphrasis of film. Though they are of course (as Morrissette points out) completely "unscientific and unsupported," Pitkin's "findings" are worthy of consideration, not only because they bear "witness to a widely shared intuitive conviction" (26), but also because the case of the Entertainment, fictional as it may be, seems to sustain them.

They might in part be explained by the fact that the filmic image (or, more to the point, the filmic stream of images and sounds), unlike the arbitrary sign-system of language, seems to be so natural. For Mitchell, "The image is the sign that pretends not to be a sign, masquerading as (or, for the believer, actually achieving) natural immediacy and presence" (*Iconology* 43). Given the way that film, more than the still image, takes in (with the uncoded appearance of photography) both movement and sound, it is reasonable to suggest that the potential believer might be even more easily taken in by the deceptive cinematic sign. Roland Barthes further explains the link between film's facade of "natural immediacy and presence" and the belief in its relative power over the written word: "I am riveted to the representation, and it is this bond which is the basis of the naturalness (pseudo-nature) of the filmed/represented scene (a bond made out of the ingredients of technique)" (3). For Barthes, it is not the "naturalness" that gives rise to the riveting power of film, but rather the "ingredients of technique," used to mask over the coded and arbitrary elements of film, that create the bond with the spectator; only then does the "pseudo- nature" of the cinema come into existence. Barthes and Mitchell both seek to reveal that which is not natural about film. Wallace, via ekphrasis, to some extent does the same, as we shall now see.

The first ekphrastic passage in the main text of *Infinite Jest*[3] comes in a section titled:

TENNIS AND THE FERAL PRODIGY, NARRATED BY HAL INCANDENZA, AN 11.5-MINUTE DIGITAL ENTERTAINMENT CARTRIDGE DIRECTED, RECORDED, EDITED, AND— ACCORDING TO THE ENTRY FORM—WRITTEN BY MARIO INCANDENZA . . . (172)

The chapter heading goes on, detailing the prize won by the film and its date, in relation to the death of James Incandenza, the father of both Hal and possibly (see 451) Mario (two years older than Hal, a physically grotesque and mentally "refracted" [314] but sincere and kind-hearted character and an aspiring filmmaker). If what follows is an ekphrasis, then the chapter heading serves the function of giving the reader the information he might, if he lived in the world of the novel, know before watching the film. Written with Wallace's typical encyclopedic maximalism,[4] it is a mixture of facts and suggestive interjections. The body of the chapter seems to be nothing more or less than an exact transcript of Hal's narration of the film.

As ekphrasis, it is rather lacking, in that, of the film's two tracks, one— the visual—is left out entirely. Its absence is to some degree compensated for (though to some degree also made all the more noticeable) by the distinctive style of the film's voiceover, in which most of the paragraphs begin "Here is . . ." or "This is . . ." (172–6). The lack of the image toward which the narration gestures assigns to the verbal track all descriptive and affective power; certainly the voiceover achieves things that the filmic image alone would have difficulty achieving (such as communicating that bandages around torn ankles should be wrapped "so tightly . . . your left leg feels like a log" [172]). Given, however, that the text of the chapter is presumably read aloud in its entirety on the film's soundtrack, the verbal representation essentially communicates nothing that the film does not, and fails to communicate a great deal that the film would seem to (not only the image track, and its editing, but also the sound of the voice reading the script as well as other elements of the sound track). Part of the effect is, by identifying the film entirely with its narration, to make clear just how much of the filmic experience is linguistic, and hence arbitrary and coded. Another part of the passage's effect is to provide a contrast with the next ekphrastic passage, which could not be more different.

It describes another of Mario's cartridges, an untitled film that uses a cast of puppets to tell the story of how the North America that the novel's readers know has transformed into O.N.A.N. (the Organization of North

American Nations, led by Johnny Gentle as dirt-phobic US President).[5] This ekphrasis is spread out over 63 pages and interspersed with descriptions of the setting of and reactions to the cartridge's screening (here, unlike in the earlier chapter, inserted seemingly at random,[6] the film is actually being shown within the world of the novel), as well as marginally- and non-related (or at least as non-related as any threads are in the novel) events. The first few pages are particularly worthy of attention. After a page and a half of scene-setting, the ekphrasis itself begins as follows:

> Mario's thing opens without credits, just a crudely matted imposition of fake-linotype print, a quotation from President Gentle's second Inaugural . . . against a full-facial still photo of a truly unmistakable personage. This is the projected face of Johnny Gentle, Famous Crooner. This is Johnny Gentle, né Joyner . . . (381)

Immediately, then, the film sets up a contrast between word and image. The word is written rather than (as in *Tennis and the Feral Prodigy*) spoken, and the image is still. As yet, then, the film described is barely film at all, but little more than a captioned photograph. This has the effect of aligning the passage with more traditional ekphrases of non-moving images, which, for Murray Krieger, serve to "interrupt the temporality of discourse, to freeze it during its indulgence in spatial exploration" (7). This idea draws on Gotthold Ephraim Lessing's *Laocoön*, which distinguishes between the so-called sister arts, poetry and painting, as a temporal and a spatial form, respectively: "succession of time is the province of the poet just as space is that of the painter" (91). The composite picture that begins Mario's film, however, is a hybrid of language and image, and so might be said to have a temporal as well as a spatial dimension. Furthermore, since the cartridge as a whole consists mostly of the moving rather than the still image, it undoubtedly has a temporal element. Thus, whether or not the ekphrasis serves to "freeze" the discourse is up for debate. One might even argue the opposite: as the passage continues from the quotation above (which ends by transitioning from ekphrastic representation of a representation—"This is the projected face"—to plain first-order representation—"This is Johnny Gentle"), Wallace spends almost two pages describing Johnny Gentle's background. There are minimal references to the progress of the film until the narrator mentions that behind Gentle is "a diorama of the Lincoln Memorial's Lincoln" (383), thus revealing that we are once again "seeing" the film as opposed to being explained its contexts. Given the amount of background that Wallace chooses to divulge, one gets the feeling that the progress of the ekphrasis is at this stage significantly slower than that of the film. Perhaps, then, it is the digression that freezes the progress of the ekphrasis, rather than the ekphrasis freezing the advancement of time within the novel.

Alternatively, we might see the digression not as freezing the narrative, but as causing it to skip backwards and forwards in time. *Infinite Jest* is by no means a chronologically linear novel, and its progress is therefore not identical with a linear movement forwards in time. Interestingly, when interviewed Wallace uses the analogy of music videos to explain the nonlinear manner in which he experiences life: "Does your life *approach* anything like a linear narrative? . . . You watch many videos? MTV videos? Lots of flash cuts in 'em. A lot of shit that looks incongruous but ends up having kind of a dream association with each other" (Lipsky 37). This works equally well as a description of this passage, and the way in which Wallace navigates seemingly "incongruous" pieces of information. As such, it would seem that novel and film (or at least music video) have the same capacity to represent Wallace's experience of life.

This reading would undermine the medium specificity thesis. Wallace's technique elsewhere in the passage, however, seems to support it. Particularly noticeable in this section is his use of punctuation, a tool basically unavailable to film apart from through the representation of text onscreen (though as Bruce Morrissette points out, there was a time when transitions such as dissolves and fades "were considered to play the role of punctuation or syntactical articulation in film language" [18]). Wallace strings together a series of 82 words with hyphens to create a kind of epic-length adjective to describe Johnny Gentle's phobias (*Infinite Jest* 381) and frequently makes uses of ellipses in dialogue to indicate silent, nonverbal communication, as well as the passage of time (385). He also uses parentheses as a method of expressing the dual tracks (sound and vision) of the film, as in the following example:

> A Johnny Gentle who was as of this new minute sending forth the call that "he wasn't in this for a popularity contest" (Popsicle-stick-and-felt puppets in the Address's audience assuming puzzled-looking expressions above their tiny green surgical masks). (383)

Not only the use of the present tense, but also the phrase "as of this new minute" represent and emphasize the constant present tense of film. The parentheses are, importantly, reserved for the visual rather than the verbal track. This has the effect of hierarchizing the relationship, making image subordinate to word.

These uses of punctuation find Wallace exploiting those things that are specific to language, following Lipsky's (later) advice, that "the best thing is to show what TV can't, to use the ways books are better than TV" (71). In the rest of the passage too, Wallace shows off the abilities that the written word affords him, varying his methods of representing speech (direct, reported, or frequently via a dialogue-only play-like format) and giving the reader behind the scenes information (identifying the organ on the soundtrack as "Mrs. Clarke's Wurlitzer" [*Infinite Jest* 384]), some gentle criticism ("It's not the cartridge's strongest scene . . ." [384]), and descriptions of the venue of the film's showing referring to senses that lie beyond film's representational capacity ("the dining hall is warm and close and multi-odored" [391]). Wallace's descriptions of the varying reactions to the film—witness the Canadian students, "chewing stolidly, faces blurred and distant," in contrast to the Americans, among whom there is "much cracking wise and baritone mimicry of [the] President" (385)— emphasize not only the cultural differences between the regions of O.N.A.N., but also the film's capacity to mean different things to different spectators, therefore bringing to the reader's attention its symbolic and coded (rather than natural) nature. The passage is undoubtedly more than just an ekphrasis, and while there may (inevitably) be certain things that a verbal description of a film cannot capture, this passage shows that there are equally many— perhaps more—things the written word can capture that film cannot.

Ekphrastic passages elsewhere in the novel often work similarly, bringing out both the differences between novel and film and the fact that the latter, like the former, operates through a set of codes rather than naturally. The description of Incandenza's nunsploitation-parody *Blood Sister* makes the reader particularly aware of the ways in which the cartridge adopts the conventions of the genre, such as in its opening, when the pre-credits action scene is frozen "in the middle of the nun's leaping kick, and its title, *Blood Sister: One Tough Nun*, gets matte-dissolved in and bleeds lurid blood-colored light down into the performance credits rolling across the screen's bottom" (701). The reader is aware that these techniques—the freezing, the bleeding of the words—are, as Wallace puts it in the David Lynch essay, "a set of allusive codes and contexts in the viewer's deep-brain core" (*SFT* 164).

This description follows Wallace's representation of the pre-credits scene, which begins, like the cartridge, "in violent medias res": "*'AIYEE!'* cries the man, rushing at the nun, wielding a power tool" (701). The two present participles here ("rushing" and "wielding") are an attempt to convey the simultaneous action onscreen that the viewer would perceive concurrently rather than serially; the complaint of *Lolita*'s Humbert Humbert is highly applicable here: "I have to put the impact of an instantaneous vision into a sequence of words; their physical accumulation in the page impairs the actual flash, the sharp unity of impression" (Nabokov 97). The inadequacy of the written word is made even more noticeable by the sentence's ambiguously placed modifier: it is not completely clear whether it is the man or the nun who is "wielding a power tool."

The ekphrasis of *Blood Sister* is also notable for its focus on the events in the viewing Room as well as onscreen. Hal, when the film begins, is alone: "I'm isolating. I came in here to be by myself" (*Infinite Jest* 702). His solitude is quickly disturbed by the entrance of first two students, then several more, who proffer reactions to the film as well as irreverent banter. The scene makes an interesting comparison with Karl Kroeber's comparison of the movie-going with the novel-reading experience:

> Each of us . . . sees for himself or herself; visual perception is private. Language, which enters into our mind through auditory systems of perception, is interpersonal, facilitating communication with others. . . . So, paradoxically, the privately created novel offers imaginative communion to a lonely reader, whereas a collaboratively constructed movie, even in an uncomfortably crowded theater, isolates each spectator. (Kroeber 57)

Kroeber's claim that the novel "offers imaginative communion" mirrors the opinion of Wallace, for whom "the point of books was to combat loneliness" (Lipsky xxii). This is not to say, however, that he believed that films always serve to reinforce loneliness: this is precisely the crime of which he accuses television in "E Unibus Pluram" (*SFT* 26), but it is not necessarily his experience of all filmed entertainment or art. When Wallace visits the cinema with Lipsky to see commercial action movie *Broken Arrow* (1996), he is "a commenting and empathizing audience," only falling quiet at the film's climax (Lipsky 122–3). Afterwards, he is not silent (like Barthes, who "does not care much to talk after seeing a film" [1]) but animated and communicative. This experience of cinema, like Hal's, is not an isolating one (despite Hal's best—or worst—intentions).

Kroeber's comparison also exhibits both the "pervasive neglect" that film words, according to Kamilla Elliott, have suffered "in film history, criticism, and theory" (3) and the common critical bias for pure arts (such as literature) over hybrid arts (such as film):

> Traditionally, pure arts have been more highly valued than hybrid ones. Therefore, in the battle for representational dominance, novels and films have been pressed toward semiotic and aesthetic purity. Pure arts are not only "better": in the case of hybrid arts masquerading as

pure arts, they can also claim territory which another hybrid art has abandoned in order to proclaim its own purity. They do this most commonly by using an analogical rhetoric, in which they speak of themselves in the language of the other. (5)

Wallace does use this "analogical rhetoric" throughout *Infinite Jest*. Whether or not it serves to proclaim the novel's aesthetic purity, though, is uncertain. We might look at phrases such as "The persons' lives' meanings had collapsed to such a *narrow focus*" (548–9; my italics) or a gun that "pans coolly back and forth" (609; this has the effect of prompting the reader to see both the literal and the metaphorical meanings when words like "shot" and "shoot" are used in relation to the gun). A particularly interesting example is Wallace's two uses of a simile involving time-lapse photography (i.e. a filmic technique). In both instances, the simile is used to describe films: Orin watches "clips of him[self] punting [that] unfolded like time-lapsing flowers" (298) and Mario's puppet film uses a montage of newspaper headlines "for a sort of time-lapse exposition of certain developments" (391). In the context of ekphrastic passages, these similes seem paradoxical and self-defeating: the film is described in words, which employ filmic terminology—if the ekphrases must rely on analogies drawn from the sphere of film to describe a film, surely the reader would be better off just watching the film rather than reading its description?

The similes also, I would argue, dilute rather than strengthen the novel's supposed semiotic purity. They acknowledge the influence of film on the novel, an admission that in interview and in his essays Wallace makes freely: of pop references in general (his example is *Gilligan's Island*), Wallace observes, "Me and a lot of the other young writers I know, we use these references sort of the way romantic poets use lakes and *trees*. I mean, they're just part of the mental furniture. That you carry around" (Lipsky 75). Similarly, in "E Unibus Pluram," he writes that the "use of Low references in a lot of today's High literary fiction," as well as helping to "create a mood of irony and irreverence" and "commenting" on "the vapidity of US culture," is most importantly a way of being "just plain realistic" (*SFT* 42–3). There are a great deal of pop/Low culture references in *Infinite Jest*, the majority of them being to film (Charlton Heston [205], Rita Hayworth [209], and Raquel Welch [371], for example) and television (for a whole host of references, see 834). In a novel set in an unfamiliar (though in many ways not discontinuous with early twenty-first-century America) future, these references provide an important connection to the reader's own experience. Their effect does not seem to be to proclaim an exclusive basis in a single semiotic sign-type.

The novel's already-undermined aesthetic purity is further disrupted by the fact that, as well as using occasional illustrations, diagrams, and graphic signifiers (see 502, 884, 891, and 1024), Wallace has a tendency to use letters and punctuation to convey meaning not only through their arbitrary, linguistic meanings, but also through their iconic meanings—that is, their pictorial resemblances. On at least three occasions he uses a capitalized v to depict not only visual objects ("T-shirt darkly v'd" [386]; "Her arms go up in a v" [760]) but also to evoke auditory effects ("the expanding white v of utter silence in the party's wake" [219]). Elsewhere, Wallace describes the eyebrows of a cat as "\/" (62) and some spilt baking soda as "a parenthesis of bright white on the counter" (236). These unconventional, quasi-hieroglyphic uses of the characters on a keyboard exhibit language's ability to represent spatially as well as temporally, brandishing a middle digit (a 1, presumably) at Gotthold Ephraim Lessing.

These devices have the effect of undermining any claims to aesthetic purity that this or any novel might have. Wallace's use of endnotes in *Infinite Jest* and footnotes throughout much of the rest of his work also emphasizes the visual and physical nature of the texts: readers of *Infinite Jest* are frequently advised to use two, or even three, bookmarks (Kottke), such is the amount of physical manipulation the book prompts with its endnotes and unconventional calendar (there is a handy explanation on 223). It should be noted that many of the more visual qualities of his (or any) books are lost when read as (semiotically "purer") eBooks, which often cannot, technologically, deal with anything but the standard array of letters and symbols. In the eBook edition of Wallace's essay collection *Consider the Lobster* (2005), the copyright page (or screen) at the book's beginning states that "'Host' is not included in this collection because it cannot be formatted as an eBook" (*Consider the Lobster*, eBook edition, 2). "Host" is, paradoxically, an extraordinarily visual essay about radio; it is filled with intricately boxed footnotes, connected to their referents with a frequently chaotic number of arrows, which occupy so much marginal space (top, bottom, and side) that page numbers are frequently elided. Wallace's writing is, then, in many different ways, extremely visual, nonsensing any claims to semiotic purity.

The final passage to be considered is one that, at first glance, might not appear to be ekphrastic at all. It is a passage in which Joelle, seated (not insignificantly) in a chair in the form of film director Georges Méliès at Molly Notkin's apartment, and preparing to attempt suicide via cocaine overdose, recalls the events immediately preceding the scene. It is a verbal representation of a memory rather than "*of a real or fictitious text composed in a non-verbal sign system*" (Clüver 26). The memory, however, is presented as if it were a film, therefore strongly associating the passage with ekphrasis. Joelle (Film & Cartridge Studies student that she is) is frequently described as experiencing life in the same way that a spectator watches a film. Here, she "reels in out of the overall voices' noise but seeing no one really else, the absolute end of her life and beauty running in a kind of stuttered old hand-held 16mm before her eyes, projected against the white screen on her side" (*Infinite Jest* 220–1). The use of the word "reels," with its connotation of reels of film, is surely no accident. This phrase frames the following two pages as an entertainment, and they play out in a constant present tense, with occasional phrases such as "an other-directed second" (221) evoking through ambiguity the language of film. Wallace aligns our visual perspective with that of Joelle: "everything milky and halated through her veil's damp linen" (221). This description recalls both the descriptions of the Entertainment (which has "a milky blur" [939] as if filmed with "a milky filter" [851]) and a nickname for Hal ("Halation," the explanation of which—"A halo-shaped exposure-pattern around light sources seen on chemical film at low speed. . . . That most angelic of distortions"—also recalls, in its references to angels and film, the Entertainment [97]). Joelle's eyes are figured as the lens of a camera, her veil a filter over it (which also serves the function of protecting her from being seen—like the camera, her vision is one way only).[7]

The language of film, then, is throughout *Infinite Jest*, not only in passages of explicit ekphrasis, but also in other, non-traditionally ekphrastic sections. Wallace's ekphrases draw attention both to the factors that distinguish the written word from filmed entertainment—such as film's pretense of naturalness, its ability to express image (and hence space) and sound, and corresponding inability to express, say, punctuation or the sense of smell, as well as writing's unavoidably sequential nature—and to the characteristics that the two media may or do share—such as the frequently nonlinear treatment of the passage of time, the potential for overcoming loneliness, and a basis in arbitrary, coded techniques rather than the simple recording of nature. The novel provokes questions regarding ideas of medium specificity and the relationship between the novel and film, whether it is complementary or rivalrous, or, as would seem to be the case, something more complicated.

In the first half of this essay, I argued that Wallace's presentation of film in the novel (whether as art or as entertainment) is consistently ambivalent, in aesthetic, intellectual, and moral terms. Film's relation to the novel, I maintained, seemed to be one more of similarity than difference. The second half took this argument further, analyzing areas of equivalence and disparity between the media, suggesting that their relationship might not be one simply of alliance or conflict, but something more complex. Perhaps most importantly, I contended that Wallace's technique and his representation of film in the novel reveal an essential element of semiotic hybridity (rather than purity) in his writing, and in writing in general. The relationship between novel and film might therefore best be characterized as intertwined.

Certainly the existence of *Infinite Jest* today in all its various forms is irreducibly hybrid, crossing the boundaries of novel and film, word and image, entertainment and art: there are many short films based on the novel (several of which were exhibited as part of Sam Ekwurtzel's project "A Failed Entertainment"), as well as paintings, graphic design projects, and music videos (The Decemberists' "Calamity Song"). Wallace's calls for a balance between leisure and work, high and low culture, and reading and spectating are arguably even more relevant today than they were in 1996, and the hybrid conception of the text for which I have argued would provide support for these calls. This essay's interpretation of the novel, then, suggests not only that *Infinite Jest* is a powerful call for balance, but also that such a call is more important than ever.

Notes

1 The term "MacGuffin" (popularized by Alfred Hitchcock) refers to a device used to drive a plot—often a mysterious object of apparently great significance, sought by the story's characters. The specific nature of the MacGuffin is typically irrelevant to the story, however: its importance usually lies solely in the fact that it gives the characters something to chase.

2 David H. Evans, in his essay "'The Chains of Not Choosing': Free Will and Faith in William James and David Foster Wallace," suggests that Marathe, as "a character positioned outside the national addiction to passive amusement" (179), is (unlike *Infinite Jest*'s American characters) able to critique the addictive pleasures of the Entertainment.

3 Earlier in the novel (64), the reader is directed to a lengthy endnote outlining the filmography of James O. Incandenza, complete with ekphrastic descriptions of many of these films. For more on this, see David Letzler's essay in this volume.

4 For more on *Infinite Jest* as an encyclopedic novel, see Letzler's essay.

5 For a comparison between this passage in the novel and Jennifer Egan's *A Visit from the Goon Squad* (2010), see Andrew Hoberek's essay, "The Novel after David Foster Wallace" (222–3).

6 Though only seemingly: despite reviews such as Michiko Kakutani's, describing *Infinite Jest* as merely a "compendium of whatever seems to have crossed Mr. Wallace's mind" (qtd. in Burn 27), the novel, as Wallace has made clear (Interview with Michael Silverblatt), is deliberately and intricately structured—specifically, in the pattern of a Sierpinski Gasket.

7 Mario Incandenza can be seen in much the same way: his head-mount camera makes the young filmmaker's field of vision almost identical with the documentaries he can frequently be found filming (*Infinite Jest* 755).

7

Encyclopedic Novels and the Cruft of Fiction: *Infinite Jest*'s Endnotes

David Letzler

In the end, the production of footnotes sometimes resembles less the skilled work of a professional carrying out a precise function to a higher end than the offhand production and disposal of waste products.
Anthony Grafton, *The Footnote: A Curious History* (6)

Endnotes and the paradox of the encyclopedic novel

In the decade and a half since its publication, David Foster Wallace's *Infinite Jest* has frequently been described as "encyclopedic" (see Cioffi 161; Burn, *Reader's Guide* 21; Aubry 208; Tresco 113). This term, probably most associated in literary studies with Edward Mendelson's 1976 essays "Gravity's Encyclopedia" and "Encyclopedic Narrative,"[1] has been used over the past five decades to categorize a genre of large, complex novels, particularly those that incorporate substantial specialized information from the sciences, the arts, and history. If we adopt Hilary A. Clark's terms and define the encyclopedic novel as a prose fiction work concerned with the "discovery," "ordering," or "retrieval" of knowledge ("Encyclopedic Discourse" 99),[2] then *Infinite Jest*'s 388 endnotes, which take up the final 97 of the novel's 1,079 pages, probably encourage that classification more than any other narrative element.[3] Just as the academic endnote has long supplied the foundation of evidentiary support for scholarly contributions to knowledge—the traditional attitude being, as Anthony Grafton writes, "the text persuades, the notes prove" (15)—the extensive supplementary information provided by *Infinite Jest*'s notes, covering subjects as diverse as pharmaceutical chemistry, calculus, political history, and tennis (including both real-world facts on these subjects and facts specific to the novel), gives contextual information to establish the workings of Wallace's strange world in a manner not dissimilar to how, say, *The Waste Land*'s do for T. S. Eliot's.

Infinite Jest's notes are not always used for this straightforwardly encyclopedic purpose, though. After all, as Gérard Genette has described, and Edward Maloney has further schematized, historically, the literary note's functions have not only included this quasi-scholarly one, but also spanned many authorial intentions and implied recipients, prominently including those notes "written" by fictional characters or playful narrators so as to layer voices for storytelling or parodic purposes, as may be seen in authors ranging from Swift and Pope to Borges and Joyce, most notably in Nabokov's *Pale Fire* (319–43).[4] This type of note also appears in *Infinite Jest*. For example, when the nutty Dr Dolores Rusk discusses something she calls the "Coatlicue Complex," a reference keys the reader to endnote 216 (516), but instead of defining this invented term—as the notes do for other inventions, like the fictional Microsoft OS *Pink* glossed in note 95 (1003)— the note's response to this phrase is merely, "No clue" (1036). Obviously, Wallace "knows" what this term means, as he created the fictional world in which it exists and thus may make of it whatever he wants,[5] so the note works not to support the narrator's authoritative knowledge but to separate his voice from that of any real or implied author (in this case, to comic effect). Elsewhere, the endnotes are used for narrative layering of other kinds, as when entire scenes are diverted from the main text to endnotes for no apparent reason: for instance, the scene depicting Michael Pemulis' expulsion (1073–6) is not only shunted to note 332, it is not even endnoted *from* anything, as the reference in the main text does not appear next to any actual word or sentence but is suspended in the white space between scenes (795).

On their own, obviously, neither use is narratively radical or troublesome. In conjunction, however, they quietly create a serious problem, because when used side-by-side, these two types of notes theoretically ought to negate each other's effects. Since scholarly notes are designed to provide authoritative support for the author's main text, layering notes' efforts toward (in most critics' eyes) "subverting the unity of the text and destabilizing, rather than affirming, the central narrative" (Fishburn 287–8) should upend the scholarly notes' informative effect. However, were we to assert that the notes primarily work in this destabilizing, cheekily unreliable way, we would have an awfully difficult time explaining why so many of the novel's notes seem simply to supply accurate information of the blandest kind. Imagine how *Pale Fire* would've read if Charles Kinbote spent most of his annotations telling us things like that "B.P.D." (251) stands for "Boston Police Department" (1000), as is the sole purpose of *Infinite Jest*'s 83rd note—his narrative would've lost its seductive pull and subversive edge within a few pages. If neither major articulation of the function of notes in literature adequately explains *Infinite Jest*'s endnotes, then, what can they possibly do that's worth adding a hundred pages to an already enormous novel?

We may begin to answer that question by observing that these two types of notes' incommensurability exemplifies the major critical conflict over the nature of encyclopedic novels themselves. In one line of criticism, encyclopedic novelists, upon mastering their cultures' vast data, use the novels to educate readers about it, as would a conventional encyclopedia. For instance, Mendelson asserts that encyclopedic novels "attempt to render the full range of knowledge and beliefs of a national culture" ("Gravity's Encyclopedia" 162), while even Tom LeClair's more poststructuralist take argues that only such "extraordinarily knowledgeable" works (1) are able to "give readers an intellectual mastery [of their culture] and, in their bulk, an aesthetic tower to counterbalance the towers of material culture" (17). In the other approach, however, the genre is conceived not as parallel to an encyclopedia but a criticism of the entire encyclopedic project. Countering Mendelson, Stephen Burn claims that, especially in the postwar era, the "mass of data exceed[s] the synthesizing powers of even [the encyclopedic novelist's] encyclopedic grasp" ("Collapse" 59), and so a good encyclopedic novelist "does not simply use the novel to store data, but rather explores the negative impact endlessly proliferating information has upon the lives of his characters" ("After Gaddis" 163).[6] Other writers in this line assert that the genre is best where it "debunks totality, highlighting a contemporary shift to fragmentation" (van Ewijk, "Encyclopedia" 220) or depicts "the encyclopaedist's despair over the impossibility of attaining to perfect knowledge" (Clark, *Fictional Encyclopedia* 37). Most conclude that we should not encyclopedize but seek more "open" approaches to knowledge: quoting *Infinite Jest* itself, Burn describes this process as "tak[ing] data pretty much as it comes" instead of succumbing to the "dangerous addiction" of encyclopedizing (*Reader's Guide* 21; also see Strecker 296; van Ewijk, "Encyclopedia" 215; and Burn, "Collapse" 61). Of the two critical approaches, obviously, the former is most compatible with the scholarly note and the latter the layering note.

However, while these approaches to encyclopedic fiction conflict with each other, more interesting, especially for understanding *Infinite Jest*'s endnotes, may be the underlying paradox they share, which reveals limitations to both. While an encyclopedia is by nature a *reference* work, fiction is (in Dorrit Cohn's words) "literary *nonreferential* narrative" (1; emphasis mine); that is, encyclopedias represent that which has existed elsewhere, while fiction presents that which does not. Referring to something as an "encyclopedic fiction," then, should be a flat contradiction in terms. An encyclopedia's value requires that it accountably and accurately represent the real world—that it is *un*original, referencing something theoretically verifiable elsewhere.[7] By definition, however, fiction's importance lies in the material that *is* original and is not contingent upon that type of reference.[8] As a result, it should seem very strange for a writer to choose the novel to communicate a "mastery" of information, given how the form disavows its text's accuracy. For the same reason, though, the novel's rejection of factual standards prevents it from directly critiquing textual knowledge in the way many critics claim it does: that one can imagine a world where all is nonsense says nothing about whether the one we inhabit is sensible, just as the disorientingly recursive, labyrinthine spaces drawn by Piranesi or Escher do not constitute critiques of the rules of architecture or physics.

What are we to do, then, with the all the vast data presented by the encyclopedic novel? In particular, what are we to do with the endnotes to *Infinite Jest*? There is no easy answer. Though often the notes serve novelistic functions independent of their nature as data—for instance, note 213's discussion of tennis's ball-retrieval etiquette is less important as information (though it is accurate as that) than it is as a characterization of Hal Incandenza and Axford (1035–6)—frequently, the information they present is minimally relevant at all, like note 296's description of the chemical makeup of the fake blood used in low-budget movies (1054). Notes of this type appear throughout *Infinite Jest*—mostly accurate (though not always), occasionally interesting, but barely relevant—and though they are characteristic of the novel's encyclopedic nature, their function is difficult to explain or justify.

To make sense of this sort of information, we need a new way to discuss the encyclopedic novel and the place of information in fiction generally. To do so, we might begin by observing an odd characteristic shared by many of *Infinite Jest*'s endnotes: many are basically pointless.

The cruft of fiction

This characterization may seem blasphemous. Many of the novel's admirers will no doubt rush to argue that note 296 is somehow necessary to fully appreciate the faux-lowbrow look of Incandenza's films. Let's grant that specific point, then, for the sake of argument, because there are more extreme examples of endnote text so extraneous that I doubt anyone could make a coherent argument for their significance. Early in the novel, for instance, when the narrator first introduces us to Enfield, he provides a categorization of its students' recreational drug preferences keyed to five separate endnotes (53). Note 8 is a representative example:

[8] I.e., psylocibin; Happy Patches[a]; MDMA/Xstasy (bad news, though, X); various low-tech manipulations of the benzene-ring in methoxy-class psychedelics, usually home-makable; synthetic dickies like MMDA, DMA, DMMM, 2CB, para-DOT I-VI, etc.— though note this class doesn't and shouldn't include CNS-rattlers like STP, DOM, the long-infamous West-U.S.-Coast "Grievous Bodily Harm" (gamma hydroxybutyric acid), LSD-25 or -32, or DMZ/M.P. Enthusiasm for this stuff seems independent of neurologic type.

  a. Homemade transdermals, usually MDMA or Muscimole, with DDMS or the over-counter-available DMSO as the transdermal carrier. (984)

How does one read this note? If one does not have a background in pharmaceutical chemistry and/or practical knowledge of synthetic street drugs, one simply can't. Since the narrator declines to explain the distinctions between, or qualities common to, the drugs he lists, the note's sequence of acronyms and Greek prefixes will be illegible to uninformed readers. At the same time, those with the knowledge to successfully differentiate these terms have nothing new to learn: for them, the passage is entirely redundant. While these respective experiences of being over- and under-whelmed by textual data may appear to be opposed, they are alike in the way they (perhaps after provoking a bemused chuckle at the note's unreadability) immediately terminate focused attention—which is to say that almost all readers will find this note boring.[9]

This junk text, simultaneously too excessive and too vacuous to be worth anyone's attention, can be found throughout *Infinite Jest*, but is not unique to it. In fact, it may be the characteristic text of encyclopedic novels: to name three other examples, similar purposelessness can be seen in the pseudo-scientific cetology chapter of Herman Melville's *Moby-Dick*, the idiotic minor-character chatter about art and economics in William Gaddis' *The Recognitions* and *J R*, and the endless catalogs of nondescript minor poets in Roberto Bolaño's novels. Given its ubiquity, we ought to name this phenomenon. I suggest we use "cruft," after the half-slang/half-technical term from computer programming. As defined by *The New Hacker's Dictionary*, cruft is "Excess; superfluous junk; used esp. of redundant or superseded code" and "Poorly built, possibly over-complex" (Raymon 135). Cruft is not "wrong" per se, but it is excessive to no clear purpose, simultaneously too much and too little. That this term can be usefully applied to the encyclopedic novel may be best seen in how the word has taken its strongest hold in the Wikipedia community, where it is used so frequently by contributors to characterize material they feel to be excessive, redundant, or distracting that the site has posted official essays addressing how and when to invoke it ("Discussing cruft"). In most cases, the information dubbed "cruft" by editors is not inaccurate, but simply of minimal use, whether because it is trivial or simply incomprehensible, as the site's wide-net approach to gathering and presenting maximum information on a subject leads inevitably to the introduction of substantial material that almost no one cares about.

Obviously, the term is pejorative, and even when we transplant it to contemporary novel theory—which has long since abandoned the Henry James/Percy Lubbock[10] model of economic, organic literary form in favor of more decentralized theories of fiction—one usually does not speak well of a novel in calling its text excessive. Nonetheless, excessiveness is exactly what draws many readers to these novels.[11] Granted, words like "excessive" and "boring" suggest subjective judgments that all readers may not share: some readers find densely written prose to be very boring and are excited by genre novels, while others feel precisely the reverse, so we should avoid calling text "cruft" simply because our tastes reject it. Yet encyclopedic novels' cruft seems often to achieve a state of near-objective pointlessness, combining both excess and emptiness, redundancy with wild innovation. Sometimes it presents long, one-off catalogs of information that have no informational use; sometimes it presents scenes that appear irrelevant to any traditional fictional elements like plot or character; sometimes it is endlessly repetitive and clichéd; and sometimes it is simply impossible to read at all. To handle such passages, we must find some way to articulate how this purposelessness may still have a purpose for readers, some cognitive benefit to processing material that appears to have minimal relevance as information. To invert Kant, we need to understand how it may have purpose*less*ness *with* purpose.

What should one do when one encounters cruft? As even LeClair admits, the usual response is to become bored, then skim or skip ahead (14–15), and in many cases this is quite necessary. As cognitive psychology has recently shown, if either the paucity or excess of stimulating material causes one to be incapable of paying attention, forcing one's focus will only lead to frustration (among other negative affects) and cognitive decline (see Carriere, Cheyne, and Smilek; Fenske and Raymond). Even those critics who insist that no committed reader could ever justify skipping a word of any work of literature—especially in an encyclopedic novel (see Moore 64–6)—should recognize that in some cases this is precisely the right approach. For instance, consider chapter IX of Mark Z. Danielewski's *House of Leaves*, a novel framed as a commentary by the 20something ne'er-do-well Johnny Truant on a manuscript by a blind old man named

Zampanó (one already loaded with notes, fragments, and comments), which purports to describe a documentary film by photographer Will Navidson (fictional, even within the world of the novel) about a labyrinthine haunted house. (If this were not enough narrative layering, there is an additional editor commenting on Truant's work.) In chapter IX, where Zampanó describes Navidson's acquaintances exploring the physics-defyingly large, but empty, labyrinth (107–52), the text's physical structure becomes overrun with marginal notes. Twenty-six consecutive pages acquire an off-center blue-outlined box that comprises one elaborate note listing types of furniture that do *not* appear in the empty labyrinth; meanwhile, each of eight consecutive left-hand pages features a marginal column detailing styles and examples of architecture with which the house has *nothing* in common, opposite eight right-hand pages with a complementary upside-down marginal column listing famous architects from the present back to Daedalus. To read thoroughly the scores of items on each of these lists would be beside the point: as even the novel's most exuberant critics admit, none but the most obsessive readers actually "read" all this text, because one might easily get lost trying (see Chanen 171–2).[12] Furthermore, those who make the attempt have little to gain. The pointlessness of the lists' text should be clear from the way two of them list things that are *not* in the labyrinth, and since we find out elsewhere that the labyrinth is empty, these encyclopedic catalogs do not even inform us of that. The text's apparent purpose is not to be read carefully but to disorient its readers, giving them the sensation of being overcome by an impossibly labyrinthine void. Once readers adjust to the labyrinth, though, they should quickly realize that this text is meaningless and should be skipped entirely. The characters themselves apparently make the same adjustment: later chapters describing their adventures in the labyrinth replace the ornate marginalia with large swathes of white space, demonstrating how little the text actually signified.

In this way, *House of Leaves*'s notes are similarly excessive and empty to many of those in *Infinite Jest*. *House of Leaves*, though, can justify this pointless text via its dazzling visual effect. Conversely, in the absence of such virtuosic images, how does one explain *Infinite Jest*'s equally pointless notes?

Monumental dullness

Unlike the artful junk in Danielewski's marginalia, there actually *is* quite a lot of important material in Wallace's endnotes, yet to discover it, one has to wade through lots of cruft. Consequently, the notes' alternate pointlessness and importance require something most critics are loath to admit in their reading processes: modulation in the rhythm of one's reading between focused attention and different levels of skimming. As far as I know, only Marshall Boswell has acknowledged that *Infinite Jest*'s notes demand this:

> Readers of the book quickly learn that the notes can provide useless information, essential information, extra but nonessential narrative, or even, at times, narrative that is more important to the ongoing novel than the passage to which the note is attached. Readers can, and even must, devise some way to read through the book that allows them to keep their focus on the story while also mining the notes for all their information, comedy, and readerly pleasure. (120)

Though Boswell mentions this merely in passing, I think he may have identified the novel's most strange and profound narrative element. How we "devise some way to read through the book" is not just an interesting side-effect of the novel's structure: it is central to the way our minds interact with the information that *Infinite Jest* (and, I believe, the encyclopedic novel generally) presents. If the novel cannot provide or critique knowledge, it certainly can test and even alter the way we process data.

Why does this require cruft, though? Why not simply load an encyclopedic novel with lots of interesting material to be processed? Wallace himself articulates this in his final, unfinished novel, *The Pale King*, which, even in its incomplete state, contains some of the most profound statements on boredom, attention, and pointless text in contemporary literature. The novel's main characters' jobs as IRS examiners place them in as pure a battle of attention modulation as can be imagined, as they must cull through endless pages of data, bureau jargon, and coded cross-references in search of hidden narratives of tax evasion. Once they become acclimated to the job, though, the examiners discover its larger implications. In Wallace's narrator's words:

> Fact: The birth agonies of the New IRS led to one of the great and terrible PR discoveries in modern democracy, which is that if sensitive issues of governance can be made sufficiently dull and arcane, there will be no need for officials to hide or dissemble, because no one not directly involved will pay enough attention to cause trouble. No one will pay attention because no one will be interested, because, more or less *a priori*, of these issues' monumental dullness. (84)

There is simply so much information to process in the digital age—and so many entertaining sources of it available to distract and hold our attention when we become bored—that any information that poses significant challenges to attention will be ignored. And why shouldn't it? Most such information—subsections to subsections of tax code, footnotes to endnotes in textbooks—is pointless and trivial, and that which isn't might require so much work to understand in comparison to its possible benefits that it would not be worth seeking. (See Wouters in this volume for more discussion on this subject.) However, this makes any breakthrough from dulling trivia to hidden discovery—whether it be tax evasion, obscured government malfeasance, hidden fine-print qualifications—even more valuable, because it is so much less likely to be found. Having understood this, one of *The Pale King*'s examiners concludes that the only essential ability in the modern world is "the ability, whether innate or conditioned, to find the other side of the rote, the picayune, the meaningless, the repetitive, the pointlessly complex. To be in a word, unborable. . . . It is the key to modern life. If you are immune to boredom, there is literally nothing you cannot accomplish" (438). To develop this ability, though, one must seek out pointless text and learn to work one's way through it—which is precisely what the encyclopedic novel's cruft forces one to do.

Becoming totally "unborable," though, is not as purely positive as that quote implies. Though Ralph Clare, elsewhere in this volume, writes that "To be able to reach a state of total concentration means gaining the possibility of transcending boredom," claiming that this state will enable us "*to parse social, political, and cultural narratives for relevance and meaning*" (see Clare 201), we should observe how its pitfalls are demonstrated by the one character in the novel who has achieved this state. As a newspaper article early in the book recounts:

> Supervisors at the IRS's regional complex in Lake James township are trying to determine why no one noticed that one of their employees had been sitting dead at his desk for four days before anyone asked if he was feeling all right.
> Frederick Blumquist, 53, who had been employed as a tax return examiner with the agency for over thirty years, suffered a heart attack in the open-plan office he shared with twenty-five coworkers at the agency's Regional Examination Center on Self-Storage Parkway. He quietly passed away last Tuesday at his desk, but nobody noticed until late Saturday evening when an office cleaner asked how the examiner could still be working in an office with all the lights off.

Mr. Blumquist's supervisor, Scott Thomas, said, "Frederick was always the first guy in each morning and the last to leave at night. He was very focused and diligent, so no one found it unusual that he was in the same position all that time and didn't say anything. He was always absorbed in his work, and kept to himself." (27–8)

This passage's significance is not that the tedium of Blumquist's work gave him a coronary—indeed, it may have functioned as did Hugh Steeply's father's singled-minded obsession with *M*A*S*H* in *Infinite Jest*, putting off an infarction that would have come sooner otherwise (646). No, it's that Blumquist's constant state of unborable attention is indistinguishable from death. To have perfect focus on something means that all else is shut out; if one spends too long with cruft, one joins it. Though Blumquist is the most extreme example of the destructiveness of pure concentration, other examiners face it too: Claude Sylvanshine, for instance, is able to focus so exclusively on analyzing how best to study for his exams that he indefinitely postpones actual studying (9, 14); by contrast, his friend Reynolds's boredom with such strategizing allows him to get to the studying itself (11), leading him to impress upon Sylvanshine the importance of "homing in on which facts were important" and casting the rest aside (16). One must not be unborable, then: instead, one must simultaneously have a high threshold of boredom *and* the ability to be bored by totally useless data so that one may skip on to more vital information.

Because there is vastly more information available in our era than ever before—and contrary to late-twentieth-century worries about the coming dominance of the image at the expense of the word, this new information is largely *text* (see Goldsmith 24–7; Koepnick 233)—we also have vastly more *pointless* information than ever before. Moreover, we have no more time in which to sort through it all. It is telling that the most emblematic technical advances of our time are directed toward getting rid of most of the unprecedented volume information to which our technology has given us access, as may be seen in the search algorithms and data mining that made Google and Facebook into corporate powers. As a result, there may be no more vital ability in the digital age than being able to recognize what data is junk and what few bits have significance—how to sort and order information. As an Advanced Tax professor in *The Pale King* tells his students, "Yesterday's hero pushed back at bounds and frontiers—he penetrated, tamed, hewed, shaped, made, brought things into being. Yesterday's society's heroes generated facts. For this is what society is—an agglomeration of facts. . . . Gentlemen, the heroic frontier now lies in the ordering and deployment of those facts" (232). How we develop methods for doing so, though—deciding what text deserves closer attention and what does not, how long to spend with any given text, when to abandon it, when to follow new paths it suggests, when to return back to the point from which we started, etc.—is incredibly complicated. We have precious little vocabulary in which to discuss it, too, though these procedures are too important for us *not* to have any method of systematically discussing and analyzing how we use them. However, the encyclopedic novel helps us develop ways to do so, serving as a kind of all-purpose gymnasium for mental filtering skills. Its expansive, messy, heteroglossic, and yet at least partly coherent structures test and pressure our systems for ordering and retrieving data.

That semi-coherence is crucial, of course. If the novel were all cruft, it could (and should) be abandoned entirely; life is too short to be spent reading nonsense. The line between a novel about the experience of pointlessness and a pointless novel, however can be a thin one, and among the many sad things about Wallace's suicide is that he was never able to fully work through the implications of this idea in *The Pale King,* which presses the issue considerably. In the state in which he left them, his experiments in cruft often test the boundaries of sheer pointlessness, frequently with little in the way of discovery behind them. We'll never know how such sections might've appeared, either individually or in context, as the novel went through further writing and revision. *Infinite Jest,* however, does include many passages that exercise this process profoundly, forcing readers not only to skim through a tremendous amount of cruft so as to avoid locking up in Blumquist-like stasis, but to be ready to modulate their attention swiftly and subtly at any moment when something important does arrive. Nowhere does it do this more rigorously than in its endnotes.

Filtering the Incandenza filmography

Note 24, James O. Incandenza's filmography, provides a microcosm for how the endnotes and the text as a whole use cruft. Taking up eight and a half pages, it comprises the production details and plot summaries of all Incandenza's 78 films. The note is loaded with cruft, the extent of which has not been fully appreciated. Even Jeffrey Karnicky, who claims that the filmography's entries reveal the work's "asignifying stasis," really argues that they *represent* (signify) that stasis via how the films' characters are made catatonically passive by the spectacles they watch (91–123). However, many entries do not even signify so much as this, such as the five that merely read "*Untitled.* Unfinished. UNRELEASED" (990, 992). These entries are pure cruft: their inclusion cannot further or enrich the novel's plot, because

Wallace tells us nothing about them, nor are they necessary for factual completeness as in a real filmography, because these unfinished films only exist inasmuch as they are invented by Wallace in the note. Such entries do not represent pointlessness—they *are* pointlessness. Other entries are barely less insignificant, like the eight undescribed, hyper-ironically self-negating and "conceptually unfilmable" works called "found dramas" (989–90).[13]

Even some more substantial entries are clearly cruft, because as Wallace's narrator acknowledges, "a lot of [Incandenza's *oeuvre*] . . . was admittedly just plain pretentious and unengaging and bad" (64). As one film critic cited in the filmography notes, Incandenza's work is almost exclusively derivative (990). Granted, much is at least purportedly parodic, yet the films seem to proliferate rather than creatively satirize the dullest elements of that which they supposedly critique. Consider this one, for instance:

> *Fun With Teeth*. B.S. Latrodectus Mactans Productions. Herbert G. Birch, Billy Tolan, Pam Heath; 35 mm.; 73 minutes; black and white; silent w/ non-human screams and howls. Kosinski/Updike/Peckinpah parody, a dentist (Birch) performs sixteen unanesthetized root-canal procedures on an academic (Tolan) he suspects of involvement with his wife (Heath). MAGNETIC VIDEO, PRIVATELY RELEASED BY LATRODECTUS MACTANS PROD. (987)

Like most of the entries, almost half of this listing comprises boilerplate technical specs, which are substantially cruft. But the film summary is not much more significant itself. Like many of Incandenza's films, *Fun with Teeth* merely reproduces its targets' overused tropes rather than generating humor from them in a novel way. Given that the entire history of Western prose satire has centered around the development of techniques by which one may mock stupidity without replicating it—consider the *reductio ad absurdum*s of Joseph Heller's *Catch-22*, which parodies a malfunctioning military bureaucracy by generating the kind of inspired, lunatic automatism that Bergson found at the root of all humor (29–33) when, for instance, an I.B.M. error accidentally dubs a character Major Major Major Major (96)—it is very odd that *Fun with Teeth* seems to *expand* rather than reduce the stupidity of the concept films it parodies. The result seems to me precisely the toothless postmodern irony against which Wallace railed in "E Unibus Pluram." If readers find any humor in this entry, it is not because the parody has found a novel way of skewering its subject (or even added insight on the Incandenza family's pervasive dental hang-ups) but likely because they acknowledge how stupendously tedious they'd find such a movie to watch, likely prompting greater skimming of the text describing it.

Other film descriptions approach cruft for other reasons. *Kinds of Light*—a sequence of "4,444 individual frames, each of which photo depicts lights of different source, wavelength, and candle power, each reflected off the same unpolished tin plate and rendered disorienting at normal projection speeds by the hyperretinal speed at which they pass" (986)—is explicitly described as so sensually overwhelming that no reader could train his imagination on it without attention breaking. Such passages' near-unreadable overload and redundancy ravages cognition while diverting reading from a main narrative—which, incidentally, has been interrupted while in the midst of its vital overview of Incandenza family history—to which they seem largely irrelevant. It becomes very tempting to skip the note and return to the main text.

Yet amidst the cruft, there are many entries that are important to examine. For instance, if one abandons note 24 at *Fun with Teeth*, deciding that the note's next six pages will likely be no more readable than the earlier notes' pharmaceutical catalogs, one does not read about *It Was a Great Marvel That He Was in the Father without Knowing Him* (992–3), a filmed version of a scene described earlier in the book wherein Incandenza posed as a therapist as a pretext for having a conversation with his 11-year-old son Hal (27–31). This entry is not mere redundancy, as it not only recounts the prior scene but adds material about Incandenza inaccessible in the main text's version. There, Incandenza comes off not only as bewilderingly overbearing but as both so poor at responding to his son (whose speech he seems at times unable to hear) and so bafflingly inept at disguising his appearance that readers would be justified in questioning his sanity. The film version, however, acknowledges that the father-therapist character is "suffering from the delusion that his etymologically precocious son . . . is pretending to be mute" (993), demonstrating both that Incandenza is not deluded as to how unhinged his own behavior appears and that he tragically understands that the failure to communicate rests largely with him and not Hal. This insight into Incandenza's recognition of his inability to communicate is necessarily incommunicable elsewhere in the novel. Other entries treat additional events in Incandenza's life similarly: *As of Yore* (991), for instance, appears to be a filmed version of a rambling monologue delivered by Incandenza's father during the former's childhood (157–69), while the passage in which Incandenza describes his inspiration in developing annular fusion (491–503) becomes fodder for the film *Valuable Coupon Has Been Removed* (990–1). Furthermore, a perusal of the films starring an actor named Cosgrove Watt—alluded to in passing only a handful of times otherwise (16, 941, 944–5, 971)—creates a sequence of filmed meditations on Incandenza's anxieties about the difficulties of family life (especially father-son communication) that is nowhere else in the novel so well articulated, not even when Incandenza tries to discuss the issue directly with Don Gately when he appears as a wraith late in the novel.

Again, discovering this portrait of an artist unable to express his emotional intelligence anywhere except in his films requires readers to dig through lots of junk data that does not contribute to it—except, perhaps, inasmuch as it demonstrates that failure to communicate on yet another level. Just "taking data as it comes" is insufficient: one needs a more disciplined method to keep moving through the endnotes' cruft without being repelled. That method, though, must allow for the modulation of attention, because trying to analyze the whole maddeningly "pretentious and unengaging and bad" filmography at constant focused attention—especially so early in the novel, before we know enough about the Incandenzas to fully contextualize all this information—would be so frustrating and overwhelming as to prevent one from seeing the honest anguish behind it. Regardless, developing such a method is necessary for managing the filmography. This difficulty in modulating between levels of attention is itself represented in the novel, during the scene in which we see how the teenaged Hal is only able to watch his father's touching (though not brilliant) film *Wave Bye-Bye to the Bureaucrat* (687–9) as part of a wallowing "weird self-punishment" (689) marathon of the latter's work, also involving *Fun with Teeth* and the putrid *Blood Sister: One Tough Nun*, whose amalgam of endless genre clichés proceeds at such excruciating, soul-sapping length as to render the movie's intent to satirize religion totally invisible to Hal and his fellow spectators, who must retreat into a mode of glazed-over, passive sarcasm to cope with its inanity (703–6, 711–14). That Hal's own mode of self-insulating irony is not sufficiently flexible to allow modulation is among the chief reasons he suffers a nervous collapse near the book's climax.

Infinite Jest's endnoted geopolitics

Furthermore, how these films test readers' cognitive processes figures how the notes work in the novel as a whole, especially regarding its political background. For instance, *The Pale King*'s comment about how sensitive political issues can be obscured by making them sufficiently boring resonates with the way that key elements to understanding *Infinite Jest*'s politics are often squirreled away in the notes. To discover the larger motives of *Les Assassins des Fauteuils Rollents*, for instance, readers must stop mid-sentence during an amusing depiction of Enfield's classroom life to read note 110, which comprises 17 pages of documents and dialogue about the Incandenzas (1004–22), only finally revealing toward the end the A.F.R.'s likely plan to force Canada to grant Québécois independence.[14] Reading note 304's description of why the A.F.R. are legless (essential to establishing their organizational mindset) (1055–62) requires an even more cumbersome sequence of steps. This note is oddly delayed until very late in the novel, only keyed at page 732 despite being *q.v.*'d in no fewer than 4 earlier endnotes: 39 (994), 45 (995), 173 (1031), and 302 (1055). When does a reader move ahead to read this important note? Should one do it immediately from note 39? If so, one risks losing concentration on not only that earlier note but on the crucial passage to which that endnote is keyed in the first place, the beginning of Marathe and Steeply's mountaintop meeting, during which time readers begin to learn about the main narrative's broader geopolitics. Should readers instead proceed to note 304 upon seeing that notes 45 and 173 do nothing but key ahead to that note? Perhaps, but one risks that one is not "supposed to" read that note yet, that the information is delayed to note 304 for some important narrative purpose and that flipping so far ahead will tangle up the story and one's ability to focus on it. As it turns out, this endnote-hopping is gratuitous: nothing in note 304 "spoils" the story or renders it inappropriate to recount at notes 45 and 173. These two notes are pure cruft, serving to make even more dull and onerous the process of learning information about the A.F.R., thus obscuring it from view. Tellingly, note 304's information is discovered by Jim Struck in an obscure journal while haphazardly researching (or, rather, plagiarizing) a paper, and the meandering process by which he comes across it renders him unable to pay enough attention to the material he plagiarizes to understand it.

How the novel's baroque politics—and complex narrative threads generally—are only visible to those who have found some way to modulate their attention to navigate between the cruft and valuable text is perhaps best exemplified by note 114, which is keyed from an otherwise innocuous description of Incandenza's father's career as the Man from Glad (313): "© B.S. MCMLXII, The Glad Flaccid Receptacle Corporation, Zanesville OH, sponsor of the very last year of O.N.A.N.ite Subsidized Time (q.v. Note 78). All Rights Reserved" (1022). In the midst of two lines of boilerplate corporatese—the kind of endnote cruft that one can usually skim past—we are suddenly and unceremoniously told that the last year that the book chronologically recounts is the final year of the O.N.A.N. Subsidized calendar. This proclamation is highly ambiguous: Has the world come to its senses and returned to the Julian calendar? Has O. N. A. N. collapsed and taken American civilization with it? Has humanity been destroyed by the *samizdat*? Yet in a book with no explicit resolution to most of its story threads, this is one of the only clues we have toward the fate of the novel's characters and imagined world. It is also entirely obscured unless one has figured out how to filter cruft.

Data detox

The ability to filter out pointlessness resonates outside the endnotes, too. Cruft's distinctive combination of expansiveness and emptiness characterizes well the thoughts of the novel's addicts. For instance, Marlon Bain describes addicts' "Marijuana Thinking" (in, what else, a footnote to endnote 269) as a tendency to "involuted abstraction" wherein smokers are hypermotivated to the point of being functionally unmotivated:

> [Addicts] Marijuana-Think themselves into labyrinths of reflexive abstraction that seem to cast doubt on the very possibility of practical functioning, and the mental labor of finding one's way out consumes all available attention and makes the Bob Hope-smoker look physically torpid and apathetic and amotivated sitting there, when really he is trying to claw his way out of a labyrinth. (1,048)

Addicts caught in this mindset are unable to terminate their attention on recursively self-negating, cruft thoughts, causing them to become paralyzed. However, recovering from the state described above—which is experienced in analogous forms by the novels' overachieving student-athletes, crazed politicians, and depressives—often causes addicts to veer into another extreme of cruft, exemplified by the novel's various recovery programs, whose clichéd mantras pointedly circumvent all critical or independent thought to the point of submerging their members into total vacuity. As one disgruntled AA member points out—again, in an endnote, number 90—"If you have some sort of Substance-problem, then you belong in AA. But if you say you do *not* have a Substance-problem, in other words if you *deny* that you have a substance problem, why then you're by definition in *Denial*, and thus you apparently need the Denial-busting Fellowship of AA even more than someone who can admit his problem" (1002). Similar nonsense assertions can be seen in the Zen formulae of Enfield's tennis instructors and the cynical, flag-waving slogans of O.N.A.N.'s ruling C.U.S.P. party.

Critical response has recognized this dialectic, but apparently without understanding that the latter cruft is every bit as empty as the former. While most understand how dangerous is the addicts' fixated, encyclopedic overthinking and consequent manic activity, their tendency to naïvely champion the 12-Step programs' attempt to break these monomanias by replacing them with communal platitudes (see Aubry; van Ewijk, "'I' and the 'Other'"; Freudental)[15] is not an adequate solution to the problem. In fact, the enthusiasm among admirers of a novel as enormous and wildly inventive as *Infinite Jest* for a philosophy that one addict, Geoffrey Day, approvingly describes as turning one's "will and life over to the care of clichés" (270–1) would be extremely puzzling. Consider Day's extended description of the program:

> One of the exercises is being grateful that life is so much *easier* now. I used sometimes to think. I used to think in long compound sentences with subordinate clauses and even the odd polysyllable. Now I find I needn't. Now I live by the dictates of macramé samplers ordered from the back-page ad of an old *Reader's Digest* or *Saturday Evening Post*. Easy does it. Remember to remember. But for the grace of capital-g God. Turn it over. Terse, hard-boiled. Monosyllabic. Good old Norman Rockwell-Paul Harvey wisdom. I walk around with my arms out straight in front of me and recite these clichés. In a monotone. No inflection necessary. Could that be added to the cliché-pool? *"No inflection necessary"*? Too many syllables, probably. (271)

Why on earth is this philosophy of simplistic language and conformity so celebrated by English professors—by *readers of David Foster Wallace*, no less? If the Wallace critics who vaunt the Ennet mindset were presented in any other setting with these notions about the evils of polysyllables and the pure good of the *Reader's Digest*, they would roll their eyes or laugh. No one who champions a work so original and thought-dense can possibly endorse Ennet's beliefs about living by clichés—just as Day doesn't really espouse them, either, as not half a page before his attack on polysyllables he has gone out of his way to describe his commitment to these ideals as proceeding "assiduously," "diligently," and "sedulously" (271).

Then why does the Ennet philosophy seem to be so persuasive to many readers of *Infinite Jest*? Likely, it's because its empty, easy clichés provide relief from the near-unreadable manic overload in the novel's other sections. It's probably not an accident that, in the Ennet House scenes, the endnotes are cut back significantly, nor that the clinic is not introduced until 200 pages have passed and we have had time to absorb how overwhelming *Infinite Jest* will be. Only after having endured the inescapable involutions of Kate Gompert's depression (68–78), the coked-up violence and semi-decipherable English in yrstruly's monologue (128–35), and the painfully detailed analysis of how Americans' endlessly reflecting physical anxieties destroyed the videophone (144–51) can the mantras that Day recites seem even remotely appealing (see Aubry 210). Such overloaded scenes may be particularly taxing to the academics who make up the majority of Wallace's critics, who by constitution are probably more initially attracted to the baroque complexities of "Marijuana Thinking" than most readers, and who thus subsequently grow all the more exhausted and repulsed by it, making Ennet House seem increasingly appealing.

Fundamentally, though, Ennet's clichés are nearly as meaningless as the addicts' overthinking; they should be accepted only as a cure for the latter's greater destructiveness. Perhaps this is best seen in how Day himself—not a week after his testimonial on the beauty of readymade mantras—goes on the rant quoted above in note 90, chastising Gately not only for recovery programs' "idiotic fallacies" but for the way they divert all criticism as "analysis paralysis," which he accurately notes is a classic "totalitarian" tactic, "interdict[ing] a fundamental doctrinal question by invoking a doctrine against questions" (1000–3). For this Gately has no response, and indeed only pages later he becomes frustrated when an AA veteran forces a similar fallacy upon him (1,004)—as it must be, in an endnote, number 100. While the endnotes always bring with them the possibility of endlessly proliferating junk, they also allow the possibility for independent critical reflection, because to read them at all requires the kind of subtle attention modulation at the basis of all higher-level thought. If readers seek to escape not just the hyperactive mindlessness exemplified by addiction but mindlessness entirely, they cannot simply be repelled by the endnotes' frequent overload but must keep returning to them, hopefully better able to skim and filter out the junk to retrieve valuable information. James Incandenza himself realized this principle late in life, understanding how AA forced its members to simply exchange one "slavish dependence" for another (706), characterized by intolerable "vacant grins and empty platitudes" (1,053). He sought to overcome both forms by addressing them in his films—as we are told most directly in an endnote, number 289—but attempting to create meaning from waste is an unstable and dangerous process, something surely known by the designer of the annular fusion program employed in the novel's Great Concavity, a multi-state trash heap that vacillates dangerously between desiccated wasteland and mutation-inducing verdancy as it processes garbage to power the continent. That Incandenza finally sticks his head in a microwave, however, is as much caused by submitting to recovery-program clichés as by resisting them, because they have rendered his mind incapable of distinguishing the language necessary to sustain a meaningful life from cruft.

Handling information in a grown-up way

We can only hope that we manage better than Incandenza and avoid his fate. Whether we actually can, though, is unclear. In his final years, the difficulties posed by the digital age to adequate data filtering increasingly disturbed Wallace. In "Deciderization 2007—A Special Report," his foreword to the 2007 volume of *Best American Essays*, Wallace chastises Americans by asserting that "There is just no way that 2004's re-election [of President George W. Bush] could have taken place . . . if we had been paying attention and handling information in a grown up way" (*BFN* 313). Yet as soon as he makes this criticism, Wallace acknowledges that this grown-up information-handling is all but impossible in the early twenty-first century. For each of the major world issues a twenty-first-century American needs to consider when making informed decisions, he notes, "the relevant questions are too numerous and complicated" to even adequately investigate. If one really wants to understand any of the important political issues of our time, each tangled in such a dizzyingly complex web of global relations, one would have to pore over so much specialized economic, historical, and sociological research in search of the core problems that "[y]ou'd simply drown. We all would. It's amazing to me that no one much talks about this—about the fact that whatever our founders and framers thought of as a literate, informed citizenry can no longer exist" (*BFN* 314). That's probably true, unfortunately.

It's also an insight that Wallace critics—trained professionally to reject the autonomous, critical subjecthood to which Wallace aspires above—have appeared reluctant to embrace. In his essay on *Infinite Jest*, Matt Tresco suggests that the encyclopedic phenomena I have identified reveal "the absence of an ordering or categorizing principle," which allows the "release and an enlargement of possibilities" in the text, favorably comparing the novel to Wikipedia in that both "are always threatening to overspill, to negate the purpose of their organizing principles" and thus challenge hierarchization (120-1). Though the similarities between *Infinite Jest* and Wikipedia that Tresco highlights—especially regarding their cross-linked structure and impressively heterogeneous scope—are important, even more important is their shared but highly divergent use of cruft. Wikipedia partisans may have an argument that the site is wider-ranging and no less accurate than other encyclopedias (Reagle 7), but as Clark notes, ordering and retrieval—critical selectivity rather than all-inclusiveness—are as important to an encyclopedia as the sum of its data. Wikipedia's frequent inability to distinguish between important and trivial information either between or within subjects—which results in proliferating and frequently unchecked cruft[16]—does little to help its users to keep from drowning in the tsunami of information of which Wallace writes: in fact, it becomes part of that tsunami. *Infinite Jest*'s much more carefully, centrally calibrated use of cruft could not be more different in this respect. Inasmuch as there is any hope of mitigating the worst effects of the dilemma Wallace highlights, it requires us to develop our abilities to filter information to their maximum capacities, and encyclopedic novels like *Infinite Jest* are powerful tools for doing so—not necessarily because they include information that is valuable itself, but because they force us to navigate around their junk to the text that is more important. Inasmuch as there is any hope of mitigating the worst effects of information overload, we must develop our abilities to order and retrieve information to their maximum capacities, and encyclopedic novels are a powerful tool for doing so, not because they include information that is valuable itself, but because they force us to learn how to navigate around their junk data to find text that is actually important.

Thanks to Judd Staley for his comments on an earlier draft of this essay.

Notes

1   Mendelson did not invent the term, though, which had been used previously by both Ronald T. Swigger and Northrop Frye (the latter of whose influence on Mendelson is apparent, though he oddly denies it).

2   I use this definition to limit the broad cultural implications with which some critics imbue the term "encyclopedic novel," which typically cause it to blend with the related "epic novel" genre (see Mendelson, "Gravity's Encyclopedia" 162; Frye 315–26; and Moretti 4).

3   Of course, many encyclopedias and encyclopedia-like volumes like textbooks do *not* have scholarly notes. However, given the criticism such omissions have provoked (see Loewen 302), it should be clear how implicated they are in the ordering and retrieval of information. (Certainly, whenever we consult the great encyclopedic project of our time, Wikipedia, we ought first to look at how rigorously endnoted is the article in question.)

4   See Fishburn for more detail on Borges, and see Benstock for a discussion of *Finnegans Wake* and its link to the eighteenth-century novel. (So much discussion of *Pale Fire* centers on the notes that there would be no point in listing references here.)

5   For that matter, anyone with some knowledge of Aztec myth can make a reasonable guess that it has something to do with associating one's mother with death and confinement.

6   Burn writes here explicitly about the work of William Gaddis. However, he appears to use Gaddis as an exemplary case for encyclopedic novelists generally.

7   Not only must it be accurate, it must accurately transmit discoveries *made elsewhere*, making it doubly unoriginal—Wikipedia's "no original research" policy sums the typical encyclopedic attitude well (Reagle 11–13). (One exception, incidentally, is the Enlightenment *Encyclopédie* compiled by Diderot and his circle.)

8   Of course, this is not to say that the more original something is, the better, a common vulgarization of modernist theories of artistic innovation.

9   We do not have time to discuss boredom and attention lapse in great depth. To review the current state of clinical studies in boredom, see Cheyne, Carriere and Smilek as well as Goldberg et al.

10 My phrase "cruft of fiction," of course, derives from Lubbock's 1921 path-breaker *The Craft of Fiction*.

11 LeClair, for instance, celebrates these novels in a book titled *The Art of Excess*.

12 These observations do not apply to all uses of notes in the novel, just these phenomena of chapter IX. Elsewhere, *House of Leaves* uses notes extensively for narrative layering and metafictional effects that do not appear to be encyclopedic cruft in the sense I discuss here, though I am not sure they accomplish anything more substantial than novelty, as their purported philosophic implications are undermined for the very reasons I described earlier.

13 In another endnote, Orin Incandenza describes these as practical jokes of hyper-naturalism in which Incandenza and his crew would simply throw a dart at a phone book page and declare whatever happened to the name it hit in the next hour and a half the "found drama," unmediated by audience, director, or cameras (1026–8).

14 Tresco also addresses this passage (118–19); the difference between our takes on it should be made clear by my conclusion.

15 To be fair, Aubry acknowledges the limits of the 12-Step philosophy and does not quite idealize it. However, in his view, the ideal blend of sincerity and irony is exemplified by an AA guest speaker (217–18).

16 Two representative examples: its article on the recent conflicts on the Georgia-Russia border quickly devolves from a disciplined overview of a key world event into an inconsistently updated and nearly paratactic day-by-day account of random events, while its article on Dr Albert Schweitzer has a lower word count than the article on *unproduced* episodes of the British TV series *Dr. Who*.

8

"A Paradigm for the Life of Consciousness": *The Pale King*[1]

Stephen J. Burn

And thus, though surrounded by circle upon circle of consternations and affrights, did these inscrutable creatures at the center freely and fearlessly indulge in all peaceful concernments . . . so, amid the tornadoed Atlantic of my being, do I myself still for ever centrally disport in mute calm.
Herman Melville, *Moby-Dick* (424–5)

Everything in art is a formal question.
Frank Bidart, "Borges and I" (11)

We are clearly still in the prototype phase of *Pale King* criticism, where the task is perhaps not yet to definitively categorize the novel, but rather to prepare a blueprint for a larger and later critical project. This project involves trying to separate our judgments from the sometimes distorted claims that since 2008 have circled around Wallace's name in the mass media, so that we can tease out the logic of what Wallace was trying to do in his final novel. For all the established orthodoxies of the intentional fallacy and the death of the author, to some extent it is only when we can start to disentangle what Wallace originally planned from the published text (heroically and painstakingly reconstructed, as it is, by his editor) that we can begin the critical project of understanding *The Pale King* in earnest, and plot its place on the rising curve of Wallace's career. As we might expect, *The Pale King* itself provides the best model that we have for this task: the end of the list poem that begins the book describes "the shapes of the worms incised in the overturned dung and baked by the sun all day until hardened . . . tiny vacant lines in rows and inset curls" and concludes with the instruction to "Read these" (4). This is, of course, an allegory for the reading process, especially the process of reading a posthumous novel— the lines of imprinted marks are not themselves the sign of a present maker, but are a message that only becomes visible once the creature that created them has passed by. At the same time the scene uncomfortably resembles a disinterment: the worms' bodies emerging from the ground; the hungry crows waiting for the carrion.

To undertake the critical project of reading the lines that Wallace left behind is not to deny that Michael Pietsch has performed a remarkable service for readers by assembling the text of *The Pale King*, but rather to recognize the novel's hybrid quality, and to begin to think about the kinds of approach that will yield a greater depth of insight as we move out of the prototype phase. Part of Wallace's importance in the history of the novel, in my view, is his skill as a narrative architect, and his fiction's layered design is often underpinned by a logic of juxtaposition that drives it forward. At the level of the sentence this logic concentrates upon the polyphonic effects sought by Wallace's prose, the contrast between different voices and the elasticity of his rhetorical register. At the level of a work's total architecture, by contrast, the same logic underpins the mosaic effect that Wallace created in each of his novels through carefully juxtaposed episodes and fragments. But because Wallace's manuscripts for the *Pale King* have not yet been made available to scholars, our reading of the book's total architecture is necessarily speculative at this stage; and it may forever be speculative. We know that Wallace left a 250-page manuscript on his desk, but Michael Pietsch told me that:

> None of the Sylvanshine chapters [were] in the partial manuscript that David had assembled as a possible portrait of work in progress. The two "Author here" chapters were first, followed by the explanation of the Personnel snafu that led to the David Wallace/David Wallace confusion. Then the "turns a page" piece and the long Chris Fogle monologue and a bunch of the childhood stories. I think David's goal was to send chapters that were very polished and that gave a sense of the book's main strands and themes. I don't believe he'd decided on a final order of presentation. ("Sylvanshine")

If a full reading of the novel's shape is likely to remain hypothetical, it is nevertheless possible to think about what Wallace was attempting in *The Pale King* by considering a number of patterns that emerge across the published text. Wallace's fiction is built less around cause-and-effect plotting, than it is around the construction of rich metaphoric nodes where multiple meanings accumulate, and by mapping some of these nodes I want to, first, elucidate the novel's genealogy, and by doing so try to identify some new reference points for our understanding of both *The Pale King* and Wallace's larger conception of the novel; second, I'm going to argue that one of the unifying mechanisms in the novel is Wallace's career-long fascination with consciousness. I'll begin this two-part task by exploring why Wallace decided to write about the IRS, though this is a question that engages with both Wallace's biography and the compositional history of his fiction.

I

One of the earliest references to the IRS in Wallace's papers comes in July 1989, when he sent a letter to his agent explaining that he had just mailed a package to the IRS and that he was, he wrote, "both confident and hopeful [that] they'll now leave me the fuck alone." The fact that Wallace was dealing with the IRS in July—that is, outside the regular timeline for tax returns— tells us that we're in fruitful territory for biographers. Something out of the ordinary was happening with Wallace's taxes and the most likely situation is that he had been audited. No doubt future biographical studies will eventually contextualize this small fragment from a 22-year-old letter. After all, over the last few years the accumulated weight of posthumous profiles and the opening of his archive in Texas have prompted a reformulation of the coordinates of Wallace's fiction, casting a fine autobiographical net over much that at one time seemed pure invention. Whatever dangers this blurring of life and work brings, one consequence of biographical readings will be to reveal that Wallace's books often had longer gestations than he acknowledged.[2] While Wallace described *Infinite Jest* (1996), for example, as a "six-year novel that got written in three years" (*CW* 91), in actual fact it appears to be a book that grew over a ten-year period, with the earliest section having been drafted in the mid-1980s.[3] Similarly, *Brief Interviews with Hideous Men* (1999), seems to have initially been proposed as a completed volume in 1997, at a time when many of the pieces that ultimately *were* included had not been written, and in their place were numerous early stories, including "Order and Flux in Northampton," "Solomon Silverfish," "Other Math," and "Crash of '62."

My purpose in making these baseline observations about the longer-than-expected life stories of Wallace's books is first to note that much of Wallace's middle- and late-period fiction accreted across time, with parallel projects bleeding into each other,[4] and this compositional technique is one way to account for what seem to be the obvious echoes of Wallace's earlier work—especially *Infinite Jest* and *Oblivion*—within *The Pale King*.[5] Reading the text that we have is like viewing a tree's trunk in cross-section: we see the visible lines marking the different years of the book's growth. Second,

I'd like to offer the currently unprovable hypothesis that *The Pale King*'s complex history may have begun in the tax frustrations he endured in early 1989. There are other clues that point to 1989 as *The Pale King*'s potential point of origin—some early notes for *Infinite Jest* (apparently from the same year) include ideas for a book about the IRS—and if this hypothesis is correct, it not only gives us an unusually long timeline for the project, but it also perhaps provides one reason why so much of the novel's action takes place in the 1980s.

Yet even as the biography helps to contextualize the novel's treatment of time, there are still problems in the novel's chronology. It is not simply that the novel offers us a counterfactual past, in a manner that mirrors the swerve into an alternative future in Wallace's first two novels; it's also the fact that time seems to have been condensed in *The Pale King*. While (as Marshall Boswell argues elsewhere in this volume) much of the novel's political argument is carefully grounded in contemporary economic policy, at the same time the novel's 1970s and 1980s are often merged with stylized scenes that could easily be mistaken for the 1950s or even earlier: all those old-fashioned hats and odes to fusty values of hardwork and self-control. In this respect, *The Pale King* resembles a work that I believe is one of its ancestor texts—B. S. Johnson's *Christie Malry's Own Double Entry* (1973)—an experimental novel that Wallace kept in his personal library. The overlaps between Johnson and Wallace are multiple and compelling. At a basic level, both writers drew upon self-consciously flamboyant vocabularies; both built their novels around formal innovations; and both worked on a novel about accounting shortly before committing suicide. It's also significant that each writer's sense of the novel's contemporary relevance was, in part, shaped by a belief that the emergence of other media had redefined the role that fiction needed to play. As early as 1973, B. S. Johnson argued that the ascendance of cinema required the novel to redirect its focus, and abandon relating certain stories that movies could treat more effectively. Within this evolving media ecology, Johnson argued that the novelist had to concentrate upon those things that a novel could do better than other art forms: "the precise use of language, exploitation of the technological fact of the book, the explication of thought" (*Rather Young* 12).

There are broad affinities between this theory and Wallace's own technical experiments and thematic obsessions, but the most instructive points of overlap and divergence are more specifically connected to *Christie Malry's Own Double Entry*. As Johnson's biographer, Jonathan Coe, has noted, *Christie Malry* is a midlife-crisis novel, a work by a writer around 40, that self-consciously attempts to reach "back into the past" in an effort to relive formative years, although autobiographical traces—as in *The Pale*

King—are stylized and distorted (316). Like Wallace's novel, *Christie Malry* takes liberties with its chronology: despite certain elements of the novel that Coe sees as direct responses to Britain's political atmosphere during the early Seventies,[6] the novel's vague temporal setting "reeks of the austere, sexually repressed 1950s rather than the early 1970s" (315–16). Perhaps most vitally, Coe argues that the novel is also a retrospective, the product of "an author taking stock, looking back over the broad outlines of an oeuvre which he already seems to believe might be nearing completion" (329).

Later in this chapter, I'm going to argue that there's a similar stock-taking exercise at work in *The Pale King*, but while Wallace seems to deliberately allude to *Christie Malry* early in his novel,[7] it's nevertheless hard to gauge the extent to which Wallace consciously considered Johnson's novel a hidden model, or to judge how fully he recognized the kinship between Johnson's artistic project and his own. Yet aside from simply noting the overlaps between the two writers, I would like to suggest that part of the importance of considering the affinities between Johnson and Wallace hinges on the difference in their treatment of accounting. In Johnson's novel, the double-entry accounting method (where every debit has to be balanced by a credit) is transposed from the realm of finance and projected into an ethical sphere: Christie, as a literal minded soul, assumes that he can apply his accounting method to life and extract a credit for every debit that life throws at him. Following this logic closely, Christie decides that because socialism has not been given a chance, the world owes him £311,398. The novel's purpose, then, is relatively clear: Johnson is trying to explode the idea that accounting can be taken as a moral system for comic effect.

The role of accountants and accounting in *The Pale King* is much fuzzier, and the buzzwords that have appeared in many reviews—boredom, attention—while no doubt relevant, do not exhaust the subject. On closer examination, Wallace's accountants seem to perform multiple roles in *The Pale King*.

II

Despite the often precise reference to dates in *The Pale King*, the novel's telescoped chronology includes a number of references that tie Wallace's accountants to the 1950s: Beth Rath, for example, shares her name with the wife of the disaffected businessman in Sloan Wilson's *Man in the Gray Flannel Suit* (1955).[8] But the novel's historical reach goes deeper than mid-century, and references to David Wallace as the "young man carbuncular" (286 n40) connect the book's environment generally to modernism's waste lands, but more specifically to the quintessential early-twentieth-century figure of the clerk. In its early usage, the title *clerk* included "keepers of accounts" (*OED*), and I'm going to argue that the figure of the clerk—as he is handed down from the early twentieth century—acts as one of the metaphoric nodes that function as building blocks in Wallace's fiction. Specifically, the clerk provides a meeting point at which general notions about morality, identity, and class cluster, while more precise concepts are tied to individual characters.

We can sketch, in brief outline, some of these general concepts. Wallace's struggle with the contemporary novel—and perhaps the larger struggle of the post-postmodern generation—was driven by a qualified nostalgia for certain values that had supposedly been lost through the decades of modernist and postmodernist innovation, and his fiction is ambivalently torn between desires to march forward and to recuperate tradition. As Kasia Boddy notes in a reading of *Girl with Curious Hair*, one instance of such division comes when Wallace is seemingly torn about whether to "pull the plug" on humanist impulses, or to "pump in oxygen and bring it back to life" (26). As earlier studies have shown, such a balancing act has historically been performed by literary representations of the clerk: in *White Collar Fictions* (1992), for instance, Christopher Wilson argues that from the turn of the century onwards, the clerk was a site where "older ideologies of thrift, sobriety, self-control, future-mindedness, and perseverance" (28) were preserved amid the flux of a changing world. In ways that are probably too obvious to require enumeration, we see a similar examination of the durability of such older value systems in a changing world in *The Pale King*, with Chris Fogle's father perhaps providing the clearest example.

Wilson also argues that the fundamental importance of subordination within bureaucracies made clerk figures "quite literally [speak] to problems of identity" (30), which were exacerbated by their existence within the so-called blurred collar-line—that is, a clerk is "not a member of management but not exactly labor either, more 'independent' financially yet with little or no autonomy or republican 'freedom to act'" (30). Once again, I think the consistency of this historical vision with Wallace's work is clear—the identity crisis provides a vital thread through Wallace's work, from Lenore Beadsman's fear that she may not really exist, through to Fogle's early meandering or Meredith Rand who offers a long account of what she calls her "total identity crisis" (504), and often the concept of freedom is a vital factor in that crisis. Yet for all these overlaps, Wallace's clerks also highlight a further bifurcation in Wallace's treatment of the past. The clerk, as John Carey argued in *The Intellectual and the Masses* (1992), emerged in parallel with "the growth of suburbs" (46) and so at the start of the twentieth century the clerk exists in a zone of negative history, divorced from any visible past or tradition. Wallace takes care to note Peoria's REC Center's location as a transitional satellite, "something between a suburb and an independent township" (256, cf. 269), but this early-twentieth-century figure is crystallized in Drinion, whose separation from his own past is literalized by his orphan status, and whose blank-slate character is indicated by the derisory nickname, Mr X. But while Wallace replicates a stock figure from the early-twentieth-century library, he also significantly breaks from past-practice—what we have of the *The Pale King* indicates a fascination with where his characters came from—especially in the cases of the long, unfolding histories provided for Steyck, Ware, Fogle, and Wallace, as they move in radial streams toward Peoria.

Yet aside from their literary historical resonance, Wallace's accountants are also suggestive of other, larger themes. First, the accountants play a central role in outlining the novel's underlying geometry, which resembles what Franco Moretti—drawing on John Barrell—called "a circular system of geography" (38). Wallace overloads our introduction to his central accountants with circular descriptions,[9] but while the association of IRS workers and circular motion has an obvious resonance, the idea of bureaucratic work as a circular routine that leads nowhere is, of course, a staid cliché, a merely procedural gesture that if taken in itself would surely represent a low point in Wallace's imaginative enterprise. Instead, we should consider the circle as another metaphorical node and explore the potentially richer resonances that emerge around the novel's loops.

As a compositional unit, the circle draws together a series of narrative overlays. First, there is the geography of the suburbs, which T. W. H. Crosland described in 1905 as: "prettily disposed in . . . rings" (15). Equally, as Rudolf Arnheim argues in *The Power of the Center* (1982), circular structures introduce the opposition between two systems that could be linked to the scalar shifts that characterize Wallace's fiction: the "cosmic" system (i.e. the circular patterns of "the vastness of astronomical space" or the earth) and the "parochial" (i.e. Cartesian grids, where the viewpoint of "small inhabitants" flattens the "curvature of the earth . . . into a plane") (vii). Yet it's notable that perhaps the highest concentration of circular structures takes place in the novel's twenty-fourth section, which charts David Wallace's arrival at the Peoria Examination Center, and within this chapter the looping structures exist at different scales, creating a pattern of concentric circles. At the largest scale, Peoria itself is "an exurban ring" (272 n17), but zooming in somewhat we're told that the center can only be approached via a "circular shape[d]" road (276). Tightening our focus further, we discover that the lower level of the building is shaped as a "wheel"

(295) with halls that "seemed curved" (289). Near the center of the pattern of ever-decreasing circles are the accountants themselves who, we're told, all work within a "circle of light" (290). Finally, at the smallest scale, there is David Wallace who describes himself as resembling a "racquetball" (296).

One way to interpret this pattern would be to invoke Chaos theory and the concept of recursive symmetry—that is the repetition of the same figure across different scales—and given the importance of order and chaos as organizing poles in any novel about bureaucracy, this is not an unreasonable approach to take. At the same time, a less esoteric interpretation is also available: the spiral pattern of expanding concentric circles swirling around Peoria also suggests that characteristically Midwestern weather system, the tornado, and—as Michael Pietsch's editor's note tells us—Wallace described the novel as evoking a "tornado feeling" (viii). Both circular structures and tornados represent one key to *The Pale King*,[10] but to clarify their importance it's necessary to explore several more specific resonances attached to Wallace's accountants, many of which circle around Claude Sylvanshine.

III

To elucidate Sylvanshine's role in the novel, we need to step back from *The Pale King* momentarily and think about Wallace's general theory of the novel. In interviews and essays, Wallace tried, to a far greater extent than many of his contemporaries, to outline a programmatic theory of the novel's function. This theory of the novel can be divided into two distinct parts that can be separated in terms of their treatment of time. The first part of Wallace's theory focused upon the novel within a time-specific context, and measured a novel's achievements in terms of its existence within the millennial media ecology: here we would encounter his well-known position on television and contemporary American fiction, in which the novel's function is not intrinsic to its own qualities, but is rather molded by the other media around it. The second part of his theory has been less rigorously examined by critics, and—in contrast to his time-bound media theories—this subset of his overall conception of the novel tried to evaluate literature in a long lens, untethered from its temporal foundations. One of the vital strands here is literature's function as "an anodyne against loneliness" (*CW* 16), which Wallace outlined in numerous interviews, but perhaps most cogently in conversation with Laura Miller:

> there is this existential loneliness in the real world. I don't know what you're thinking or what it's like inside you and you don't know what it's

like inside me. In fiction I think we can leap over that wall itself in a certain way. But that's just the first level, . . . A really great piece of fiction for me may or may not take me away and make me forget that I'm sitting in a chair. [But] there's a kind of Ah-ha! Somebody at least for a moment feels about something or sees something the way that I do. (*CW* 62)

Unlike his media ecology theory, the battle against loneliness is timeless, and it is not original to Wallace. I want to try to trace the ancestry of this defense of the novel in a way that articulates its importance to *The Pale King*, by concentrating upon its derivation from two sources.

Among Wallace's notes for *The Pale King* are scattered references to Walker Percy's nonfiction, specifically to his volume *The Message in the Bottle* (1975), which is a comparatively overlooked influence on Wallace's work. A collection of 15 essays, *The Message in the Bottle* is framed by an overarching exploration into the coexistence of increased levels of profound sorrow alongside advances in education and prosperity in the contemporary world. "Why does man feel so sad in the twentieth century?" Percy asks, when "he has succeeded in satisfying his needs and making over the world for his own use?" (3). The answer Percy proposes stems from the centrality of language to human personality. There are marked affinities between Percy's broad argument and the Wallace who conceived of *Infinite Jest* as an attempt to explore the "stomach-level sadness" that characterizes a technologically advanced America (*CW* 59), but the essay from Percy's book that most directly engages with *The Pale King* is "The Man on the Train," a title that itself evokes the clerk's diurnal motion.

Percy begins the essay by identifying his focus upon the "literature of alienation," which is of course the title of a class Fogle takes (184). But Percy's argument is that this body of literature is, in fact, an inverted category. Percy writes:

There is a great deal of difference between an alienated commuter riding a train and this same commuter reading a book about an alienated commuter riding a train. . . . The nonreading commuter exists in true alienation, which is unspeakable; the reading commuter rejoices in the speakability of his alienation and in the new triple alliance of himself, the alienated character, and the author. His mood is affirmatory and glad: Yes! that is how it is!—which is an aesthetic reversal of alienation. (83)

In this imaginative union, I'd suggest, there's a clear precedent for Wallace's own belief in fiction's ability to invert loneliness, and while there are other connections between "The Man on the Train" and *The Pale King*, I'm going to suggest that the other primary source for Wallace's theory of the novel is C. S. Lewis. Wallace identified *The Screwtape Letters* (1942) as his favorite book when he contributed to J. Peder Zane's volume, *The Top Ten* (128). But the work that most profoundly shaped Wallace's conception of the novel as a timeless achievement is Lewis's later monograph, *An Experiment in Criticism* (1961). Like Percy's conception of the literature of alienation, *An Experiment in Criticism* is itself a product of a reversal: Lewis sets out by proposing that criticism has traditionally worked by assuming that any evaluation of the act of reading stems from qualities inherent to the books themselves. Bad reading, therefore, is simply the act of reading a bad book. Lewis's experiment is to reverse this picture, to argue that reading is not a singular activity and that different kinds of reading should define a book's quality. Therefore, he defines "a good book as a book which is read in one way, and a bad book as a book which is read in another" (1).

For Wallace scholars, however, the vital component of *An Experiment in Criticism* is less Lewis's larger argument, than the epilogue, in which Lewis (after some complaint) finally agrees to establish what constitutes his conception of the value of literature. As in *The Pale King*, the notion of attention is an important component of Lewis's theory—"if it is worth . . . reading at all," Lewis tells us, it is "worth doing so attentively. Indeed we must attend even to discover that something is not worth attention" (132). But underpinning attentive reading is a solution to the metaphysical loneliness we suffer within the prison of ourselves. Lewis writes:

> Each of us by nature sees the whole world from one point of view with a perspective and a selectiveness peculiar to himself. And even when we build disinterested fantasies, they are saturated with, and limited by, our own psychology. . . . We want to see with other eyes, to imagine with other imaginations, to feel with other hearts . . . One of the things we feel after reading a great work is "I have got out." Or from another point of view, "I have got in"; pierced the shell of some other monad and discovered what it is like inside . . . [we have got] out of the self, to correct its provincialism and heal its loneliness. (137–8)

Clearly Wallace's own defense of the novel closely parallels Lewis's conception, but the epilogue to *An Experiment in Criticism* is not a bequest that is simply handed down to *The Pale King* without some productive mutation. At this point, we have to turn our attention in earnest to Sylvanshine.

When Sylvanshine is first introduced in the novel's second section, Wallace presents him amid an overwhelming cluster of imagery that on one level simply extends the novel's stock association of accountants and looping structures. His anxious exchanges with teachers are described as "a loop" (9). He can't help but recognize that his regional flight is just one part of a perpetual circle performed by the plane that goes "up and back again and again all day" (20), and, significantly, our final glimpse of Sylvanshine in this section features him spinning in circles "turning 360° several times . . . trying to merge his own awareness with the panoramic vista" (24). Even his last name involves the looping movement of reflected light.[11]

In Pietsch's arrangement, Sylvanshine is the first accountant we meet, and he remains a prominent presence throughout the book, appearing in eight chapters. Yet despite his multiple appearances, he seems to be insufficiently integrated into the novel's proposed arc. While Wallace's notes and asides indicate relatively clear developmental arcs for David Wallace, Drinion, and Rand, those notes connected to Sylvanshine's place in the novel's plot appear to be in flux more than most: he wants to be CID, he wants to become a CPA, he wants to get out of the service, he may be in a homosexual relationship with Reynolds (540, 544). Sylvanshine is left in the paradoxical position of being central in the published novel but largely an adjunct to its putative development. When we see him through Fogle's focalized narration, for instance, in the penultimate chapter, he is little more than a stock comic character who seems almost entirely divorced from his earlier appearances.[12]

Yet despite Sylvanshine's apparently amorphous position in the novel's early drafts, Lewis's *An Experiment in Criticism* nevertheless helps to explicate his function in the novel, and suggests that his role is less closely tied to narrative development than it is to Wallace's conception of narrative as a whole. Sylvanshine initials are the same as C. S. Lewis's first two initials, and it's notable that the qualities that make him a member of Lehrl's "strange team of intuitive and occult ephebes" (80) are broadly those that both Wallace and Lewis saw as the hallmarks of a novel's function. While our general experience of other minds is closed off to the point that "I don't know what you're thinking. I don't know that much about you" (*CW* 16), because Sylvanshine has Random-Fact Intuition syndrome he is able to leap over the wall of self to experience the minds of those around him. So, in section 15, Wallace tells us an RFI-sufferer knows "the middle name of the childhood friend of a stranger they pass in a hallway. The fact that someone they sit near in a movie was once sixteen cars behind them on I-5" (118). Such examples place heavy emphasis on the *random* nature of the intuitions, but elsewhere in the book, Sylvanshine's read on those around him suggests a much more controlled access to particular minds: in section seven, for instance, the narration is focalized through Sylvanshine as he evidently takes careful account of Bondurant's mind, noting that the agent is "having some kind of wistful memory and was cultivating the wistfulness, reclining a bit in it as one would in a warm bath" (51).

Just as B. S. Johnson conceived *Christie Malry* as a reflection upon his own total body of work, so Sylvanshine plays a vital role in making *The Pale King* a similarly summative work,[13] as he acts as the stand-in for the Lewis-Wallace conception of the novel, a model for the novel within the novel that is rehearsed and tested. But Wallace brings this model into dialogue with the contemporary field in section fifteen, which is really the point at which the knot between the two strands of Wallace's theory of the novel is tied. In working out the contrast between the novelists' function in the nineteenth century (as represented by Leo Tolstoy) and the novelist's function in the age of media overload, Wallace told David Lipsky:

> I imagine Leo getting up in the morning . . . Sitting down in the *silent* room . . . pulling out his quill, and . . . in deep tranquility, recollecting emotion. . . . I received five hundred thousand discrete bits of information today, of which maybe twenty-five are important. And how am I going to sort those out? (37–8)

As Wallace explains in section fifteen, the RFI-sufferer "lives part-time in the world of fractious, boiling minutiae that no one knows or could be bothered to know even if they had the chance to know" (120); or to put it more briefly, Sylvanshine lives in Wallace's world, not Tolstoy's, or even Lewis's. To be a writer in this world, to live part-time through other people's minds is summed up by the final word of the RFI-chapter: "overwhelming" (121). On one level, then, Sylvanshine's role in the incomplete phase of the drafting process may have been to dramatize the difficulties that Wallace was experiencing with his novel, to productively explore the load-bearing threshold of the conception of narrative that he had carried forward from Lewis. This explains, to some extent, why Sylvanshine is so often present in the novel, and yet so often trapped in a frustrating stasis, a combination of bodily presence and mental dispersion that we might read as a figure for writer's block.

At the same time, however, Sylvanshine is not simply an overarching model for the novel as a genre; he is also, more precisely, the model for *this* specific novel, *The Pale King*. In contrast to Reynolds' rifle focus, Sylvanshine's mind is described as a shotgun (16), and irrespective of Pietsch's editorial hand, it seems clear that the novel's structure would ultimately have been centrifugal. Similarly, the logic that underlies many of the short fragments that interrupt the longer narrative seems to be the same logic that drives a Random Fact Intuition: sometimes these miniature chapters are simply data, bureaucratic scraps irrupting into the novel. Other times they're shards of conversation, but shards that often initially seem contextless: bereft of names, locations, or other narrative ballast that would ground them in some way that might allow us to assimilate them into the larger story.

C. S. Lewis's conception of narrative is not the only model at play in Wallace's novel. Toni Ware, for example, seems to represent Bret Easton Ellis's shock-based aesthetic, an approach that Wallace felt was antithetical to his own, which might help explain why Toni has a first name that yields the anagram of *NOT I*.[14] But perhaps it is because of Sylvanshine's very closeness to Wallace's conception of the novel that he also seems to have a key role in negotiating a vital further resonance to *The Pale King*'s circular structures that returns us, once again, to the novel's unusual treatment of time. As I suggested at the beginning of this chapter, the opening section has funereal overtones as it traces a journey downwards, from "skylines of canted rust" into the ground, where bodies are being consumed by crows (3). More specifically, however, the movement is heavy with mythic overtones, and the "very old land" is not simply the rich Midwestern soil, but also the imaginative geography of Ancient Greek myth (3). The first sentence seems to make this clear as it traces a bleak journey that carefully alludes to both a stygian darkness and the coins that must be paid to Charon to ensure a safe crossing, as Wallace moves "past the tobacco-brown river overhung with weeping trees and coins of sunlight" (3).

The novel's second section replicates this downward movement— beginning in midflight and descending to ground level where Sylvanshine experiences "Total Terror" (24)—and it's perhaps this parallel movement, as well as the Sylvanshine-like sensory overload of the opening section, that persuaded Pietsch to place the two sections together. In this first introduction to Sylvanshine, Wallace layers further underworld imagery: the propellers' sound is "otherworldly" (10); another passenger's appearance is "skull-like" and resembles an "omen of death" (11); and, significantly, the boy that Sylvanshine sees before boarding the flight extends the underworld theme while also connecting it to government, with his "Sympathy for Nixon" (9) shirt. Later, this link is solidified when Sylvanshine thinks of Erebus (119)— the shadowy realm between Earth and Hades in Homeric myth.[15]

Certainly if one dimension of the novel is taken to be Sylvanshine's journey into the underworld it would help explain not just the ghosts at the Exam Center, but also that why "much of the info" about the ghosts comes "from Claude Sylvanshine" (315). At the same time, there's an echo, here, of *The Screwtape Letters'* vision of hell as a bureaucracy—the "Lowerarchy" (102)—and it's worth noting that the bar the IRS agents frequent is decorated with "fake flames" casting a "red light" (473n). In general, however, the resonances here are perhaps initially harder to parse. Wallace was perhaps playfully considering the IRS's economic judgments as a modern counterpart for the moral evaluations handed out in Hades, which would seem on one level a cosmic joke, and on another an extension of his long-term fascination with the way contemporary structures substitute for religious belief. At the same time, it's notable that looping structures are no less prevalent in the voyage into the underworld—the worms in the opening incantation, for instance, are trying to form themselves into loops, though "head never quite touches tail" (4)—and the system of concentric circles in Peoria resembles both the looping river Styx, which encircles Hades seven times, and the circles of Dante's inferno.

IV

Like *The Pale King* itself, my focus so far has been diffuse: accumulating different meanings and pointing toward a variety of sources without perhaps drawing these strands together into a sufficiently unified whole. But there is such a unity within the fragmentary novel that binds together the tornado structure, Wallace's reflections upon the novel, the voyage into the underworld, and the novel's treatment of time, though to make this unity more visible the novel has to be placed back into the context of Wallace's working library.

My title is taken from the prose poem that provides the novel's epigraph, and, as Wallace adapts and recontextualizes a fragment from the poem, he blurs the meaning of "forms" to spread it between *bodily form* and *bureaucratic forms*. The animating ideal, here, is the analogy, which in large part is also the concept that underlies my description of *The Pale King*'s metaphoric nodes. On the subject of analogies, Herman Melville noted halfway through *Moby-Dick* that: "not the smallest atom stirs or lives in matter, but has its cunning duplicate in mind" (340). In the final part of this chapter, I'm going to argue that the unifying analogies in *The Pale King* reverse Melville's dictum, to search in the external world for "a paradigm for the life of consciousness" (Bidart 9).

While Wallace's own comments about *The Pale King* invoke the tornado as an analogy for the novel's form, references within the book forge a connection between the novel's structure and cognition, when

Sylvanshine describes Bondurant's thought patterns as "tornadic" (51). Sylvanshine's role in the book is also linked to the mind: while his initials point us toward C. S. Lewis, CS is also the abbreviation that Freud used for *consciousness*, and it's worth noting that the Underworld—especially in Freudian iconography—stands for the unconscious mind. In fact, the epigraph for *The Interpretation of Dreams* was taken from Virgil: "If I cannot bend the higher powers, I will move the infernal regions" (Freud 604 n1). A fascination with how "the mind works" (259) provides a unifying thread through these disparate elements, and what I believe Wallace was trying to do in *The Pale King* was to make—in William Gass's words—the "book . . . a container of consciousness" (327), that is a concrete model in which numerous analogies might dramatize different aspects of cognition.[16] The problem of the novel as embodied by Sylvanshine, for example, is its tendency to be overloaded by the multifarious information that makes up other peoples' mental lives. The qualities of fiction that Lewis and Wallace champion devastate Sylvanshine, and he needs Reynolds to act as a kind of filter. On one level, then, Reynolds stands to Sylvanshine as the brain stands to consciousness, because, as Aldous Huxley argued in a passage that Wallace underlined in his copy of Joseph Campbell's *Myths to Live By* (1972):

> The function of the brain and nervous system is to protect us from being overwhelmed and confused by this mass of largely useless and irrelevant knowledge, by shutting out most of what we should otherwise perceive or remember at any moment, and leaving only that very small and special selection which is likely to be practically useful. . . . To make biological survival possible, Mind at Large has to be funneled through the reducing valve of the brain and nervous system. What comes out at the other end is a measly trickle of the kind of consciousness which will help us to stay alive on the surface of this particular planet. (261)[17]

This conception of consciousness as a thin slice of the brain's total mental activity is more precisely explored by Timothy Wilson in *Strangers to Ourselves* (2002), which Wallace read while working on *The Pale King*. Acknowledging but also diverging from Freudian thought, Wilson's model of the mind is divided between the "narrow corridor of consciousness" (4), which is a "limited capacity system" (8), and the adaptive unconscious. "At any given moment," Wilson observes, "our five senses are taking in more than 11,000,000 pieces of information" but "the most liberal estimate is that people can process consciously about 40 pieces of information per second" (24); the remaining 10, 999, 960 pieces of information are processed in the unconscious, while a "nonconscious filter . . . examines the information reaching our senses and decides what to admit to consciousness" (28). Reading *The Pale King* next to Wilson's study, suggests that Sylvanshine's descent into the underworld symbolizes the fact that his RFI syndrome has immersed him in the "blooming, buzzing, confusion" (William James qtd. in Wilson 28) of the nonconscious mind. In this sense his initials are a double pun: he is C. S. Lewis's model encountering sensory overload, while he is also consciousness unduly open to the flux and minutiae of the adaptive unconscious.[18]

But to return to one of my first questions in revised form: why did Wallace turn to accounting to provide the skeleton that would hold his model of the mind? To some extent, Wilson again provides a vital clue. In another passage marked by Wallace, Wilson introduces his position by explaining that:

> the mental processes that operate our perceptual, language and motor systems operate largely outside of awareness, much like the vast workings of the federal government that go on out of the view of the president. If all the lower-level members of the executive branch were to take the day off, very little governmental work would get done. (21)[19]

The Federal government, for Wilson, is an analogy for the working mind, but for Wallace the tornadic tax system—a mere fragment of the federal machine—stands as a more accurate model, perhaps because tax figures so prominently in American lives as the generating force driving the national economy without its minute details ever being fully brought into consciousness. Reversing the analogy to think about how the mind informs Wallace's treatment of the IRS, it seems that the novel equates the IRS with a nonconscious filter that either saves us from being overwhelmed or blinds us to the realities of economic policy.[20]

Yet while the adaptive unconscious protects us from sensory overload with a nonconscious filter, the mind also protects us from the power of an individual sensation—say profound grief, or excitement—through what Wilson calls the "psychological process of ordinization," which "weaves [extraordinary sensations] into our knowledge of ourselves and the world, in a way that makes" them seem "normal, ordinary, even expected" (158, 151). This process is linked to the novel's chronology, because in our experience of time, ordinization blinds us to the persistence of the past, keeping our focus only on that which is novel.

Bearing in mind the work carried out by Wallace's accountants and the overall thematic focus on attention, the term that I would suggest best characterizes *The Pale King*'s treatment of time is: *concentration*. The book's temporal arrangement—compressing so many disparate periods—is, then, carefully designed to recapitulate one of the novel's thematic obsessions.[21] At the same time, however, the novel's concentrated time seems to be an attempt to reverse ordinization. While Chris Fogle feels as if he's "trapped in the present" (154), *The Pale King* attempts to present time through a negative psychology that inverts our habituation processes, that is, it creates a timeframe that replaces the shiny veneer of the present with a deeper liquid time in which the submerged signs of the past—from Ancient history to the early-twentieth century—can float to the surface and coexist with our contemporary fascinations. Abstracting from this principle also helps to explain on one level why *The Pale King* is a kaleidoscopic text, one in which we can see the outlines of Wallace's evolving career: the echoes of the earlier books, his evolving style, and a condensed rehearsal of his theory of the novel.

Across nearly 20 years, Wallace talked with Jonathan Franzen about the utility of fiction, that is, how they could justify sitting in their "rooms and struggling with fiction when there [was] so much wrong with the world" (Franzen, "Art of Fiction" 73). While *Strangers to Ourselves* presents a frame for the exploration of Wallace's earlier work, it also sketches a picture of the mind that—crucially—urges us to depart from traditional self-examination in a way that perhaps provided one answer to the utilitarian question Wallace had explored with Franzen. Because the adaptive unconscious presents a model of the mind in which we have access to only a fragment of our total cognitive activity, Wilson argues that we are fundamentally blinded to our own personalities but *can* assess more accurately other people's characters. This division stems from a tendency to attribute our own behavior to the marginal activities of consciousness, but to assess other people's motivation in terms of the full range of their actions, which are likely to reflect both conscious and nonconscious processes. According to the experiments that underlie his account, self-reports of motivation yield unreliable predictions of behavior, while we can generate more accurate predictions about others precisely because we are not privy to their self-delusions. This theory is, of course, a reversal of C. S. Lewis, which might explain both why Sylvanshine is in crisis through much of *The Pale King*, and why the "David Wallace" figure is so obviously a counterfactual Author rather than a serious attempt to record Wallace's character: we learn more about ourselves, Wilson argues, by looking not at what William James calls the "warmth and intimacy" of our own consciousness (242), but by looking at other people, and deducing the boundaries of our nonconscious self.[22] Such a process arguably equips us to lead less ruinous lives. The array of characters and the administrative structures that comprise Wallace's last novel might, then, be seen as an attempt (in Tor Nørretranders's words) to "cut consciousness down to size" and create a dissociative projection of the mind that dramatizes the workings of the adaptive unconscious—with its filtering, and protective strategies—as well as our conscious delusions, in his final effort to explore why humans "did what they did" (52).

Notes

1   The text was originally delivered on September 22, 2011, as the opening keynote presentation at the University of Antwerp's *Work in Process: Reading David Foster Wallace's The Pale King* conference.

2   Moving in a different direction, Toon Staes's essay, "Rewriting the Author," engages with the explosion of interest in Wallace's biography, mapping his relevance to novels by Jeffrey Eugenides and Jonathan Lethem, and employing a narratological approach to Wallace's work.

3   The earliest section seems to be the monologue beginning "Wardine say her momma aint treat her right" that appears on pages 37–8 of the published novel.

4   If this model of Wallace's compositional procedures is correct, then accounts that see his creative history as a "struggle to surpass *Infinite Jest*" (to take the subtitle of D. T. Max's profile) mistakenly ascribe a linear sequence of discrete projects, rather than emphasizing a series of parallel compositions enlivened by creative cross-fertilization. Indeed, Max's biography of Wallace—published after this paper was delivered in Antwerp—makes some concessions to this perspective, seeing in *Infinite Jest*, for example, a collation of "all three of Wallace's literary styles, passing through his infatuation with postmodernism at Arizona, and ending . . . in Boston" (159).

5   As one example of the blurring of the edges between works, Michael Pietsch notes that both *Oblivion*'s final story and the opening of *The Pale King* are preoccupied with shit, art, and death.

6   Coe historicizes *Christie Malry* by noting that the Tories rise to power, the fate of the Angry Brigade (a terrorist group Coe describes as a "a loose-knit assembly of malcontents . . . brought to trial for offences related to explosives" [312]) all "weighed heavily on Johnson's mind as he began to think about his sixth novel" (315).

7   See page seven, when Sylvanshine traces the origin of the "double-entry method" to the "Italian Pacioli" (cf. *Christie Malry* 17).

8   Though Wilson's novel is more explicitly referenced later in *The Pale King* (145, 215), in light of the shared names, it may not be coincidental that the novel begins with a first sentence that moves past "the flannel plains" (3).

9   In the first chapter devoted to Toni Ware she is drawing "circles within circles" around her name (58). When we first see Lane Dean at work we're told that he's desperately fighting the urge to run "in circles . . . flapping his arms" (123, cf. 125). Given Chris Fogle's love of "doubling" effects, it's probably appropriate that his long epiphany is catalyzed by a double reference to circular motion—he's spinning a ball while he's watching *As the World Turns* (221). Even Drinion, we're told, has an unusually "round head" (451).

10 Paul Quinn offers a detailed and persuasive reading of the many ways that tornadoes might seem a key to the novel—and to Wallace's larger body of work—in his essay, "'Location's Location': Placing David Foster Wallace."

11 Reflection is central to the REC's geography—the center's building is "back-leased through . . . Mid West Mirror Works" (265), and seems to be built upon "one square acre of hidden mirror" (312).

12 The way this scene inverts the viewpoint through which we're used to seeing Sylvanshine in the novel is indicative of one of the novel's consistent techniques, that is to relativize perspective by alternating between internal and external views of characters, often by replaying the same scene. Compare, for instance, the divergent reflections of the Davids Wallace and Cusk upon their shared journey to the Peoria REC (285, 318).

13 This dimension of Wallace's novel is further emphasized by the source text for *The Pale King*'s epigraph—Frank Bidart's "Borges and I"—since Rosanna Warren describes Bidart's poem as itself a "small *ars poetica*" (96).

14 Though sections of Toni's narrative are often read as stylistically tied to Cormac McCarthy's example, from the perspective of narrative incident it's worth noting that Wallace argued that Ellis's aesthetic could be reduced to the basic desire to "affect people" borne out of the urge "to make sure that people don't ignore you" (*CW* 16). Late in *The Pale King*, Toni's MO is "concerned entirely with whether the" people are around her "could be affected" (511).

15 It is not coincidental, in the context of *The Pale King*, that Erebus was also the son of Chaos in Greek mythology.

16 It may be worth noting that—as part of Wallace's overall inheritance from DeLillo—this attempt to model consciousness has some affinities with DeLillo's conception of *Underworld* as (in its own words) a "living likeness of the mind's own technology" (496).

17 Another way to read the importance of filtering in the novel is through the concept of Maxwell's Demon and the novel's overall interest in "uncontrolled heat" (96).

18 For further exploration of *The Pale King*'s investment in non-conscious processes, with attention to another aspect of the novel's obsession with circular structures—eyes and optical function—see Burn, "Toward a General Theory of Vision in Wallace's Fiction."

19   Following Daniel Dennett, Wilson later qualifies this position to see consciousness as the "press secretary" rather than the president (47).

20   Next to the novel's civic exploration is, of course, a fascination with bodily waste: Toni's "standard-colored clot of mucus" (514), the catalogue of shit stories (347–55), and the double-entendres encoded in both the abbreviation for tax payers (TP) and Fogle's description of the Jesuit who "had himself firmly in hand" (208). To some extent, the references to bodily waste similarly serve to draw our attention to activities that are frequently refined out of conscious attention.

21   The use of the novel's chronological rearrangement to suggest a thematic node is an example of what I've elsewhere described as *temporal form* (see Burn, *Jonathan Franzen at the End of Postmodernism* [78–81]).

22   This approach adds a further resonance to Wallace's choice of epigraph, as Warren argues that Bidart's poetry is involved in a similar attempt to displace "an ego-bound conception of self" (96).

9

"What Am I, a Machine?": Humans and Information in *The Pale King*

Conley Wouters

A measure of disorder

In his book-length study of David Foster Wallace's *Infinite Jest*, Stephen Burn notes that the beginning of that novel "sets up a tension between an excess of information and unexplainable selfhood that is elaborated throughout the rest of the book" (*Reader's Guide* 40). Focusing on Hal Incandenza, the more linguistically voracious of the novel's two protagonists, Burn writes, "no matter how expansive your vocabulary, or how careful your description, a list of words is not enough to make a self" (40). For Burn, much of *Infinite Jest*'s circular narrative unwinds so that its characters—particularly Hal, but also, for instance, Kate Gompert, whom Burn points out is at least once referred to as a "data cleric"—have multiple opportunities to locate and try to retain authentic selves in the face of a flood of external input, whether drugs, entertainment, or other easily obsessed-over stimulation.

This chapter proceeds from Burn's convincing contention that many of *Infinite Jest*'s most commonly discussed themes all derive from the timeless question of *Hamlet*'s opening line: "Who's there?" (*Reader's Guide* 40). My reading of *The Pale King* assumes that the unfinished, posthumous novel builds on thematic concerns established in *Infinite Jest*. Beyond Hal Incandenza's scarily urgent quest to prove that he "is in here"—that he is more than a body surrounded by heads—*Infinite Jest*'s characters constantly struggle to identify the most fundamental signs of their own interior selfhood, of proof that they exist, even as they embark on external challenges such as beating addiction in a halfway house or making it to the Show, the prevailing entertainment-infused euphemism for professional tennis among Enfield Tennis Academy's young athletic prodigies.

The Pale King is overtly concerned with the meaning and consequences of all-pervasive boredom, which, as Ralph Clare demonstrates elsewhere in this volume, has not only a rich history, but the potential, in the hands of federal bureaucracies, to become "a political tool." This exploration of boredom reprises many of *Infinite Jest*'s questions concerning the self and the subject, and it does so, I will argue, in a different ontological arena than the one in which the latter is set. *The Pale King*'s characters constantly struggle to locate themselves in the face of an excess of material that they can be sure is *not* the self, which, in the late twentieth century, often takes the shape of data, information, entertainment, or some cross-section thereof. At first glance, the avalanche of data that greets new IRS examiners like Lane Dean seems to be nothing but "numbers that connected to nothing he'd ever see or care about" (*TPK* 379). However, in keeping with the way *Infinite Jest* persistently positioned information in an antagonistic relationship to both humans and subjects, many of the details that *The Pale King*'s data clerks handle turn out to be a barometer of the self or lack thereof. As the Compliance Training Officer proclaims to a room full of agents, "'[i]nformation per se is really just a measure of disorder'" (342).

Claude Sylvanshine, an agent whose head "pops up" at this aphoristic definition of information, had, "at age eight . . . data on his father's liver enzymes and rate of cortical atrophy, but he didn't know what these data meant" (341). Information in *The Pale King* does not merely threaten to obscure humanity, as it did in *Infinite Jest*. It also actively and in some cases aggressively works to replace humanity, as in the unusually explicit case of Sylvanshine's father, who, through his bodily disorder, becomes an unintelligible pile of data, or the IRS agents, who "'are all,'" a supervisor tells them, "'if you think about it, data processors'" (340). I rely on the work of Wallace scholar Paul Giles and his reading of N. Katherine Hayles' influential *How We Became Posthuman* in my attempt to show that *The Pale King*'s characters possess an ambivalence in the face of these information avalanches that is at times healthy and at other times consuming. Though it varies from character to character, it seems that the existential dread and uncertainty that is often the primary consequence of these information onslaughts becomes the most threatening obstacle Wallace's agents face. Given Wallace's track record for thoroughly exploring paralyzing self-conscious and its attendant despair, this may not come as a surprise.

Additionally, I argue that despite the multiple examples of humans in danger of becoming machines, and the characters' varying reactions to this contemporary vulnerability, the book's singular structure overrides the fears and anxieties that appear throughout the narrative, suggesting through its very existence that humans and information can and do coexist naturally, in some kind of millennial harmony. The novel is obviously unfinished, taking on its final, published form thanks to the efforts of Wallace's longtime editor Michael Pietsch. But the manuscript's notes, directions, and precise presentation suggest that elements of its incomplete composition that were previously ascribed to chance, and to the tragedy of Wallace's death, might in fact not only be deliberate, but cues to consider the possibility that *The Pale King* might exist in some generic limbo—not quite a novel or a pure work of fiction, but obviously not a book of facts, either.

What follows attempts to position *The Pale King* as a kind of technological prequel to *Infinite Jest*, one that suggests that with the right political-philosophical tools, we might still be able to retain a traditional, liberal-humanist selfhood in the face of informational avalanches. If *Infinite Jest* documented uniquely contemporary dangers associated with an information overload, *The Pale King* asks variations on the questions Wallace originally posed in his 2005 commencement address to Kenyon College (e.g. *This Is Water*)—that is, how to be aware of our surroundings, and how best to choose what to give ourselves to—but with a much keener eye for our own more mechanical water.

Riding the crest

A hilarious, profound exchange on a broken elevator in *The Pale King*'s nineteenth section begins this way: "'There's something very interesting about civics and selfishness, and we get to ride the crest of it'" (130). The statement tentatively introduces the ideas floated over the course of the next 20 pages' political debate, but it also works as an autonomous encapsulation of Wallace's complex stance toward America's political foundations. DeWitt Glendenning, director of the Midwest Regional Examination Center, congratulates himself for tracing these foundations back to principles of the European enlightenment articulated in Rousseau's *The Social Contract*. As they are presented in *The Pale King*, these ideas are at a critical, late-twentieth-century impasse, and the section in which characters valiantly attempt to confront them illustrates one of the broad implications of Marshall Boswell's concluding essay: It might be time we conceive of Wallace as a political novelist, one who grappled with not only the content, but the form, of our national conversations in the ways "the Jonathans Franzen and Safron Foer are regarded" as doing (211).

I want to focus on the word "selfishness," which functions in *The Pale King* as a pun, and might be a single-word entry point into one of these conversations. The first sense of the term—devotion to one's own advantage at the exclusion of regard to others, to paraphrase the OED—is what Glendenning clearly intends here, but this denotation is the antithesis of the Rousseauian social pact that is referenced throughout *The Pale King*. The social contract as it exists without "everything that is not essential to it ... comes down to this: 'Each one of us puts into the community his person and all his powers under the supreme direction of the general will; and as a body, we incorporate every member as an individual part of the whole'" (Rousseau 61). What Rousseau outlines here is exactly what the agents fear is suddenly, scarily obsolete: "We don't think of ourselves as citizens—parts of something larger to which we have profound responsibilities. We think of ourselves as citizens when it comes to our rights and privileges, but not our responsibilities" (*TPK* 130). From where the agents stand, US citizens' refusal to give themselves over to a civic collective impedes and threatens to revoke their very citizenship.

This is where the second sense of "selfishness" comes in. If the first meaning is written all over consumerist culture, the second is its much more malignant consequence. I contend that Wallace uses the word "selfish," rather than a more precise or political synonym like "entitled," because he wants to communicate the idea of an incomplete or malformed self; something that's not quite a self, but self-*ish*. If this seems far-fetched, we might consider the fact that the Peoria Processing Center at which all of the characters work is situated on "Self-Storage Parkway" (27), which should suggest that the concept of the self is important enough to explicitly manifest throughout the novel, and that Wallace was not afraid to pun on it. The two significations of the word are intimately connected. By "abdicating our civic responsibilities to the government" (130)—responsibilities which, as Rousseau claims, are "in the first place, [that] every individual gives himself absolutely" (Rousseau 60)—many of these characters are left with a gaping void that often manifests as loneliness or personal dysfunction, both concrete correspondents to a primarily self-ish existence.

Glendenning voices a paradox that perpetuates this state of affairs when he says, from his dual position as citizen and federal employee, "'As citizens we cede more and more of our autonomy, but if we the government take away the citizens' freedom to cede their autonomy we're now taking away their autonomy'" (130). By waiving their responsibility and thrusting it on their government—by expecting the government, which Glendenning points out "'*is* the people ... but we split off and pretend it's not us'" (134–5), to give of *it*self—individuals abdicate their prerogative to give themselves to the collective. Paradoxically, it is by not giving themselves that the citizens lose part of themselves.

To disown these civic duties and thrust them onto the government, one still sacrifices one's self to the collective that Glendenning calls "'some threatening Other'" (134), but in this case one does so incorrectly, almost forcing an infringement on one's rights and, ultimately, whole being. By refusing to participate in one of the fundamental covenants of democracy (sacrifice of the self to the benefit of the collective), Americans do not just invite but catalyze some near but still-unspecified form of tyranny, by forcing their government to take from them that which they have the power to give.

If the American TPs, as the agents refer to average taxpaying citizens, refuse to give themselves to their government, and indeed resent the very suggestion that they might perform such a sacrifice, to what do they offer themselves, their attention, and their respect? This is another question that hangs over at least the latter half of Wallace's career, but one potential answer that *The Pale King* suggests is, ultimately, nothing. Rousseau puts it most plainly when he writes of slavery: "To speak of a man giving himself in return for nothing is to speak of what is absurd, unthinkable; such an action would be illegitimate . . . because no one who did it could be in his right mind. To say the same of a whole people is to conjure up a nation of lunatics . . ." (54).

When Glendenning, in the same winding conversation, says, "I think Americans in 1980 are crazy. Have gone crazy. Regressed somehow" (*TPK* 135), it is to the unthinkable insanity of a "whole people" who have given their very selves in return for nothing that he refers. The character identified only as X's well-intentioned but inaccurate paraphrase of the assessment— "'The quote lack of discipline and respect for authority of the decadent seventies'" (135)—is met with this exasperated threat: "'If you don't shut up I'm going to put you up on the roof of the elevator and you can stay there'" (135). If the problem were merely a lack of respect, it might be one with an easy solution.

Instead, Glendenning seems to be motioning toward something like the paradox of self-inflicted slavery that might be Americans' undoing, an unthinkably destructive political maneuver that is uniquely post-industrial and, in this novel, dependent on machines and information. After considering Paul Giles' essay "Sentimental Posthumanism: David Foster Wallace," I'll examine three separate IRS employees, all of whom face Rousseau's void-like nothingness in different yet related ways, to try to reveal the connection between this self-destructive impulse and the social landscape of late-twentieth-century America.

What am I, a machine?

Drawing on the work of N. Katherine Hayles, whose *How We Became Posthuman* details a shift away from the prevailing liberal humanism of the past two centuries, Paul Giles speaks of a recently arrived phenomenological arena in which "computation, rather than possessive individualism or biological organism" is deemed the "ground of being" (329). For Giles, much of Wallace's work fits firmly under the posthumanist umbrella, which, he notes, "as Hayles emphasizes, does not mean the end of . . . humanity; rather, it takes issue with comfortable liberal assumptions about the sovereignty of the human subject" (329).

In 2012, the year after a surprisingly charismatic computer defeated two human prodigies in a *Jeopardy!* tournament, posthumanism as Giles and Hayles describe it might seem to have necessarily ambiguous beginnings. Is it a critical-theoretical response to an outdated set of beliefs and practices, or is it simply a way to formally articulate the experience of our increasingly computerized day-to-day existence? Wallace's tentative division of humans and machines in *The Pale King* seems to suggest the latter. Giles' swift dissection of the posthumanist elements that flourish throughout Wallace's body of work turns on a contradiction in terms that begins with the essay's title and gets reinforced throughout the piece—namely, the idea that something called "sentimental posthumanism" could exist as an abstract idea, let alone a set of thematic and stylistic principles to be developed over the course of Wallace's career.

For Giles, Wallace's texts "reflect a condition of confusion where . . . the . . . distinction between human and non-human is becoming ever less self-evident" (328), but they ultimately "[seek] to open up spaces within [abstract] grids of information technology where emotion and identity can be explored" (341). In other words, he concludes that Wallace simultaneously affirms and questions the centrality of the human subject. Wallace writes posthumanist fiction that retains and affirms humanism at the same time it acknowledges and grapples with twenty-first-century social and cultural milieux that are hostile to that same humanism. *The Pale King*, set during the dawn of our current, post-industrial information age, traces the beginnings of the way humans give themselves to computational tasks. One of the questions this trajectory opens up is whether the rote tasks and machine-like existence which many of the characters confront are an instance of the agents giving themselves *to* such self-ish existences (in place of Glendenning's body politic), or a sinister symptom of the technology itself. Much like it was during the elevator debate, the issue is one of agency.

This is a particularly difficult problem, since the novel's superficial treatment of the collapsing distinction between humans and machines is ambivalent or even contradictory at times. In §14, an initiative aims to "humanize . . . the Service . . . [and] help citizens understand . . . that [the agents are] not hostile or machines" (100), while later on, an agent identified only by the SSN 928514387 says he likes his work because "' . . . it's like you're a machine that know it's running well and doing what it was made to do'" (115). Chris Fogel, a character whose entry into the Service marks the culmination of a spiritual awakening, partly describes his early, recreational drug experiments as "'a sort of emergence . . . [a]s though I was a machine that had suddenly realized it was a human being and didn't have to go through the motions it was programmed to perform over and over" (182). In notes published in the book's appendix, Wallace clearly intends this division to be one of the book's central thematic concerns: "Big issue is human examiners or machines" (545). All of these examples point toward an increasingly dubious categorical distinction, but none address the question of process, of how people might become machines. The next three sections I examine all offer competing visions of what this process might look like, and how threatening it may be.

The story of Lane Dean, a brand new husband and returns examiner, indicates that self-ish-ness can be thrust upon people by requiring them to perform work that explicitly asks them *not* to think, and that being coerced into becoming a cyborg[1] is now a viable threat. Lane's struggles concern, first, family, and then work, and in his separate sets of problems, we find an antagonistic distinction between liberal humanism and posthumanism. Ultimately in line with what Adam Kirsch, in an article for *The New Republic* called "The Importance of Being Earnest," points out are "a number of conservative tropes" that "Wallace takes obvious pleasure in rehearsing" (25), *The Pale King* suggests that the capacity to ethically engage in situations is what might barely rescue humans from mechanization. This morality sometimes takes the form of earnest Midwestern value systems that Wallace seemed alone among his contemporaries in embracing.

We first meet Lane in what is essentially a pastoral retelling of Hemingway's "Hills Like White Elephants" that was originally published under the title "Good People." Lane and his young, newly pregnant girlfriend Sherri sit atop a picnic table "at the one park by the lake" (Wallace 36), letting the specter of a probable abortion hang between them while they mostly fail to discuss it. Throughout the story, a quiet sentimentalism builds to the edge of incredibly tense personal tragedy, all the while employing borderline-cliche imagery and dialogue. Kirsch notes that the way Lane finally comes to decide to marry Sherri and support her decision to have the baby (all while acknowledging to himself that he doesn't love her) is to "[ask], literally, what would Jesus do," and he posits that with this question, Wallace is "daring you to roll your eyes" (25). As important as the method by which Lane comes to reconcile himself to a potentially loveless marriage is the fact that the section ends on notes of extreme uncertainty:[2] "Why is one kind of love any different? What if he has no earthly idea what love is? What would even Jesus do? . . . What if he is just afraid, if the truth is no more than this, and if what to pray for is not even love but simple courage, to meet both her eyes as she says it and trust his heart?" (Wallace 42–3).

These questions are all left unanswered, but somehow still instill a sense of comfort and closure, especially when one contrasts them with Lane's query-free work life. The inability to ask questions like these is what ultimately threatens to undo Lane Dean in §33. In the park, they serve as proof that Lane is "good people," a term that, in addition to its vernacular meaning, suggests a fundamental, functional humanity, a humanness that falls squarely in line with liberal humanism's sovereign self and that, in this novel, is opposed to a cybernetic, partially mechanic existence. Good people are not self(-)ish. Sherri and Lane are good people because they are capable of even conceiving of a "right thing," something that seems out of reach for Lane's already-defeated coworkers.

The opening of §33 finds Lane sitting "at his Tingle table in his Chalk's row in the Rotes Group's wiggle room" (376), working through a day's worth of returns in a monotonous routine that "made the routing desk at UPS look like Six Flags" (377). If we contrast Lane's first day at the processing center with his interior monologue at the park, it becomes clear that Wallace injects his precarious humanity with a much more threatening quality than he does the potentially fatal boredom. Unlike the episode with Sheri in the park, which ended with a kind of comfortably uncertain, carefully weighed conclusion, Lane's capacity as "IRS rote examiner" (377) now makes him guardian of a different kind of truth—rigid, lifeless data that leaves no room for interpretation or engagement.

Indeed, in the slew of information Lane now faces, uncertainty occurs not in the data itself but in the physical medium on which it is collected: "Crosschecking W-2s for the return's Line 7 off the place in the Martinsburg printout where the perforation if you wanted to separate the thing's sheets went right through the data and you had to hold it up against the light almost and sometimes guess . . ." (377) Lane records each return's minutiae and errors, issues which he deems "almost unbelievably meaningless and small" (381). But as boring the work may be, it is his inability to engage with it that threatens to doom him to a somehow subhuman existence. His job as a processor—as, essentially, a sentient computer—becomes dangerous when it precludes some element of interpretation or wonder, of human qualities that Wallace positions not as social luxuries but as biological necessities.

Showing a still-intact capacity for this kind of wonder, Lane tries, in a Thoreau-like way, to "envision the inward lives of the older men to either side of him, doing this day after day. Getting up on a Monday . . . knowing what they were going out the door to come back to for eight hours" (377). Compare his vision of the men outside of their work to the brief attention the narrator gives these minor characters, through which we learn that "[n]either man . . . seemed to fidget or move except to reach up and lift things onto the desk from their Tingles' trays, like machines, and they were never in the lounge during break" (381). Lane's ostensible reason for constructing the men's after-work lives is to ascertain how someone so terminally bored can have any sort of interior life, but his true motivation is to try to deny the prominent evidence that these men are no longer even men, not beings capable of any type of extraprofessional activity. Their limited physical activity has been mechanized, ensuring their only movement meets the minimum requirements of a literal paper pusher. Their absence in the break room supports the frightening possibility that anything beyond base, rote functionality—that is, anything human—has been eliminated from their existence.

This elimination is a consequence of the work, not an inborn personal defect. In a defense of his stylistic tendencies that also implicitly condemns the repetitive work of the examiners ("I am about art here, not simple reproduction" [259]), "David Wallace" reminds the reader that, "What renders a truth meaningful, worthwhile . . . is its relevance, which in turn requires extraordinary discernment . . . to context, questions of value, and overall point—otherwise we might as well all just be computers downloading raw data to one another" (259). Emotionally uninterpretable data, like the kind the examiners work with, is dangerous because it does indeed turn them into data-swapping computers. It removes the possibility that they might choose which information deserves their attention, and it makes it impossible to, as Wallace put it in *This Is Water*, the published version of his speech to Kenyon College, "exercise some control over *how* and *what* you think" (52).

Lane's coworkers seem to be the culmination of a dystopian version of the "machines [who have] learned to think" that James Gleick, in *The Information*, writes Alan Turing and Claude Shannon dreamed of. While the two scientists discussed the nearly limitless potential for thinking machines, Turing, according to Gleick, exclaimed, "'No, I'm not interested in developing a *powerful* brain. All I'm after is just a *mundane* brain . . . '" (205). The mundane brains on either side of Lane Dean square with much of what Wallace was interested in and seemed to fear late in his life and career. *This Is Water* lays out a way to live on a setting other than our default autopilot, and to be aware enough of our surroundings to engage with them emotionally and spiritually, but returns employees remain on their default settings, or get downgraded against their will to a newly redundant default.

In addition to the human calculators that flank him on either side, the fact that a ghost, a haunting approximation of a man "with a seamed face and picket teeth" (382), visits a half-asleep Lane further signals the center's hostility toward coherent, intelligible selfhood. In the park, Lane and Sheri both are spiritually absorbed in their dilemma by the section's end, and the last sentence evokes a stylistic mode that seems, in its unabashed and almost excessive sentimentality, to exist partially in order to provide a human counterpart to the frighteningly soulless dynamics of Lane's office. In fact, Wallace inserts a unifying figure that explicitly connects §§6 and 33. Early on we learn that other than Sherri and Lane, "the only other individual nearby was a dozen spaced tables away by himself, standing upright" (36). This "older individual stood beside his picnic table, he was at it but not sitting, and looked also out of place in a suit coat or jacket and the kind of older men's hat Lane's grandfather wore in photos as a young man . . . If he moved, Lane didn't see it" (37).

This "man in the suit and gray hat" (41) is almost certainly the wraith that appears to Lane in the office later on,[3] only here his humanity is possibly still intact. Though his staid appearance might foreshadow Lane's imminent, sober professionalism that is a direct result of what transpires in the park (i.e. he takes the job to support Sherri and the child she decides to have), the fact that he does not either engage with Lane or threaten him—but that his presence is still noted, in an otherwise anachronistically uninhabited pastoral landscape—suggests both Lane's potential fate and a silent, subtle affirmation of the deep humanity with which this section is imbued. The irony, of course, is that it is by following *This Is Water*'s prescriptions to a tee that positions Lane Dean, Jr in danger of relinquishing the very humanity that made possible his family in the first place. Again there is the suggestion that external, environmental factors drive the existential dilemmas many of *The Pale King*'s characters face, since Lane seems the epitome of a "good," human person.

David Cusk's childhood tribulations are a less obvious but equally significant case study of the consequences of realizing one's very humanity might suddenly be at stake. Cusk remains unnamed in §13, when the reader is first introduced to him and his debilitating, humiliating condition. Though he reappears later on as an adult and IRS employee, the narrator in §13 refers to him only by the third-person pronoun, or, at best, as "this boy" (91), tagging him with an objectifying anonymity that hints at the way his humanity will soon be under siege. Though this section is primarily concerned with the boy's embarrassingly excessive sweating and his inability to control it, as well as the fact that his high school years were the period in which he "learned the terrible power of attention and what you pay attention to" (91), the particular language that communicates Cusk's plight betrays thematic threads that parallel Dean and Sylvanshine's stories.

Through his disorder, and his desperate, largely unsuccessful attempts to treat it himself, Cusk is presented as more machine-like than human, a kind of terminally malfunctioning apparatus that bewilders its owner into bouts of self-loathing. The most insidious aspect of the sweating is not that Cusk cannot control it, or cannot stop it once it has begun; instead, it is that he can only partially (or barely) understand it. In this way, we might begin to see it not as some psychological or physiological impairment, but rather a mechanical malfunction, something that cannot be understood in terms of human breakdown:

> It was by far the worst feeling he had ever had in his life, and the whole attack lasted almost forty minutes, and for the rest of the day he went around in a kind of trance of shock . . . and that day was the actual start of a syndrome in which he understood that the worse his fear of breaking into a shattering public sweat was, the better the chances [of it happening]—and this understanding caused him more . . . inner suffering than he had ever before even dreamed . . . somebody could ever experience, and the total stupidity and weirdness of the whole problem just made it that much worse. (94)

As will hopefully become more clear in a moment, the description of the "stupidity and weirdness" of the episodes is an understatement we can chalk up to the characteristically conversational tone that Wallace's narrator takes here. In reality, the problem's "weirdness" is probably something closer to totally alien, terrifyingly foreign due to its complete hostility to any type of human intervention. Additionally, it is important that while the syndrome is defined by a vague connection to Cusk's thoughts and emotions (it can be exacerbated by natural fear), it is not directly or logically influenced by either. The disorder is removed from the realm of mental illness when it is ultimately separated from Cusk's consciousness. It exists on a much scarier, because much more unreachable, plane, a place where the disorder can torment him from some invisible distance, deep inside of himself.

The narrator goes on to describe Cusk's coping methods for his ailment, which, notably, "he thought of . . . as *attacks,* though not from anything outside him but rather from some inner part of himself that was hurting or almost betraying him, as in *heart attack*" (96). The image is of one part of a whole gone haywire, a stubbornly dysfunctional cog in a larger machine it usually helps run. The coping methods themselves are also important: "His main way of dealing with being constantly primed and preoccupied with the fear of it all the time at school was that he developed various tricks and tactics for what to do if an attack of public sweating started . . ." (97). Cusk's only defense against the thing that threatens to unwind his mental and emotional stability are "tricks and tactics," workarounds that depend on luck insofar as they are, by their nature, partly unreliable. Because of the unknowably alien nature of his affliction, he has no real tools with which to attack it. Instead, he relies on makeshift maneuvers (such as running to the next classroom at a precise pace that guarantees him a spot away from the furnace, but isn't fast enough to induce between-class sweating) akin to banging on an errant TV set, or blowing on a broken game cartridge. Cusk's pathetic pain management system never moves beyond ill-conceived strategies that are self-defeating in their absurd complexity and ultimate unreliability.

Additionally, at least one of these tactics almost makes explicit the inhuman nature of Cusk's strange condition: "This was one of the tricks—to cough or sniff and feel uncomfortably at his glands if he feared an attack, so if it got out of control he could hope people would maybe just think he was sick and shouldn't have come to school that day. That he wasn't weird, he was just sick. It was the same with pretending he didn't feel well enough to eat his lunch at lunch period . . . That way, people might be more apt to think he was sick" (97). This desperate desire to appear "sick" requires the reader to make a distinction between "sick" and "weird," and to determine why one is to be preferred over the other.

I hope I have already supplied a believable answer: the idea that if we can extrapolate "weird" to encompass foreign, alien, and even inhuman, then it becomes obvious why "sick" is a more attractive alternative. If Cusk's classmates buy his coughing and sniffing, he has a chance of appearing to suffer from a mundanely human malfunction. Otherwise, he is something else, something more sinister in its mystery. The uncomfortable, almost tragic image that concludes the section confirms that it is the possibility of being fundamentally, ontologically different—of being a malfunctioning machine—that Cusk so fears, rather than just the sweating:

> [he] faked being sick at Easter so he could stay home . . . and [try] to jump-start an attack in the mirror of his parents' bathroom instead of driving with them to Easter dinner . . . he felt a bit sad about it, as well as relieved, plus guilty about the various lies of the excuses he gave, and also lonely and tragic . . . but also creepy and disgusting, as though his secret inner self was creepy and the attacks were just a symptom, his true self trying to literally leak out—though none of all this was visible to him in the bathroom's glass, whose reflection seemed oblivious to all that felt as he searched it. (99)

In the way that Cusk immediately cycles through a litany of emotions, Wallace subtly reinforces the thin line between person and machine. On the one hand, these human feelings might theoretically counteract Cusk's implied fear of becoming mechanical, but in their misfiring appearance and overwhelmingly chaotic deployment, they once again recall the way inhuman machines can suddenly—and, at least to the layperson, mysteriously—implode. The language also explicitly suggests that some other, creepy "inner self" is constantly on the verge of escaping through Cusk's external, ostensible humanity.

While Cusk himself is one of many examples of people slouching toward posthumanism, other agents must contend with less abstract instances of machines' looming dominance. In a section in which Claude Sylvanshine and Reynolds Jensen Jr discuss the potential for UNIVAC and IBM computers to begin replacing humans agents' duties, Sylvanshine repeatedly describes employees' physical appearance to Reynolds, insisting that the relevant details of potential employees like Julia Drutt Chaney are the fact that she is a "'[b]ig, big woman. Large'" (357), or that Gary Yeagle has "'Tolkien-like eyebrows'" and a "'very intense smile he feigns into trying to make it look like a wicked grin or grimace by drawing these incredible brows down'" (358). When he describes a "'[c]risp little woman, dry tight little face'" with a "'[s]weater over her shoulders like a cape,'" (363), Reynolds chides him for the seemingly irrelevant excess information: "'He's running to Region a lot already? You wait till now to include this and when you do it's an aside on the secretary's sweater?'" (363).

The way Sylvanshine weaves the important information through the fabric of seemingly mundane human details resonates with storytelling techniques that Wallace will employ elsewhere in the novel, which I will discuss shortly. Additionally, though, the compulsive listing of physical traits and personal characteristics highlights the very humanity that's at stake in the two men's staffing decision, something Reynolds does not seem to grasp at first. Indeed, his exasperated reaction to all of this comes in the form of a valid complaint and important question: "'Hey Claude, seriously, is there some process by which you decide I want to hear aesthetic appraisals? ... Don't strain now, but think about it and tell me the process by which you decide I have to wait through incidentals on dress and carriage before I hear material that's going to help me do my job here'" (360).

Sylvanshine's reasoning for reciting bodies and their material accessories seems obvious when the task is to decide how to delegate work between a new batch of agents and two singular machines. Sylvanshine, who shares his first name and last initial with Claude Shannon, the father of information theory and data's first great disciple, works to underscore the workers' humanness, something that, at the processing center on Self-Storage Parkway, can no longer be taken for granted. So when Sylvanshine asks, in the section's last words, "'What am I, a machine?'" (370), it is clear that while the question is intended as a lament about being overworked, it also doubles as a genuine inquiry, one that hangs unanswered at the top of a mostly blank page as well as throughout the unfinished novel.

All of this is true

Before trying to account for the larger significance of the human/machine dichotomy that recurs throughout the narrative, I want briefly to suggest that the topology of the novel, the Midwestern landscape as it is described at the outset of the story, symbolizes a relatedly tenuous distinction. The first section, written in the second-person imperative and ending up as a kind of lush plea to stay human and aware, begins with a description of a place "[p]ast the flannel plains and blacktop graphs and skylines of canted rust, and past the tobacco-brown river overhung with weeping trees and coins of sunlight through them on the water downriver, to the place beyond the windbreak, where untilled fields simmer shrilly in the A.M. heat" (3) before hitting an abrupt colon and breaking off into a list of "shattercane, lamb's-quarter, cutgrass, sawbrier, nutgrass, jimsonweed, wild mint, dandelion, foxtail, muscadine, spine-cabbage, goldenrod, creeping charlie, butter-print . . . vetch, butcher grass, invaginate volunteer beans, all heads gently nodding in a morning breeze like a mother's soft hand on your cheek" (3).

Already in the novel's first sentence, Wallace has synthesized the epochal shift that both precedes and runs concurrent with many of the characters' internal struggles to locate a human subjectivity. After the first few lines, the sudden introduction of what is essentially a bulleted list of natural fauna—that is, the organism as datum—suggests that our technologically driven, human-organized present has somehow already superimposed itself on an eternal environment, one with a "shapeless" horizon that has existed the same way forever.

The "very old land" (3) contrasts sharply with "the shush of the interstate off past the windbreak" (4), yet the fact that traffic sounds are audible from this vast, isolated, expanse of plains points toward an affirming coexistence of, on the one hand, land that seems to go on forever, and on the other, densely populated highways, full of either people or information. Finally, the firmly gentle imperative to "[l]ook around you," and the insistence that "[w]e are all of us brothers," (3) immediately recalls and foregrounds themes that constantly run through Wallace's fiction and nonfiction: the continual, dual, and sometimes related struggles of staying aware of your surroundings and of connecting to other human beings, both clearly the concerns of a humanist. In both its form and its content, the brief prose poem (originally published as "Peoria" in *TriQuarterly*) that opens *The Pale King* serves as a clear example of how the contradiction inherent in the idea of "sentimental posthumanism" might play out in the real world, and its quietly affirmative poetic consonance belies the anxiety—and in some cases, outright terror—of the rest of the novel, after the human players enter the picture.

One of the book's only other depictions of scenery or landscape serves as the reader's introduction to Toni Ware, a victim of multiple sexual trauma who eventually comes to work for the Service. §8 recounts her violent childhood travels with her mother, and it begins in an exhaustive manner that echoes §1's laundry list of natural data:

> Under the sign erected every May above the outer highway reading IT'S SPRING, THINK FARM SAFETY and through the north ingress with its own defaced name and signs addressed to soliciting and speed and universal glyph for children at play . . . and then hard left along the length of a speed bump into the dense copse . . . along the north park's anafractuous roads . . . skirting the corrugate trailer where it was said the man left his family and returned sometime later with a gun and killed them all as they watched *Dragnet* and the torn abandoned sixteen-wide half overgrown by the edge of the copse where boys and their girls made strange agnate forms on pallets. . . . (53)

The human tragedy embedded in all of this factual input might easily be glossed over due to the run-on quality of the passage, and the noticeable lack (even for Wallace) of punctuation. The tragically mundane murder that people at least associate with this location fades into the landscape, becoming a directional landmark rather than an event unto itself. On the one hand, this seems like an extreme example of §1's poetic conflation of uninhabited landscape and inevitable human intervention and destruction. The murder occurs in the trailer, but the trailer becomes a single point on a map of interconnected points of interest that spans highway entrances, bugs, and "saplings' branches" (53). But it also portends, early on in the story, a way to conceptualize the book as other than a novel proper (and other than an unfinished novel proper, whatever that may look like), as foreign as that may at first seem.

The passage that opens §8, almost by some stylistic sleight of hand, folds human drama and tragedy into the middle of one of many lists, not only surrounding the event with unrelated data but transfiguring it into mere data itself. This might prefigure the way Toni Ware will end up in the numerical comfort of the Service after a lifetime of violence and abuse. Additionally, however, the embedded quality of the murder is the first hint that *The Pale King*'s treatment of posthumanism goes further than merely exploring the similarities and sometimes-overlapping trajectories of humans and machines. It also attempts to tell very human stories in a form we might assume to be hostile to such stories. It shows how human lives and constructed subjectivities are merely data, too, and how, perhaps surprisingly, the two modes of existence are not mutually exclusive. Instead, one can both encourage and elicit the other.

In an editor's note, Michael Pietsch writes of the challenge of stitching together a work whose degree of incompleteness is ultimately "unknowable" (viii). Pietsch describes the "hundreds and hundreds of pages of [a] novel in progress, designated with the title 'The Pale King'" (vi) that Wallace's widow and agent discovered in his garage shortly after his death, as well as "a neat stack of manuscript, twelve chapters totaling nearly 250 pages" which Wallace had marked with the question, "'For [Little, Brown] advance?'" (vi). Despite its under-construction, piecemeal quality, Piestch notes that the manuscript's contents seemed to comprise "an astonishingly full novel . . . gorgeously alive and charged with observations" (vi).

Additionally, however, the editor found a noticeable lack throughout the scattered manuscript, one that I want to argue is intentional and important. According to Pietsch:

> Nowhere in all these pages was there an outline or other indication of what order David intended for these chapters. There were a few broad notes about the novel's trajectory, and draft chapters were often preceded or followed by David's directions to himself about where a character came from . . . But there was no list of scenes, no designated opening or closing point, nothing that could be called a set of directions or instructions for *The Pale King*. As I read and reread this mass of material, it nevertheless became clear that David had written deep into the novel, creating a vividly complex place. . . . (vi–vii)

For a writer as painstakingly precise as Wallace, a "perfectionist of the highest order" (ix), according to Pietsch, it seems not just unlikely but impossible that this complete absence of generic formal trappings of a novel is due to oversight or accident, especially when what Bonnie Nadell and Karen Green found of the manuscript was so carefully preserved and presented. Instead, the conspicuously absent set of "directions or instructions," of starting points or narrative landmarks, may be a larger-scale example of the data-narrative melding I argued for earlier in the passage from §8.

Rather than a novel, it may be helpful to think of *The Pale King* as resembling something closer to an almanac, or a narrative compendium. If nothing else, I believe this would help account for some of the book's more opaque sections (such as §25, wherein nearly everyone "turns a page," but nothing else happens) not as mere illustrations of the pervasive boredom that blankets the IRS, but as matters of narrative record, or examples of novelistic datum. In the same way many readers and critics were able to see *Infinite Jest* itself as emulating many qualities of the fatally enthralling Entertainment that catalyzed that novel's plot, we might see *The Pale King*, with its section headings instead of chapter titles, its "tornadic feel" that Wallace spoke of, and its "central story" that "does not have a clear ending" (viii) as an enactment of the increasingly sketchy binaries of information and organisms, humans and machines, that I have argued the novel is interested in thematically. I am not insisting, as the narrator David Wallace does, that the book itself be officially classified as something other than novel, but I am suggesting that we should try to account for his insistence on *The Pale King* as "more like a memoir than any kind of made-up story" (67), and as something other than the "clever metafictional titty-pincher" (69) he goes out of his away to disavow.

There is a wonderful indeterminacy to the way this narrator classifies the book that, despite its apparent uncertainty, I believe is once again deliberate. If the book is "more like a memoir than any kind of made-up story"—that is, it resembles a memoir more than a novel, but is not quite either one—then here the narrator-cum-"author" lends credence to the idea of the book as a kind of fictionalized record of truth, a "true" account of biographical information and personal trajectories of people that never existed. The comically insistent claims that "All of this is true. This book is really true" (67), as well as the absurdly complex explanation of why certain legal limitations force *The Pale King* to be marked and marketed as a novel speak to a real belief that the book might exist in some liminal space between fact and fiction, record and novel.

Of course, this is not to say that anything in the novel is true. As obvious examples, we know that David Foster Wallace never worked as an IRS agent, and that the claim that "the only US citizens . . . whose Social Security numbers start with the numeral 9 are . . . employees of the [IRS]" (66) is patently false. Instead, the ostensible confusion enacts, on a book-wide scale, a condition that many of its characters confront throughout their own personal narratives. In crafting a tornadic document that mirrors a tax return form in its labyrinthine layout and disjointed, swappable collection of narratives (not to mention a sizable element of complete structural chance, which Michael Pietsch admirably confronted when he ordered these sections), Wallace pushes the novel firmly into data-driven territory, an area usually reserved for cold facts and humanless input. This compression, however, is one borne of a hopeful, humanist impulse. *The Pale King* is full of characters who fear and struggle with information's exponentially unfolding presence. Its form, though, illustrates a way lived experience can become objective data, and vice versa. *The Pale King* sustains this unlikely combination for its 538 pages, overriding its characters' anxieties to suggest that cohabitational harmony between consciousness and information, human and machine, is both possible and productive.

Notes

1   Here I intend to convey a selective snippet of Donna Haraway's definition of *cyborg*: "a hybrid of machine and organism" (2269).

2   Many of the sections examined in this essay end on question marks, which helps cultivate an aura of uncertainty. I would argue that this uncertainty, like nearly everything else Wallace does, is calculated and deliberate. It exists not to denote a failure to find answers, but as an acknowledgment of the primary quality of these characters' existence.

3   He's also a clear allusion to a famous twentieth-century literary office drone, *The Man in the Gray Flannel Suit*.

10

The Politics of Boredom and the Boredom of Politics in *The Pale King*

Ralph Clare

As the reviews poured in for David Foster Wallace's posthumous and unfinished *The Pale King*, it became evident that most reviewers took an almost perverse glee in declaring the book was "about" boredom. Michiko Kakutani's review of the novel for the *New York Times*, for instance, claims, "[n]ot surprisingly, a novel about boredom is, more than occasionally, boring" and wonders if Wallace, at times, "wanted to test the reader's tolerance for tedium." In a long piece for *The London Review of Books* praising Wallace and his work, even Jenny Turner admits, "much of *The Pale King* I found completely deadly." Perhaps Sam Anderson, writing for the *New York Times Magazine,* puts it most succinctly: "Wallace seems to have posed, to himself and to his readership, a sadomasochistic challenge: a novel devoted to the world's least-appealing-possible subject." These responses are fairly representative of many of the major reviews of *The Pale King* that were quite positive in their assessment of the novel but continued to muse upon what ways, to borrow the words of the purported narrator David Wallace, the novel says "something about dullness, information, and irrelevant complexity. About negotiating boredom as one would a terrain, its levels and forests and endless wastes" (85).

Numerous questions follow from this statement, such as: what does it actually mean to write about boredom? What does Wallace mean by "boredom"? How does Wallace's take on boredom fit into a larger literary and cultural context? In what ways does boredom function within the work-in-progress that is *The Pale King*, and how does it resonate in Wallace's *oeuvre* as a whole? It might be fair to admit from the outset that there are myriad ways to understand boredom and that Wallace's work, and *The Pale King* in particular, puts several of these into play. Ultimately, Wallace's treatment of boredom resonates with some of his earlier themes concerning depression and anxiety, which are most fully developed in *Infinite Jest*, and both extends and challenges them in what was, is, and must remain uncharted territory. Wallace is primarily interested in exploring the roots of "boredom" as a specific historical formation of late capitalist American life. What Wallace does in *The Pale King* is conduct a thorough analysis of how boredom has functioned, and continues to function, socially, culturally, and politically in the age of neoliberal capitalism, which dawned in the mid-1970s and is currently in crisis. In doing so, Wallace engages in a kind of "aesthetics of boredom" by examining boredom in both the novel's form and content, and offering a possible solution to the apparent malaise of post-industrial life.

The construction of boredom

It may seem like a simple task to define boredom, but it is actually more complicated than one might imagine. Studies of "boredom" itself, for instance, are a rather recent phenomenon in literary studies. Earlier understandings of what we, today, might call boredom arose out of analyses of "ennui," "melancholy," or a similarly distinguished sounding concept. The most recent theorizations of boredom, however, are unique in their attention to the history of boredom, as well as to the rhetoric or discourse of boredom itself. That boredom is given numerous forms and representations in *The Pale King* only reinforces the difficulty of defining boredom once and for all, but it does imply the distinction of a typology of postmodern boredoms.

Still, a history of boredom exists. A radically condensed version[1] would mention that there is a notion of boredom in Greek thought, but that its true roots can be found in the experiences of the first Christian hermits, the Desert Fathers, who lived alone in caves and prayed rigorously all day. Perhaps due to their extreme isolation, they would sometimes experience a despair that they referred to as *acedia*, "the noontide demon," which prevented them from fulfilling their spiritual duties. By the Renaissance, *acedia* had given way to the secular concept of "melancholy" and the theory of the Four Humors, according to which the melancholic suffers from an excess of "black bile." In the eighteenth century, the rise of Romanticism gave birth to the modern concepts of "spleen" and "ennui," or a general exhaustion with life itself, which is primarily a psychological and social phenomenon. These notions of boredom were expanded upon by writers and poets, such as Baudelaire, Kierkegaard, and Flaubert until eventually the existential abyss was fully opened up in the twentieth century. On this point, theorists concur that boredom has explicit ties with modernity and marks a radical change in how subjects experience the world and boredom itself.

These theorists, moreover, are keen to underscore the specificity, linguistically and historically, of boredom's many forms. In *Melancholy and Society*, Wolf Lepenies remarks that "[m]elancholy and boredom belong together, even etymologically; 'ennui' is not the only term to cover both" (87), while Patricia Meyers Spacks claims, in *Boredom: The Literary History of a Sate of Mind*, that "[b]oredom was not (*is* not) the same as ennui, [which is] more closely related to acedia. Ennui implies a judgment of the universe; boredom, a response to the immediate" (12). No matter how each definition is drawn, its parameters are always somewhat ambiguous. In *A Philosophy of Boredom*, Lars Svendsen writes that not even "a clear distinction can be made between psychological and social aspects when dealing with a phenomenon such as boredom" (12). Thus, as Barbara Dalle Pezze and Carlo Salzani write in their introduction to *Essays on Boredom and Modernity*, "[w]hat these and other authors want to emphasize is that boredom is not an inherent quality of the human condition, but rather it *has a history*, which began around the eighteenth century and embraced the whole Western world, and which presents an evolution from the eighteenth to the twenty-first century" (12). In short, they continue, "modern boredom is certainly more 'democratic' [than its earlier forms]" and is "a mass phenomenon" (8). In turn, it has become, Spacks writes, "a remarkably useful, remarkably inclusive explanatory notion" (6). Nevertheless, no matter how boredom is defined, notes Svendsen, it is usually judged "to be an evil" (18). Boredom is, quite simply, a modern problem, and this is something *The Pale King* attempts to investigate in all of its facets.

Despite the trouble with defining boredom as a concept, it is possible to differentiate between types of boredom by establishing a range including what might be called "common boredoms" (such as waiting for a train or bus); more "complex" forms, such as the boredom of modern life (the dead-end career or endless commodity consumption); existential ennui (contemplating the meaninglessness of existence); and lastly, perhaps even some forms of depression. Indeed, one could add any number of categories to this list, but the key for contemporary theorists of boredom, and for reading boredom in *The Pale King*, is to understand this list as composing a continuum, and not a hierarchy, of boredoms. In short, this means being careful not to privilege one form over another, as well as to recognize the blurred boundaries between these so-called forms.

Reinhard Kuhn's *The Demon of Noontide: Ennui in Western Literature*, which offers a wonderful literary history of "ennui," is exemplary of an earlier literary analysis of boredom that subsumes boredom under a grander term, in this case "ennui." Although Kuhn parses "a great many forms of boredom," he selects "ennui" as his totalizing term in order "to distinguish it from the more general concept" (5). According to Kuhn, ennui is distinct from the common boredoms mentioned above, which Kuhn finds unworthy of study. Yet for all this, even Kuhn admits that such common boredoms "are often confused with ennui because they can never be completely divorced from it" (9). Thus while Kuhn's privileging of "ennui" passes over these more "common" forms of boredom, even he must admit that the delineation between the "grander" and more "common" boredoms is not a clear one.

Unlike Kuhn's work, *The Pale King* refuses to privilege one type of boredom over others and, in fact, embraces the common forms of boredom, as when David Wallace wonders whether "dullness is associated with psychic pain because something that's dull or opaque fails to provide enough stimulation to distract people from some other, deeper type of pain that is always there, if only in an ambient low-level way, and which most of us spend nearly all our time and energy trying to distract ourselves from feeling" (85). The likening of existential angst and death to an "ambient low-level" noise is akin to Don DeLillo's description of death in *White Noise* as the "dull and unlocatable roar, as of some form of swarming life just outside the range of human apprehension" (36). Much as DeLillo's novel examines notions of death from a postmodern perspective, *The Pale King* treats boredom as a peculiar contemporary phenomenon and not as a timeless and universal experience. As David Wallace comments, "I can't think anyone believes that today's so-called 'information society' is just about information. Everyone knows it's about something else, way down" (85).

As such, *The Pale King* documents a variety of boredoms—from the existential life-crisis to those of the daily grind and to those resulting from stultifying political and economic systems—and suggests the links between them. The anonymous narrator who recounts his dream in §23 brings all three of these "boredoms" together in detailing his nightmarish vision of an office in which he sees "rows of foreshortened faces" bent over their desks hard at work, while "[a]t the edges were office workers bustling at the endless small tasks involved in mailing, filing, sorting, their faces blankly avid" (253). As he reflects upon this dream, which "was my psyche teaching me about boredom," the narrator explains how he was "often bored as a child, but boredom is not what I knew it as—what I knew was that I *worried* a lot" (253). He goes on to describe how on "wet distended Sunday afternoons" he often "felt the sort of soaring, ceilingless tedium that transcends tedium and becomes worry. I do not recall the things I worried about, but I remember the feeling, and it was an anxiety whose lack of a proper object is what made it horrible, free-floating" (252–3). Connecting this to his primary educational experience, the "petrified bureaucracy of the Columbus School System," he concludes he and the other students were "locked tight inside themselves and an institutional tedium they couldn't name but had already lost their hearts to" (255).

In this short chapter, Wallace gives us a representation of at least three distinct types of boredom. Yet instead of presenting each in an isolated fashion or privileging one kind of boredom over another, he demonstrates how they inform one another. First, there is the daily boredom of the child, whether he is at school or sitting around the house on a lazy Sunday, who has nothing to do or would rather be elsewhere. This is the kind of boredom Kuhn found beneath studying. For Wallace, however, it is a starting point for analyzing boredom. Wallace immediately links this simple boredom of foot tapping and clock watching to a state of anxiety, which quickly balloons into a second type of boredom, that of full existential terror, the "horrible, free floating" kind, and one worthy of even Kuhn's study. Essentially, the untreated simple boredom grows to become a revelation of the reality of existential Time. Lastly, Wallace is careful to use the novel's setting—here the spatial representation of boredom in the rows and rows of work and school desks that bookend the chapter, respectively—to introduce a third kind of boredom produced by the rote, regimented, systematized postmodern world. Even the so-called simplest subjective psychological boredom, then, is directly connected to the other forms and ultimately to the world outside the subject's own psychological suffering.

In §33, Lane Dean Jr's despair while at work expands on this notion of a particular kind of postmodern boredom:

> He felt in a position to say he knew now that hell had nothing to do with fires or frozen troops. Lock a fellow in a windowless room to perform rote tasks just tricky enough to make him have to think, but still rote, tasks involving numbers that connected to nothing he'd ever see or care about, a stack of tasks that never went down, and nail a clock to the wall where he can see it, and just leave the man there to his mind's own devices. (379)

That Lane Dean's conception of hell is not of a carefully ordered, Dantean hierarchy of suffering but includes a lone cubicle, subject to empty time and filled with infinite and useless tasks, offers a fitting spatial representation of a post-industrial hell.[2] His work "connected to nothing he'd ever see or care about" signals the larger structural forces that keep Lane Dean at his desk. Moreover, whatever order or meaning there is to this system remains ultimately unknowable from Lane Dean's point of view, and it is certainly not an order insured by a God but by a bureaucratic system. Clearly,

Wallace's exploration of boredom is more nuanced, in its fashion, than is Kuhn's.

In *The Pale King*, Wallace's notion of boredom is much more in line with contemporary theorists' views in showing a careful consideration of the concept's linguistic and historical realities. It is in the midst of the despair mentioned above that Lane Dean is visited by Garrity, one of the two office ghosts and a former mid-twentieth-century line inspector at a mirror factory before his suicide. Their interaction is key to understanding the way Wallace is exploring boredom as a historical construction specific to our times. After Lane Dean enters into a near trance-like state, which is earlier called "a certain threshold of concentrated boredom" (314), Garrity's ghost perches on his desk and delivers a lengthy monologue on boredom, during which he informs Lane Dean that the "word [boredom] appears suddenly in 1766. No known etymology. The Earl of March uses it in a letter describing a French peer of the realm" (383) and "*Bore*. As if from Athena's forehead. Noun and verb, participle as adjective, whole nine yards. Origin unknown, really. We do not know" (384). In the middle of this century-spanning etymological and rhetorical history lesson, which includes references to Pascal, Kierkegaard, and Fritz Lang's *Metropolis*, Garrity concludes:

> Philologists say it was a neologism—and just about the time of industry's rise, too, yes? of the mass man, the automated turbine and drill bit and bore, yes? Hollowed out? . . . Look for instance at L.P. Smith's *English Language*. . . . Posits certain neologisms as *arising from their own cultural necessity*—his words, I believe. Yes, . . . the word invents itself. . . . Smith puts it as that when anything assumes sufficient relevance it finds its name. The name springs up under cultural pressure. Really quite interesting when you consider it. . . . (384–5)

Ghost or not, Garrity gives the reader of *The Pale King* a true material and historical grounding of the word bore, which, in turn, suggests the degree to which language creates or constructs reality.

In order to compose his lecture on boredom, Garrity's ghost may have picked up (as Wallace almost certainly did) Spacks's text on boredom, referred to above. At times Garrity's lesson reads like a summary of Spacks's introduction (though Garrity refers to Smith), which provides a kind of archaeology of the word. Garrity's stress on the linguistic creation of boredom, for example, clearly echoes Spacks's request that her readers "conceive boredom as an invention, an idea that became both useful and necessary only at a relatively recent historical moment" and to wonder "[w]hat social and psychological conditions would require the construction of boredom as a concept?" (9). So too does Elizabeth Goodstein, in *Experience without Qualities*, argue that the construction of boredom marks "less a new feeling than a new way of feeling" and thus "[a]s a discursively articulated phenomenon, . . . boredom is at once objective and subjective, emotion and intellectualization—not just a response to the modern world but also an historically constituted strategy for coping with its discontents" (3). Wallace, in *The Pale King*, is exploring the concept of boredom in a similar way to these thinkers: as a specific historical construction and discourse that can be evidenced both objectively and subjectively, sociologically as well as psychologically.

Spacks also offers several conditions, what Garrity calls "cultural pressure," that necessitated the invention of boredom at the advent of modernity. These include "the development of leisure as differentiated psychic space [due to capitalism]; the decline of Christianity; the intensification of concern with individual rights; and the increasing interest in inner experience" (24). And while "[n]one of these developments can be taken as a definitive cause for *boredom* the word or boredom the experience, nor do all together suffice as total explanation" (24), they do establish some grounding, as does *The Pale King* in its representation of post-industrial life, to what otherwise may seem a timeless and universal experience.

It is important to emphasize that Wallace wants to look at boredom as a particular type of discourse in *The Pale King* because this point can easily be passed over by merely translating the thematic of boredom into the thematic of existential angst or depression. Like Kuhn, James Lasdun moves in this direction in his review of the novel for *The Guardian* wherein he claims that "[a]t a certain point it becomes impossible to resist the thought that under all the high talk about the place of boredom in modern life, what Wallace was really writing about was depression." Yet this is precisely what the reader of *The Pale King* needs to resist, the facile equation that boredom=depression. The novel, and all of Wallace's work, is far too complex to reduce in this fashion. Moreover, it takes away from the novel's pointed examination of how boredom functions and is understood in late capitalist American life.

The temptation to equate boredom with depression lingers, however, and is evidence of the continuing influence of *Infinite Jest* on Wallace's work. Although *Infinite Jest* is hardly a boring novel and its central action surrounds several groups' pursuit of "The Entertainment," it is, like *The Pale King*, a novel about boredom. Boredom within the pages of *Infinite Jest*, however, takes on an existential quality and is often linked to depression, clinical and otherwise. Indeed, *Infinite Jest* provides the fullest treatment of Wallace's themes of existential angst, depression, and addiction. Numerous characters in the novel suffer a kind of existential dread—sometimes referred to as "The Howling Fantods"—that is often related to their own sense of loss, depression, and neuroses. In *Understanding David Foster Wallace*, Marshal Boswell discusses the existential concerns raised in the novel and conducts a compelling reading of the "existentialist"[3] philosophy found in Kierkegaard's *Either/Or* as it relates to the "aesthetes" (Kierkagaard's term for hedonists inadequately protected from depression by their sophistication and irony) in *Infinite Jest* who attempt to escape the self through hip irony (Boswell 137–41, 143–5). As Boswell argues, after quoting Hal's reference to Kierkegaard and Camus at the start of the novel, "Hal, like all of Wallace's despairing drug addicts, bears the stamp of Kierkegaardian aesthetic despair" (139).

This despair even makes a visual appearance in the novel, most dramatically in Geoffrey Day's childhood memory of practicing violin one day when he experienced "a large dark billowing shape [that] came billowing out of some corner of my mind" (649). He tells Kate Gompert, "it was total horror. It was horror everywhere, distilled and given form. It rose in me, out of me" (649). Worst of all is that the horror was "[s]hapeless. Shapelessness was one of the horrible things about it. I say and mean only *shape, dark,* and either *billowing* or *flapping*. . . . The shape of horror" (649). This free-floating angst (similar to the "free-floating" anxiety suffered by the narrator of §23 in *The Pale King*), depression, or existential dread made tangible here affects nearly every character in the novel, in one way or another.

But while *The Pale King* still gives credence to the existential horror of existence, which may or may not be linked to clinical depression,[4] the novel is more interested in setting this kind of boredom in a revealing context. In one of the novel's key chapters, in which several IRS employees find themselves stuck in an elevator, Stuart Nichols puts the existential terror of Day and *Infinite Jest*'s characters into perspective during his discussion of America, civic responsibility, and freedom.[5] At one point, Nichols goes on an existential tirade for nearly a full page (and with only one interruption) about "the individual US citizen's deep fear, the same basic fear that you and I have and that everybody has except nobody ever talks about it except existentialists in convoluted French prose. Or Pascal" (143). As Nichols layers detail upon detail about "our insignificance and mortality" and reminds us "that we are tiny and at the mercy of large forces and that time is always passing, . . . that everything we see around us all the time is decaying and passing, it's all passing away, and so are we, so am I" (143), his monologue becomes a light parody of existential thought. By rant's end, he is predicting that "if I'm cremated the trees that are nourished by my windblown ash will die or get cut down and decay, and my urn will decay, and before maybe three or four generations it will be like I never existed" (143). If Nichols's over-the-top existential angst is not hilarious enough in its flurry of linguistic exaggeration and jab of self-indulgent solipsism, the punch line from one of his fellow trapped elevator interlocutors adds the final blow: "This is supposed to be news to us. News flash: We're going to die" (144). Ironically, Nichols's own desire to get to the bottom of "your own responsibility to civics" (141) is somewhat undercut by this extreme (and to some degree self-aware) pursuit of (un)happiness and privatized "self-interest" in his own death. The point here is that anyone could come to the same nihilistic conclusion as Nichols, thus not arriving at a sense of a civic duty that outweighs the individual citizen's selfish needs and demands a careful consideration of what personal "freedom" entails.

An even more damning comment on this older existential discourse occurs in the middle of Chris Fogle's story of personal conversion from "wastoid" to IRS devotee and wiggler. Fogle describes taking, ironically enough, a "Literature of Alienation" course during his "nihilistic" years at UIC. Fogle's failure to get through Camus' *The Fall* is partly ironic in and of itself, but his ability "to totally bullshit my way through the Literature of Alienation midterm" (186–7) suggests that there is something outdated or clichéd about "alienation" and existential thought in the postmodern era. Whether or not the "B" Fogle received on the exam is really indicative of "a meaningless bullshit response to meaningless bullshit" (187), it does reveal the limitations of any literature of alienation. Instead of finding something of value in existentialist literature (for which, considering his nihilistic outlook on life at the time, he would appear primed), the younger Fogle finds it a waste of time and can easily mimic its familiar discourse.

Thus, the more personal existential angst of *Infinite Jest* is subtly critiqued, recontextualized, and broadened in *The Pale King*. Anxiety and angst are not just privileged, possibly hackneyed, existential ponderings or even real forms of depression, but are entangled with the notion of boredom, which is a concept that Wallace allows to open "outward" onto the world, as it were, instead of shrinking "inward" to the individual. To be more precise, *The Pale King* brings a historically informed understanding of boredom, which lay nascent in *Infinite Jest*, and maps it on to the drastic political and cultural developments in America during the neoliberal era.

Boredom and neoliberalism

The Pale King also establishes a different relationship with history than does *Infinite Jest*, in which the history retold relates mostly to its own fantastical world. While *The Pale King* remains closely tied to actual twentieth-century American history,[6] *Infinite Jest*, for example, is very much a millennial novel of the '90s. Writing during the Clintonian Golden Age and amidst the apparent fruition of neoliberal economics—that is, the "globalization" that many were trumpeting (the world was now run by "the Electronic Herd" [Friedman, 1999] and we had reached "the end of History" [Fukuyama, 1992])—Wallace cast his neoliberal dystopia in the near future. Here, Wallace warns, is the result of this kind of consumer capitalist utopia: sadness, waste, and addiction, emptiness in a world full of things. *The Pale King*, in contrast, was written *during* the exhaustion of the unfulfilled neoliberal promise (the very time period in which the action of *Infinite Jest* mainly occurs) yet returns to the era's historical roots in the 1970s and its rise in the 1980s to explore the subtle shifts in American culture that helped form the world of *Infinite Jest*.

Much of the change in America over these decades is a result of the rise of neoliberalism.[7] As David Harvey defines it in *A Brief History of Neoliberalism*, neoliberalism is "a theory of political economic practices that proposes that human well-being can best be advanced by liberating individual entrepreneurial freedoms and skills within an institutional framework characterized by strong private property rights, free markets, and free trade" (2). The neoliberal changes to the American economy (and the world's) began in the 1970s in response to the energy crisis triggered by the Arab Oil Embargo of 1973 and an overall stagnation of the post-World War II economic model. Neoliberalism's response to this economic stalling-out was to recommend the "liberalization" of capital itself, chiefly through deregulation (of industries and financial markets), privatization (of former publicly held industries), tax breaks and concessions (especially to large corporations), a severe disciplining of labor (union busting), and a call for "smaller" government (to ease regulation, though a strong military and defense spending is a must). Added to this was a commitment to cutting social spending, thereby dismantling LBJ's "Great Society." Though some of these policies were initially enacted under the Carter administration, it would be Ronald Reagan's commitment to these policies, and more importantly to the principles on which they are founded, that would sweep him into office in 1980 and radically transform America's understanding of the role of government in economic development and the lives of its citizens. Since then, Harvey writes, neoliberalism has "become hegemonic as a mode of discourse" and a part of "the common-sense way many of us interpret, live in, and understand the world" (3).

Wallace weaves the history of neoliberal economics into *The Pale King*'s narrative by tying its most spectacular element—the Presidency of Ronald

Reagan—to its least noticed—the changes in the tax code that completed Reagan's Tax Revolt. In doing so, Wallace is able to show the intricate relationship between culture, politics, and economics that developed in the neoliberal era. Wallace's ideas about boredom, too, will be added to the mix. In this sense, the novel is, as Tom McCarthy puts it in his astute review for *The New York Times Sunday Book Review,* "a grand parable of postindustrial culture or 'late capitalism.'"

A crucial window into the decade during which neoliberal ideology begins to take root comes in §22, in which "irrelevant" Chris Fogle's conversion-from-nihilism narrative gives us a fascinating reconstruction of the 1970s, in part from the perspective of his younger self, a nonvoting, drug-taking, and adrift teenage college student. Fogle neatly sums up the decade with a catalogue of pop cultural, political, and social fragments. Among his cataloguing, he remembers "[r]italin versus Ritadex, Cylert and Obetrol, Laverne and Shirley, Carnation Instant Breakfast, John Travolta, disco fever, and children's tee shirts with 'Fonz' on them. And 'Keep on Truckin'' shirts" (158), as well as "a lot of wood-pattern designs on things that were not wood" (164), "something about Carter's brother turning out to be a wastoid" (164), and the fact that "Edward Muskie cried in public on the campaign trail" (166). Wallace is careful here not only to underscore the one-time drugged-out Fogle's memories that "almost feel like some other person's memories" but also to reproduce the very signs, commodities, and apathetic feeling that the decade embodies for Fogle. This is clearly a decade of anxiety and boredom (witnessed by the new drugs, which are meant to "focus" the distracted user), entertainment (TV shows, movies, and commercials), trends (disco), commodification of "culture" (shirts of *Happy Days* [itself a '50s nostalgia show] and of the '60s via underground comics [Robert Crumb]), signs and simulacra (fake wood paneling), and "spectacular" media events masking as political intrigue (Carter and Muskie).[8]

At this point one might accuse Wallace of reducing history to a superficial set of signs, although this is certainly not the case. There is, of course, the fact that Fogle's nickname is "irrelevant," hinting at his own piling on of (possibly) useless details and information. Yet Wallace's placement of concrete facts throughout Fogle's hazy recollection subtly recreates the economic and political realities underlying the times, especially when Fogle mentions "the energy crisis and recession and stagflation" (162), New York's 1976 fiscal crisis (162), the decade's "high inflation [and] high deficits" (194), and that "pretty much every red-blooded American in [the] late-Vietnam and Watergate era felt desolate and disillusioned and unmotivated and directionless and lost" (213). The hard political and economic reality of the times, combined with the cul-de-sac cultural attitude, would help lay the foundation for the neoliberal revolution in economic and political thought that Reagan would lead.

The resonance with the theme of boredom is made abundantly clear when Fogle remembers how "Jimmy Carter was ridiculed for calling [the state America was in a] 'malaise' and telling the nation to snap out of it" (223). This infamous "malaise" (a word Carter never actually used in the speech), or what Fogle calls nihilism, is another way of conceiving of boredom, of which Fogle's experience and the entire decade of the 1970s appear exemplary. It is Garrity's ghost who, amid his comparative etymological reflection on the word boredom, announces that "[t]he French of course had *malaise*" (383). Boredom is thus a symptom, in *The Pale King*, of an entire generation's attitude toward the world.

It is precisely this boredom as cultural "malaise" that leaves people desperate for stimulation in the form of ever-newer products and images, and makes them more susceptible to going along with the cash flow, so to speak. In the stalled elevator scene, Glendenning's surmise that in response to "some sort of disaster—depression [or] hyperinflation" Americans will "either wake up and retake our freedom or we'll fall apart utterly" (131) is troubling because there was no such awakening in response to the social and fiscal crises of the 1970s, during which depression and hyperinflation were rampant. Instead, as is often the case, writes Naomi Klein in *The Shock Doctrine*, "if an economic crisis hits and is severe enough . . . leaders are liberated to do whatever is necessary (or said to be necessary) in the name of responding" (175). Thus, an economic "shock" or crisis gives leaders *carte blanche* in terms of enacting solutions.

Not surprisingly, it is Ronald Reagan's election that, for Wallace, typifies the result of such apathy. After summing up their (mostly Nichols and Glendenning's) elevator discussion about freedom, individuality, and responsibility, Nichols foresees how Reagan will triumph:

> we'll have for a president a symbolic Rebel against his own power whose election was underwritten by inhuman soulless profit-machines whose takeover of American civic and spiritual life will convince Americans that rebellion against the soulless inhumanity of corporate life will consist in buying products from corporations that do the best job of representing corporate life as empty and soulless. We'll have a tyranny of conformist nonconformity presided over by a symbolic outsider whose very *election* depended on our deep conviction that his persona is utter bullshit. A rule of image, which because it's so empty makes everyone terrified. . . . (149)

In the end, it is the "rule of the image" that matters. And this battle for political power, as Nichols points out, will "be played out in the world of images" (146). So it was that the character of "President Reagan," performed so well by former actor Ronald Reagan, projected a seemingly unifying, but ultimately obscuring, image over a fractured, post-industrial America— and an image that nonetheless fed off the nihilistic boredom and "rebellion" of the burnt-out '70s. For, as Harvey makes clear in *The Condition of Postmodernity*,

> [t]he mediatization of politics has now become all pervasive. This becomes, in effect, the fleeting, superficial, and illusory means whereby an individualistic society of transients sets forth its nostalgia for common values. The production and marketing of such images of permanence and power require considerable sophistication, because the continuity and stability of the image have to be retained while stressing the adaptability, flexibility, and dynamism of whoever or whatever is being imaged. (288)

In the wake of the American people's failure to take back their freedoms, the "rebel" image of Reagan conveniently allows them cede even more of these freedoms while indulging in a cultural nihilism packaged and sold as rebellion.

By centering *The Pale King*'s critique of neoliberal institutions on the new IRS, Wallace is able to bring together economic, political, cultural, and social explanations as to why the neoliberal revolution came to be. For instance, Reagan "the rebel" gained national political prominence by courting the New Money of the post-industrial economy that was basking in the Sun Belt, and gained much of his initial popularity in his run for governor of California by leading a voter "tax revolt" (Kleinknecht 62–70). So it should come as no surprise that it is the tax code, as explored by the novel, which becomes representative of the quiet and unnoticed neoliberal revolution.

In the novel, the politically driven tax code restructuring under Reagan comes as a result of the fictitious "Spackman Memo or Initiative" that Kenneth Hindle mentions in his interview. The Spackman Memo "appeared to describe a politically more appealing way to ameliorate the rock-and-hard-place of unexpectedly low tax revenues, high defense outlays, and an uncuttable base floor in social spending" (109). David Wallace outlines the result of these changes within the halls of the IRS itself: "the struggle here was between traditional . . . officials who saw tax and its administration as an arena of social justice and civic virtue, on the one hand, and those more progressive, 'pragmatic' policymakers who prized the market model, efficiency, and a maximum return on the investment of the Service's annual budget" (82–3). To put it in blunt terms, as Hindle does, "[a]t root, the Spackman report was intensely anti-bureaucratic. Its model was more classically free-market. . . . This, after all, is an era of business deregulation" (113). Here, the Spackman initiative reads like Reagan's neoliberal creed— deregulate industries, cut social spending, and liberalize capital for the creation of new markets and the expansion of old ones.

In using the IRS as representative of neoliberalism in general, *The Pale King* is able to connect neoliberalism back to boredom in an illuminating way. This becomes evident when David Wallace remarks that "[t]he real reason why US citizens were/are not aware of these conflicts, changes, and stakes is that the whole subject of tax policy and administration is dull. Massively, spectacularly dull" (83). Thus it is that boredom and apathy become a kind of political tool, or a sure bet to manufacture consent, since "if sensitive issues of governance can be made sufficiently dull and arcane, there will be no need for officials to hide or dissemble, because no one not directly involved will pay enough attention to cause trouble" (84). It would seem, then, that choosing not to pay attention to such "boring" things as political and economic issues does not mean one will lead a life "free" of constraint, but that one will pay off this debt with the freedoms that were granted long ago.

Paying attention: The cost of happiness

While boredom in *Infinite Jest* leads almost exclusively to existential terror, addiction, and solipsism, the expanded notion of boredom in *The Pale King* holds out the possibility that boredom can lead to something positive, perhaps even constructive, even if it has been one of the underlying conditions for the neoliberal revolution. For "[b]oredom," Peter Toohey reminds us in *Boredom: A Lively History*, "has its uses" (33).

The hope that boredom can be converted into something productive is entangled with the novel's preoccupation with concentration. As Wallace writes in one of his notes regarding Drinion, "[i]t turns out that bliss—a second-by-second joy + gratitude at the gift of being alive, conscious—lies on the other side of crushing, crushing boredom" (546). "Paying attention" and the ability to concentrate are held up as virtues in an entropic world typified by the endless flow of data and information. Wallace only leaves hints as to how his theory of attentiveness might have looked and how it could "solve" the problem of boredom, but suffice it to say that this theory is modeled after his own literary aesthetic, which demands an attentive reader. Furthering this aesthetic, *The Pale King* engages in an "aesthetics of boredom" that examines the concept of boredom in both its form and content.

It is for this reason that *The Pale King* is full of characters that have an extraordinary ability to concentrate, no matter how they struggle with it, and who demonstrate an awareness of the qualities of this ability. Lane Dean battles daily at his Tingle with nightmarish visions of a bureaucratic hell (376–85); the unfortunate sweat-prone David Cusk learns early in his life about "the terrible power of attention and what you pay attention to" (91); Fogle puts his transformation down to "something to do with paying attention and the ability to choose what I paid attention to" (187); Drinion is happy because of his "ability to pay attention" (546); and upon arriving at the "Immersives Room" in the Midwest REC and seeing the wigglers hard at work, David Wallace admits that, as a child, "I . . . felt ashamed about how easily I got bored when trying to concentrate" (292). That many of these characters are being brought together by either Glendenning or Lehrl (it makes no difference, in this case) underscores that their ability to concentrate, which the novel connects to extrasensory perception, is a sort of latent "power."

To be able to reach a state of total concentration means gaining the possibility of transcending boredom. It is unclear what this entails exactly, but Wallace perhaps had something mystical in mind. For instance, the contortionist's story in chapter 36 could be a warning tale of narcissism and solipsism, as this "one particular boy's goal was to be able to press his lips to every square inch of his own body" (394), until we consider that the boy's ability to concentrate and stay disciplined is juxtaposed with stories of supposed religious miracles, as well as the acts of saints and holy men (396–7, 399, 401–2). Wallace implies some sort of connection between the ability to concentrate and the possibility of transcendence here, as he also does in entertaining the possibility that Fogle has hit upon a "string of numbers that, when held in serial in his head, allows him to maintain interest and concentration at will" (541). Wallace goes so far as to make this idea of transcendence literal in the scene in which Drinion is so engrossed by Meredith's story of her courtship by her husband that he begins to levitate, though he is "unaware of the levitating thing by definition, since it is only when his attention is completely on something else that the levitation happens" (485).

That it is during the act of storytelling that Drinion's literal transcendence occurs is highly suggestive of the power of narrative to counteract boredom and thus transforms the Meredith-Drinion conversation into an allegory of the relationship between author and reader in *The Pale King*. Drinion, in this sense, is the perfect reader since his ability to transcend boredom is directly related to his listening skills, which include paying close attention to a narrative and sorting through details to establish meaning. In response to Meredith's self-conscious question as to whether her story is boring him, Drinion replies, "'[b]oring isn't a very good term. Certain parts you tend to repeat, or say over again only in a slightly different way. These parts add no new information, so these parts require more work to pay attention to'" (501). Such a take on repetition as being potentially negative unless countered by a measure of concentration is interesting in that Wallace is clearly commenting on his own prose style here, which is sometimes composed of a flow of information that is, in fact, densely layered, carefully repetitive in detail, and frequently cross-cuts between objective description and subjective reflection. In this sense, the reader must, as Wallace once said in his interview with Larry McCaffery, "do her share of the linguistic work" (*CW* 34) to glean meaning from the text. As any "close reader" like Drinion knows, one must discriminate as to which parts of a text's narrative hold more relevant information or evidence of a certain theme than others. This means, above all, paying attention to the act of reading itself, especially if it may, at times, seem repetitive or boring.

Repetition, though it may risk boring the reader, is not necessarily always a bad thing. As Drinion clarifies his comments to Meredith, he adds that her tendency "to recast" her story "in many different ways" helps "to assure yourself that the listener really understands you" and thus "'it coheres in an interesting way with the surface subject of what Ed, in the story you're telling, is teaching you, and so in that respect even the repetitive or redundant elements compel interest and require little conscious effort to pay attention to'" (502). This *meta*-meta-moment in Wallace's narrative proposes that there is, as Orrin E. Klapp states in *Overload and Boredom*, a "social function of redundancy for continuity" since it "surround[s] us with familiar cues assuring us that things are, and will continue to be, what they seem; that people are known and reliable; that debts will be paid, money is good, and so on. Our social world in this sense *is* redundancy" (72).

The difficulty lies in finding the right balance between redundancy and relevant information without overwhelming the reader. This can be seen in the case of Sylvanshine, whose clairvoyance or "shining," called "Random Fact Intuition," leaves him subject to a host of random data: "abundance, together with irrelevance and the interruption of normal thought and attention, composes the essence of the RFI phenomenon" (118).[9] However, Sylvanshine's supposed blessing is really a curse since the facts, quite literally, do not add up. True, "[s]ome are connected, but rarely in any way that yields what someone with true ESP would call meaning" (120). Sylvanshine's situation, then, is representative of the situation many Americans encounter in the information age, in which, "factoids are just one more distraction . . . to shake off" (119). What has meaning and what is just a distraction is a true dilemma. As Sylvanshine struggles, unsuccessfully, to concentrate on reviewing for the CPA exam at the novel's beginning, even he recognizes the truth of "Reynold's dictum . . . that reality was a fact-pattern the bulk of which was entropic and random" (16). The "trick" to dealing with this entropic fact-pattern is "homing in on which facts were important—" (16), provided one can pay attention and not get distracted.

One such flood of seemingly irrelevant, repetitious, and boring information comes to us in §25, Wallace's parody of double-entry bookkeeping. In fact, §25 becomes an instructive readerly allegory for understanding how the theme of boredom plays out in *The Pale King*, both formalistically and conceptually, and typifies Wallace's "aesthetic of boredom." It would be all too easy to nominate this chapter as a candidate for one of the "most boring" parts of the novel due to its double-columned reproduction of the tedium of IRS workers' daily tasks. A closer look at this section, however, unearths two minor gems in this respect. Buried within this properly post-industrial truncated catalogue of American workaday life (a disturbing inversion of its one-time Whitmanian cosmic expansion) are the sentences "[d]evils are actually angels," and later on "[e]very ghost story is really a love story" (312).[10] These sentences (appearing, oddly enough, in the middle of a litany of repetitive tasks) reward the attentive reader. Skim through this chapter's pages, as some readers may be wont to do, and you'll miss these two seeming non-sequiturs. In any event, what becomes clear is that just as the reader's possible boredom is turned into surprise here, so too does the possibility arise for the novel's characters in this section and elsewhere, laboring as they are at their dull, purgatorial jobs, to perceive "devils as angels." Once again, the mechanism that metamorphosizes one into the other remains shrouded in mystery and tinged with mysticism.

In a strange way, this mysticism returns us to the original theme of boredom when we consider how the novel treats one mystic in particular, Saint Anthony. "Who is St. Anthony?" Wallace wrote in his notes, as he considered creating a Peoria district named after him (545). We do not know how Wallace would have answered his own query, but we do know that Saint Anthony was the first of the Desert Fathers to popularize monasticism. These forerunners of the first monks were, of course, the first to experience and condemn *acedia*, "the noontide demon," or the boredom of its day. These hermits condemned acedia and considered it immoral and a sin because the afflicted lost interest in spiritual matters. Nonetheless, writes Kuhn, "for certain thinkers acedia is almost a precondition for a life of eternal bliss" (45). Since, for Wallace, "bliss . . . lies on the other side of crushing, crushing boredom," the possibility of transcending boredom or turning it into its opposite remains, even here. Noteworthy, too, is the fact that the situation of each IRS wiggler, working away in isolation and sometimes visited by demons or ghosts that upsets her routine, resembles that of the early monks, each alone in his cell.

For Saint Anthony and the Desert Fathers, giving in to acedia, or boredom, was a sin; in the secular world of *The Pale King*, giving in to boredom is ultimately irresponsible and childish—but, in both cases, boredom is an ever-present temptation and succumbing to it is a choice. It is therefore the subject's will that can transform "devils into angels" by being aware that one has the choice of what to attend to, or as Wallace put it in *This Is Water*: "[t]he really important kind of freedom involves attention, and awareness, and discipline, and effort" (120). If this sounds a little "monkish" then aptly so, for acquiring this "habit" is simpler in theory than in constant practice. It is for this reason that Drinion's nickname, "Mr. X," is ironic; for although he appears unexciting to others, he holds the elusive X factor in terms of paying attention and being interested in the world.

Nevertheless, the careful consideration that the reader must give *The Pale King*, which is put to the test by Wallace's "aesthetics of boredom," is analogical to the attention that American citizens must pay toward civic duty and maintaining their freedoms. This means paying active attention to economic and political policy, not being easily distracted by the latest consumer trends and entertainment, and realizing that opting to "rebel" by cynically withdrawing from the world is a choice to cede one's opportunity and freedom to change that world. As Glendenning remarks to one of the stalled elevator's unidentified occupants, who complains that the discussion of civics and freedom is boring, "[s]ometimes what's important is dull. Sometimes it's work" (138). In short, *The Pale King* reminds us that it takes work to pay attention, to recognize responsibilities that go beyond the immediate self, and to parse social, political, and cultural narratives for relevance and meaning. If such a message is a boring one to have to hear, suggests Wallace, then so much the better.

Notes

1 This list is indebted to the structure of Reinhard Kuhn's *The Demon of Noontide: Ennui in Western Literature*. Later theorists working on "boredom" tend to retrace Kuhn's map with mostly minor additions or subtractions. See Toohey (107–42), Spacks (7–24), Healy (15–36), Svendsen

(49–81), Pezze and Salzani (7–15), and Goodstein (3–4). For Lepenies's purposes, he begins in the Middle Ages.

2   Earlier in this volume, Stephen Burn points out the larger "underworld theme" of the novel, in § 2, in which "Peoria resembles both the looping river of Styx . . . and the circles of Dante's inferno" (382–3).

3   Kierkegaard, of course, would have never considered himself an existentialist as the term did not exist until the mid-twentieth-century. Even then, Kierkegaard's Christianity would never have gelled with the atheistic existentialism of, say, a Jean-Paul Sartre. Nevertheless, Kierkagaard, like Dostoyevsky, effectively kicked the rug out from under Christian certitude, even while simultaneously leaping faithfully to safety and a-voiding the void revealed beneath. For more on Wallace's debt to Kierkegaard, see Allard den Dulk's essay earlier in this volume.

4   In *Infinite Jest*, Kate Gompert reflects upon the relationship between existential angst and clinical depression when she meditates upon the complexities of "anhedonia" (694–8). Perhaps the best example of this relationship, however, lies not among the residents of Ennet House or the students at Enfield Tennis Academy but in Wallace's (erstwhile controversial) "The Depressed Person" from *Brief Interviews with Hideous Men*. The story braids the main character's recursive thoughts, anxiety, melancholy, and clinical depression together in a way that makes them inseparable—no matter how narcissistic she may ultimately be.

5   This is a radical simplification of Wallace's take on "freedom." For a deeper examination of Wallace's engagement with the history of American democratic ideals see Adam Kelly's deft contribution to this volume.

6   However, the relationship between the novels is a complicated one that cannot be ignored. Adam Kelly makes the connection between the two, and the earlier *Broom of the System*, by seeing Wallace as a novelist of ideas, "with each novel addressing conceptual questions remaining from before" (4). Burn stresses the actual overlap in Wallace's writing projects as significant (151). It would also be fair to say that *The Pale King* is *Infinite Jest*'s other half, its "logical sequel," as Anderson writes, because, Kakutani points out, it "demonstrates that being amused to death and bored to death are, in Wallace's view, flip sides of the same coin." Yet the dialectic these novels form is a dynamic one, suggesting cross-novel influences backward as well as forward in time. The relationship between the novels is thus chiastic, and makes it tempting to suggest that, if anything, *The Pale King* pre-dates *Infinite Jest*. For if *Infinite Jest* works under the sign of "Entertainment" and *The Pale King* under that of "Boredom," we would do well to remember one of the final points Garrity's ghost makes to Lane Dean: "[n]ote too that [the word] *interesting* first appears just two years after *bore*. 1768. Mark this, two years *after*. Can this be so?" (385). I would argue that any serious critical consideration of *Infinite Jest* from this point on in Wallace studies must always take the earlier/later novel, *The Pale King*, into account, and vice versa.

7   In "Trickle Down Citizenship: Taxes and Civic Responsibility" in *The Pale King*, Marshall Boswell also points to the historical underpinnings of the neoliberal era in *The Pale King* by way of a rigorous look at "the Reagan tax cuts of 1981 and the subsequent ascendancy in American political discourse of so-called 'supply side economics' as a pivotal and damning moment in postwar American history" (210). While Boswell focuses his keen analysis mostly on the effects of the Reagan tax cuts, I am more interested, as is Kelly, in the broader economic, social, and cultural effects of neoliberalism, of which tax cuts and distrust of government are surely a part.

8   Wallace is even sure to make the decade's illegal drugs—and especially Fogle's drug of choice, Obetrol, significant of the narcissism of the times. On Obetrol, Fogle gains a "self-awareness, which I used to privately call 'doubling'" (180) that "felt like . . . a sort of emergence, however briefly, from the fuzziness and drift of my life" because "[w]hat became more intense was my awareness of my own part in it [experience], that I could pay real attention to it" (182). Yet this supposed self-awareness is nothing short of solipsistic escapism. His aversion to cocaine, the '80s stimulating drug *par excellence*, is telling in this respect (177). The 1970s drugs reflect the solipsistic and apathetic social mood of Fogle and America itself, as even Hunter S. Thompson saw in his whatever-happened-to-the-'60s novel, *Fear and Loathing in Las Vegas*, in which Raoul Duke remarks that "'[c]onsciousness Expansion' went out with LBJ . . . and it is worth noting, historically, that downers came in with Nixon" (202). Thus, even seemingly irrelevant cultural objects become invested with social importance.

9   The particular style of some of Sylvanshine's more chaotic sections fit what Andrew Warren calls the "Spontaneous Data Intrusion model" that is "compelled to run us up against the data mass's implicit infinitude" (401). However, this data is not always a "pure, threating Outside without order or meaning" (399). Often, as in the Meredith-Drinion section, it is Wallace's own narrative "data," so to speak, that is, once generated, recycled throughout a particular narrative section in a way that does not necessarily lead to the creation of traditional meaning-structuring themes or motifs but does build a sort of database of thick or dense description.

10 A possible third gem lies in the line "[t]wo clocks, two ghosts, one square acre of hidden mirror" (312), though it is a description (of the examination room, or the unseen in the room?) and not a statement. The strange declaration that "[d]evils are actually angels" could allude to a line spoken in the film *Jacob's Ladder* (1990) that a character in the film attributes to the medieval German mystic, Meister Eckhart, though it is not a direct quotation and instead an interpretation of one aspect of his thought. In the film, Jacob is plagued by demons and his dead son, and sees conspiracy everywhere. Unbeknownst to him and the viewer (until the

film's end), Jacob is actually a soldier dying in Vietnam, who is fantasizing the entire film (after the manner of Ambrose Bierce's "An Occurrence at Owl Creek Bridge"). Offering advice, his friend and chiropractor Louie tells him,

> Eckhart saw Hell too. He said: The only thing that burns in Hell is the part of you that won't let go of life, your memories, your attachments. They burn them all away. But they're not punishing you, he said. They're freeing your soul. So, if you're frightened of dying and . . . and you're holding on, you'll see devils tearing your life away. But if you've made your peace, then the devils are really angels, freeing you from the earth.

What commences from this buried and borrowed line, then, is something old and something new. What returns here is Wallace's familiar theme of the imprisoned self, which, in refusing to recognize its limitations, turns inward and constructs a more elaborate and labyrinthine prison in order, impossibly, to escape from itself. The Funhouse becomes a Haunted House, a saving grace is turned into damnation, and thus angels appear to be devils. Set within the post-industrial hell, however, the secularized setting gives a new twist to the suffering subject.

11

Trickle-Down Citizenship: Taxes and Civic Responsibility in *The Pale King*

Marshall Boswell

The Pale King is conspicuous in David Foster Wallace's *oeuvre* in being the only one of his three novels not set in the future. Although *The Broom of the System*'s cartoonish 1990s America is almost indistinguishable from the mid-Eighties world of the novel's creation, and *Infinite Jest*'s post-millennial America was clearly imagined from the vantage point of the actual early Nineties, both novels take place in a fully replete alternative reality that seems to have branched off from the reader's world and pursued its own quirky, though plausible, path. This playfully proleptic strategy frees Wallace to exaggerate and alter the details and contours of our workaday world for the purposes of comic and thematic emphasis. Nevertheless, both novels achieve an almost a-historical and, at times, even spectral quality that, whether intended or not, sometimes obscures the historical contingency of their signature themes. Conversely, *The Pale King* takes place in a carefully reconstructed historical past, with May 1985 through June 1986 carved out as of primary interest, as this marks the 13 months during which a one David Wallace allegedly worked for the Internal Revenue Service as a lowly G-9 in the Regional Examination Center in Peoria, IL. In very deliberate ways, Wallace portrays the IRS as this novel's alternative reality. In a paragraph-long section early in the novel, the third-person narrator describes the IRS as a "parallel world, both connected to and independent of this one, operating under its own physics and imperatives of cause" (*TPK* 86).

This dramatic shift in approach feeds directly into what I wish to submit is one of *The Pale King*'s more striking agendas. More so than any of his other major works, *The Pale King* wrestles directly with matters of real world politics and—here we have one of the novel's key words—civics, while the philosophical and ethical issues it engages are grounded firmly in a series of concrete historical particulars that Wallace rightly identifies as key to understanding what Salon.com journalist Steve Kornacki, in an internet postmortem on the colossally stupid "debt ceiling debate" of summer 2011, identified as "the hopeless politics" of our current political era. *The Pale King* zeroes in specifically and relentlessly on the Reagan tax cuts of 1981, and the subsequent ascendancy in American political discourse of so-called supply-side economics, as a pivotal and damning moment in postwar American civics history, and it builds its elaborate inquiry into taxes, bureaucratic heroism, and civic responsibility atop this decisive event which, in the words of Dewitt Glendenning, might very well "bring us down as a country" and signal the "end of the democratic experiment" (132). These concerns all converge with dramatic force in IRS agent Chris Fogle's lengthy account of his surprise conversion from 1970s "wastoid" to devoted IRS "wiggler." Fogle's monologue operates as both a quasi-religious narrative grounded in the work of American pragmatist William James's *The Varieties of Religious* as well as a focused dramatization of the novel's more diffuse analysis of post-Reagan conceptions of taxes and civic responsibility.

One would not necessarily know any of this from a cursory reading of the voluminous press that greeted the novel's Spring 2011 publication. Most of the book's initial reviewers described the book as, primarily, an IRS novel about boredom. Some of this blindness to one of the book's central concerns may be inadvertently credited to Michael Pietsch, who undertook the Herculean task of compiling the published book from Wallace's copious drafts and notes. Nowhere in his introduction does he touch upon the novel's political concerns. Rather, he argues that "David set out to write a novel about some of the hardest subjects in the world—sadness and boredom—and to make that exploration nothing less than dramatic, funny, and deeply moving" (ix–x). To be sure, this description of Wallace's primary purpose limns seamlessly with the unfortunate popular conception of Wallace as a technically dazzling and intellectually sophisticated writer of self-help narratives designed to "save us" from solipsism, loneliness, addiction, and so on, an image calcified by the book publication of his Kenyon graduation speech, *This Is Water*. But a brief glance through the "Notes and Asides" included at the end of the published text of *The Pale King* clearly confirms that the novel was to have what Wallace describes as "2 Broad arcs," which he describes thusly:

1. Paying attention, boredom, ADD, Machines vs. people at performing mindless jobs.
2. Being individual vs. being part of larger things—paying taxes, being "lone gun" in IRS vs. team player (545).

This second "broad arc"—which the novel treats as unavoidably political— has thus far received very scant attention, perhaps because Wallace is not generally thought of as a political novelist, per se, at least not in the same way that, for instance, the Jonathans Franzen and Safron Foer are regarded. And yet, Wallace's shift to more politically engaged work can be traced back directly to his 2003 *Rolling Stone* article on the John McCain campaign, a condensed version of which, titled "Up, Simba," he would later collect in *Consider the Lobster* alongside such other politically motivated pieces as "The View from Mrs. Thompson's," about the 9–11 attacks, and "Host," Wallace's devastating portrait of right-wing radio personality John Ziegler, who has since gone on to make an obsequious documentary about Sarah Palin. Around this same time—that is, November 2003—Wallace, in an interview in *The Believer*, weighed in passionately about his disgust with the country's rigidly partisan political discourse, singling out in particular the then-current bloodbath between Bill O'Reilly and now Minnesota Senator Al Franken. He went on to ask,

> How can any of this possibly help me, the average citizen, deliberate about whom to choose to decide my country's macroeconomic policy, or how even to conceive for myself what that policy's outlines should be . . . ? Questions like these are all massively complicated, and much of the complication is not sexy, and well over 90 percent of political commentary now simply abets the uncomplicatedly sexy delusion that one side is Right and Just and the other Wrong and Dangerous. Which is of course a pleasant delusion, in a way—as is the belief that every last person you're in conflict with is an asshole—but it's childish, and totally unconducive to hard thought, give and take, compromise, or the ability of grown-ups to function as any kind of community. ("Interview," *The Believer* 87)

Although there is no way of knowing how deep Wallace was in his composition of *The Pale King* when he made this statement, he nevertheless seems to be speaking very much in the language of the novel, primarily in his questions about "macroeconomic" policy and his description of this fundamental issue as "massively complicated" and "not sexy." *The Pale King* directly seeks to address this massively complicated and not sexy issue in a way that does not devolve to the childish delusion he outlines above.

Part of the elusiveness of the novel's political underpinnings is no doubt deliberate. In the justly celebrated "Author's Foreword," Wallace's persona describes the changes in the IRS that grew out of the 1981 Reagan Tax cuts—changes, he goes on to emphasize, "that today directly affect the way citizens' tax obligations are determined and enforced" (83)—as having been almost universally overlooked, even though these changes occurred in the bright light of full and open disclosure. The cause of this public blindness, he goes on to argue, arises directly out of the very nature of tax policy itself: "The real reason why US citizens were/are not aware of these conflicts, changes, and stakes," he proclaims, "is that the whole subject of tax policy and administration is dull. Massively, spectacularly dull" (83). Note, for instance, the reuse of the word "massively" from the interview passage above. This dullness, David Wallace concludes, sits at the heart of what he calls "one of the great and terrible PR discoveries in modern democracy, which is that if sensitive issues of governance can be made sufficiently dull and arcane, there will be no need for officials to hide or dissemble, because no one not directly involved will pay enough attention to cause trouble" (84). Similarly, the novel's treatment of the Reagan tax cuts, both their origins and their consequences, is arcane and, at times, dull, and has also been largely overlooked by many of the book's initial readers, even though the material is right there in front of our faces.

The 1981 tax cuts are the impetus behind one of the novel's central plot devices, namely the mysterious and probably fictional "Spackman Initiative," the clearest description of which is provided by Kenneth ["Type of Thing Ken"] Hindle in his excerpted video Interview included in §14. Without naming Reagan directly, Hindle explains the background of the Initiative as arising directly from "the incoming administration's . . . belief that marginal tax rates could be lowered, especially in the top brackets, without causing a catastrophic loss of revenue," because, according to the theory being promulgated at the time—that is "trickle-down economics" in Reagan's nomenclature, "voodoo economics" in the words of his rival and later Vice President George Herbert Walker Bush—"lower marginal rates would spur investment and increased productivity, type of thing, and there would be a rising tide that would cause an increase in the tax base that would more than offset the decrease in marginal rates" (107). Of course, that is not what happened. As one character remarks in response to yet another articulation of Reagan's "trickle-down" explanation, "Even a child could see the contradiction in that" (148). What happened, instead, was the largest federal budget deficit in history. Journalist Jonathan Chait, in *The Big Con,* a fascinating takedown of "trickle-down economics" and its pervasive and corrosive effect on macroeconomic policy since Reagan's first term, about which more anon, quotes David Stockman, Reagan's own budget director, as admitting, on record, "By 1982, I knew the Reagan Revolution was impossible." Stockman goes on to admit that the Administration needed to address the massive budget deficits created by the cut—and concurrent increases in military spending—"in order to reduc[e] the size of the nation's fiscal disaster" (qtd in Chait 33).

In *The Pale King*, one of the ways the Administration addressed this disaster was to change the culture of the IRS in accordance with ideas laid out in a policy paper written between 1969–70 by the mysterious Spackman. Spackman argued that "increasing the efficiency with which the Service enforced the tax code would provably increase net revenues to the US Treasury without any corresponding change in the code or a raising in the marginal rates" (109–10), the final option being, in Hindle's terms, politically and ideologically "unacceptable" to the new Administration. As a direct result of implementing the Spackman Initiative, the IRS, in Wallace's depiction, transforms from an institutional bureaucracy once regarded as "the nation's beating heart," or, more specifically, "the heart . . . of these United States as a team, each income earner chipping in to share resources and embody the principles that make our nation great" (101), and into "a business—a going, for-profit concern type of thing"—with the profits here being "revenues" collected through aggressive and targeted audits. Put another way, the Initiative launched a "struggle," as the character David Wallace puts it, "between traditional or 'conservative'"—the latter term glossed in a footnote to mean "confusingly, classically liberal"— "officials who saw tax and its administration as an arena of social justice and civic virtue, on the one hand, and those more progressive, 'pragmatic' policymakers who prized the market model, efficiency, and maximum return on the investment of the Service's annual budget" (82–3). Even more confusingly—a confusion Wallace invites for important thematic reasons, as will be shown—the "conservative" officials above might be viewed as more in line with current progressive advocates for higher marginal tax rates at the top end, with the "progressive" policymakers corresponding with today's supply-side, free market, tax-cut advocates, not to mention the militantly misinformed members of the House of Representative's Tea Party caucus, the whole of whom actively sought to force a default on the nation's debt obligations rather than concede to the merest, most insignificant increase in tax revenue.[1]

Although the Spackman Initiative appears to be a fanciful invention, Wallace is on very solid ground in his treatment of the Reagan Tax Cuts of 1981 as Year Zero of our current political morass. As I was writing the previous sentence on my laptop—the day of composition being August 15, 2011—an email popped into my inbox from *The New York Times* trumpeting a link to an editorial by billionaire investor Warren Buffett titled "Stop Coddling the Super-Rich," in which Buffett advocates quixotically for a return to high marginal tax rates for the nation's top earners (Buffett A21). The very fact that someone like Buffett feels compelled to take to the pages of *The New York Times* to make such a plea attests to the bewildering but also occult power Reagan's "trick-down economic" debacle still exerts over our political landscape, this despite the fact that the theory, so called, has been resoundingly refuted, over and over again, for 30 years. And yet, a massive majority of the Republican party—as well as many in the Democratic party—continue to believe—or claim to believe—despite a mountain of evidence to the contrary, that lowering the marginal tax rates for the super wealthy results in job creation and increased tax revenues over all, and that, conversely, increases in tax rates for the wealthy result in job loss and lower revenues.

Chait provides a fascinating account—perhaps apocryphal—of how supply-side theory took over the Republican party, an account that, in many ways, sounds like a scene from a David Foster Wallace novel. The theory was the brainchild of a disgraced economist from the Nixon era named Arthur Laffer who, around the same time that Spackman was writing his soon-to-be influential white paper, began arguing that "it was possible to simultaneously expand the economy and tamp down inflation by cutting taxes, especially the high tax rates faced by upper-income earners" (Chait 14). He illustrated his counterintuitive theory via a simple graph that has since become known as—and here the truth is better than the fiction—"the Laffer Curve." According to Chait, Laffer first outlined the Curve on a cocktail napkin while explaining his theory, over lunch, to then Chief of Staff for the Ford Administration, Dick Cheney. The Curve purported to show that,

> If the government sets a tax rate of zero, it will receive no revenue. And if the government sets a tax rate of 100 percent, the government will also receive zero tax revenue, since nobody will have any reason to earn any income. Between these two points—zero taxes and zero revenue, 100 percent taxes and zero revenue—Laffer's curve drew an arc. The arc suggested that at higher levels of taxation, reducing the tax rate would produce more revenue for the government. (Chait 15)

One of the clear virtues of the Laffer Curve, and a key factor in its success as a piece of political rhetoric, is its simplicity, a quality that Hindle also attributes to the Spackman Initiative: "At root," Hindle explains, "the paper's proposal was said to be very simple and, of course the current executive"—this would be Reagan—"approves of simplicity, arguably because this administration is somewhat of a reaction type of thing, or backlash, against the complex social engineering of the Great Society, which was a very different era for tax policy and administration" (109). In other words, complexity, which requires attention and threatens boredom, is antithetical to both the Laffer

Curve and the Spackman Initiative. Conversely—and this point is key—complexity is absolutely essential to the governing ethics of *The Pale King,* a fact which should dispel another popular notion of Wallace as a writer whose "principal goal," according to Hubert Dreyfuss and Sean Dorrance Kelly in their deeply offensive exploitation of Wallace's suicide in *All Things Shining: Reading the Western Classics to Find Meaning in a Secular Age,* "is to resuscitate the truths living within . . . clichés" (37). The simplicity of the Laffer Curve certainly appealed to Dick Cheney, who, Chait reports, was instantly converted, right there, at the lunch table. And "convert" is precisely the term used not only by Chait but by many of the country's most virulent supply-siders, such as Irving Kristol, who is quoted as saying, "It was [Laffer advocate] Jude [Wanniski] who introduced me to Jack Kemp, a young congressman and recent convert. It was Jack Kemp who, almost single-handedly, converted Ronald Reagan" (qtd in Chait 16). The language of "conversion" helps, I think, to explain the current thinking among members of the Republican party, for whom there is apparently no situation—not a war, not a massive, crushing national debt—that might justify raising taxes. As columnist Peter Wehner put it in a 2011 piece published in *Commentary,* "If taxes cannot be raised under any circumstance —then we have veered from economic policy to religious catechism" (Wehner).

Incidentally, former Republican presidential candidate Michele Bachmann, who between 1988 and 1992 worked as a lawyer at the I.R.S. Office of Chief Counsel in Saint Paul, MN, routinely lists Arthur Laffer as the primary intellectual architect of her own economic policy (Lizza 60).[2]

Yet inasmuch as the novel is very clear and specific in designating the historical budget deficits following the 1981 tax cuts as the impetus for the Spackman Initiative, Wallace, as already evidenced above in his slippery use of the terms "conservative" and "progressive," takes great pains to contextualize the rise of Reaganomics in a way that skirts a simplistic partisan dialectic. The two places where Wallace lays out his own analysis as to how the American electorate became "primed"—another key word in the novel—for the supply-side scam can be found in §19, which details the elevator debate about civics between Glendenning, Drinion, and others, and §22, which consists of Chris Fogle's remarkable monologue.

§19 lays out a fascinating, nuanced, and, in the end, quintessentially Wallace-esque analysis of the effect of the 1960s counterculture on the psyche of the American electorate that led to the conservative triumph of the Reagan-Bush era. The § consists of a roundtable debate datable to spring and/or summer 1980 and organized without dialogue tags[3]—a technique Wallace adopted from William Gaddis and which has been a feature of his novels from the very beginning of his career—with the primary voice belonging to DeWitt Glendenning, whom the existing material paints as, overall, a positive figure. David Wallace, in §43, declares that he "didn't know a person at the Post who didn't like and admire DeWitt Glendenning" (433), while an interesting entry in the notes indicates that Glendenning, described as an "Old School IRS-as-Civics believer," was to be pitted against Merrill Lehr, who, by inventing something called Automated Collection Systems, seeks to replace "human Examiners with computers" in order to transform the IRS into a "corporate entity" as opposed to "a *moral* one" (543). As such, Glendenning, who announces himself in this § as a conservative who "voted for Ford" and who will "likely vote for Bush or maybe Reagan and . . . feel solid about [his] vote" (134), should be considered a positive figure, the bulk of whose views Wallace appears to advocate. As one of the characters points out, the term "conservative" must not automatically be considered a putdown in the context of the novel's political engagement. "There are all kinds of conservatives," the speaker observes, "depending on what it is they want to conserve" (132), a line that calls to mind Wallace's famous, and perhaps overly fetishized, call, in "E Unibus Pluram," for a new breed of literary "*anti*-rebels" who have the "childish gall actually to endorse and instantiate single-entendre principles" (*SFT* 81).

In fact, this section of *The Pale King* in many ways replays, and deliberately updates and expands, Wallace's youthful analysis of how television successfully co-opted, and hence diluted, the techniques and strategies of literary postmodernism. In both that essay, and the oft-quoted interview with Larry McCaffery that preceded the essay's original appearance in the Summer 1993 issue of *The Review of Contemporary Fiction*, Wallace associates the revolutionary strategies of post-World War II postmodernism—defined in "E Unibus Pluram" as "involution," "absurdity," "sardonic fatigue" "iconoclasm," and "rebellion" (*SFT* 64)—with the 1960s countercultural movement. He describes his generation's relationship to this long-term rebellion as "a bit like the way you feel when you're in high school and your parents go on a trip and you throw a party. . . . For awhile it's great, free and freeing . . . [b]ut then time passes, and the party gets louder and louder, . . . and you gradually start wishing your parents would come back and restore some fucking order in your house" (*CW* 52). The "civics" debate in *The Pale King* directly reprises this description of the 1960s as a "free and freeing" period that eventually inspired a childish desire for parental authority. Yet whereas in both "E Unibus Pluram" and its accompanying interview, Wallace contextualizes that desire in terms that invoke Harold Bloom's *Anxiety of Influence,* in *The Pale King*'s updating of this analysis of postwar culture, Wallace confronts directly the very real political rebellions, and concurrent expansion of rights and opportunities, of the 1960s and the insidious way that corporations co-opted this rebellious impulse for the purposes of marketing, much the same way Wallace analyzed how television successfully seized upon and atrophied the hypocrisy-exploding power of postmodern self-reflexivity.

Glendenning begins the debate by contrasting "civics" with "selfishness," the very same terms that form the fulcrum of the novel's second "broad arc." Glendenning worries aloud that Americans in the year 1980 no longer "think of [them]selves as citizens—parts of something larger to which we have profound responsibilities" (130). He goes on to assert that this conception of citizenship directly informs both the Constitution and the *Federalist Papers*, which he describes as "an incredible moral and imaginative achievement" (133). The Founding Fathers, Glendenning opines, "were geniuses of civic virtue" (133) who "assumed their descendants would be like them—rational, honorable, civic-minded" (134). Although Wallace is careful to complicate Glendenning's portrait of the Founders with pointed interruptions by various other speakers regarding Jefferson's hypocrisy on the manner of slavery and the Founders' original decision to enfranchise only wealthy landed educated males and so on, Glendenning's core point remains. Starting in the Sixties, Glendenning continues, we as Americans stopped thinking "of ourselves as citizens in the old sense of being small parts of something larger and infinitely more important to which we have serious responsibilities" (136). This change occurred partly because "here was a whole generation where most of them now for the time questioned authority and said that their individual moral beliefs about the [Vietnam] war outweighed their duty to go fight if their duly elected representatives told them to," to which one of the other speakers amends, "In other words that their highest actual duty was to themselves" (132).

Glendenning's problem is not with the Vietnam protests per se. It lies with the way corporations learned to transform real rebellion into a fashionable pose that could be used to market products. As he explains, "Whatever led to it becoming actually fashionable to protest a war opened the door to what's going to bring us down as a country" (132), namely, an end to the belief that good citizenship entails shared sacrifice. That view has been replaced by "individual citizens" adopting "a corporate attitude. That our ultimate obligation is to ourselves. That unless it's illegal or there are direct practical consequences for ourselves, any activity is OK" (136). The danger here lies precisely in treating corporations as if they were people, since corporations "can't vote or serve in combat," they "don't learn the Pledge of allegiance," and they "don't have souls." Rather, they "are machines for producing profit" and a way to "allow for individual reward without individual obligation" (136).

Mere days after I reread this section of the novel for the purposes of writing this essay, 2012 Republican Presidential candidate Mitt Romney, at a campaign stop in Iowa, declared, "Corporations are people, my friend" (Parker A16).

Anyway, as a result of this shift in the conception of citizenship, Glendenning and his fellow debaters agree that Americans now expect the government to take care of the civic functions that used to be everyone's shared responsibility, a shift in perspective that puts the government in the role of the parent of children who can't take care of themselves, "with all the ambivalent love-hate-need-defy charges that surround the parent-figure in the mind of the adolescent . . . in its twin desire for both authoritarian structure and the end of parental hegemony" (147). And the aspect of civic life where this dynamic "gets revealed in the starkest of terms" is taxation. According to one of the speakers, taxation will also be the place where then Presidential candidate Ronald Reagan will focus his campaign pitch, primarily by setting up the IRS "as the blackhatted rapacious Big Brother he secretly needs" in order to portray himself as an outsider and a rebel. The IRS, in other words, will become the enemy: the national symbol of the government as repressive parent that individualist Americans need to defy.

Final real-life interpolation: a week after I wrote that last paragraph, Republican Presidential candidate Michele Bachmann declared on the stump that the reason she agreed to join the IRS was because, in her words, "the first rule of war is 'know your enemy'" (Sargent).

At one point in the dialogue, Glendenning admits, "[I]t's probably part of my naiveté that I don't want to put the issue in political terms when it's probably irreducibly political" (136), a view I imagine Wallace shared. But there's no getting around it: the issue is irreducibly political, and it is to Wallace's credit that he chose not to shy away from this fact. That being said, Wallace was not a political scientist; he was a novelist, and the job of the novelist is to express abstract ideas, including "irreducibly political" ones, in concrete and dramatic form, and the place where he does this most effectively in *The Pale King* is in Chris Fogle's monologue, which Michael Pietsch wisely placed more or less immediately after Glendenning's civics debate, a move that permits close readers to recognize and appreciate the clear and surely intentional echoes in vocabulary, imagery, and theme that link the two §s.

Throughout his lengthy account of his dissolute college career in the late 1970s, Fogle repeatedly refers to himself as a "wastoid" and a "the worst kind of nihilist—the kind who isn't even aware he's a nihilist" (154). Wholly without "initiative"—that word again—he simply drifts from one empty enthusiasm to the next, his tepid rebellions against the so-called establishment consisting entirely of consumer choices and pointless drug use. As he puts it, "I was like a piece of paper on the street in the wind, thinking, 'Now I think I'll blow this way, now I think I'll blow that way,'" (154), an image that directly invokes an earlier passage from the civics debate §, in which one of the characters quotes De Tocqueville as regarding "the democratic citizen's nature to be like a leaf that doesn't believe in the tree it's part of" (141), to which another character amends, "Not even on a tree but more like leaves on the ground in the wind, blown this way and that by the wind, and each time a gust blows it the citizen says, 'Now I choose to blow this way; this is my decision'" (142). Fogle, who, like Wallace, generationally sits at the cusp between the baby boomers and Generation X, is set in direct contrast with his clean-cut father, a child of the Depression and a member of the "Silent Generation" whom Fogle regards as "a robot and a slave to conformity" and "one hundred-percent conventional establishment, and totally on the other side of the generation gap" (167). Conversely, Fogle's mother, who has left the family to pursue her own enlightenment as a 1970s feminist with a same-sex lover, is presented as his spiritual ally, as someone who is "changing and growing up right there with me, both on my side of the generation gap" (166).

Wallace pointedly portrays Fogle's transformation from wastoid to IRS agent as a conversion experience, even a religious one, and this conversion is the exact obverse of the conversions to Laffer economics that changed Dick Cheney, Jack Kemp, and Ronald Reagan. Wallace sources his treatment of this conversion back to American pragmatic philosopher William James, the title of whose essay "The Moral Equivalent of War" is projected onto an A/V screen in the accounting class into which Fogle accidentally stumbles late in his narrative. In a letter to Miss Frances R. Morse, James explained that in *The Varieties of Religious Experience* he sought to "defend (against all prejudices of my 'class') 'experience' against 'philosophy' as being the real backbone of the world's religious life" (James, "Experience and Religion" 740–1). Granting that "the special manifestations of religion may have been absurd," he endeavors to analyze what religious experience actually *feels* like, and to affirm its positive function in human life. As such, James defines religion to mean "the feelings, acts, and experiences of individual men in their solitude, so far as they apprehend themselves to stand in relation to whatever they consider the divine" (James, "Circumscription of the [Religious] Topic 744). Moreover, religion is "a *serious* state of mind" whose "universal message" is that "'All is *not* vanity in this Universe, whatever the appearances may suggest'" (748). As for the divine, James defines that loaded concept as any "such primal reality as the individual feels impelled to respond to solemnly and gravely, and neither by a curse nor a jest" (749). Given the context, I'm particularly grateful to Mr James for that final word. In a nod forward to the later essay already referenced, James even compares the religious life to that of a soldier in a war:

> A life is manly, stoical, moral, or philosophical, we say, in proportion as it is less swayed by personal considerations and more by objective ends that call for energy, even though that energy brings personal loss and pain. This is the good side of war, in so far as it calls for "volunteers." And for morality, life is a war, and the service of the highest is a sort of cosmic patriotism which also calls for volunteers. (754)

This war imagery will return later in Fogle's narrative. Finally, in the conclusion to *The Varieties*, James asserts that, as an outgrowth of the religious experience, one may experience "a new zest which adds itself like a gift to life, and takes the form either of lyrical attachment or"—and here is a phrase that speaks very directly to Chris Fogle's own experience—"of appeal to earnestness and heroism" (759).

Fogle's "conversion" from wastoid to tax assessor corresponds directly to the Jamesian formula, even to the extent of borrowing some of James's own language. But the conversion is not instantaneous. Rather, Fogle is "primed" for the conversion by two earlier episodes in his narrative, much as his roommate's Christian girlfriend, in *her* conversion narrative, was "primed" to take a minister's vague pronouncements as directed precisely at her. As Fogle explains in a passage that has an unavoidable Jamesian ring,

> I think the truth is probably that enormous, sudden, dramatic, unexpected life-changing experiences are not translatable or explainable to anyone else, and this is because they really *are* unique and particular. . . . This is because their power isn't just a result of the experience itself, but also of the circumstance in which it hits you, of everything in your previous life-experience which has led up to it and made you exactly who and what you are when the experience hits you. (214)

So although Wallace wants us to understand that Fogle's conversion arrives as a product of his 20 years as a Seventies wastoid and nihilist "wandering aimlessly in the psychological desert of our younger generation's decadence and materialism and so on and so forth" (211), he does have Fogle single out two key moments that "prime" him for this sudden, dramatic, and unexpected life-changing experience. Significantly, both involve his father.

In the first episode, Fogle's father returns home early from a business trip to find Chris and his friends splayed out in the living room after a three-day debauch, with bongs and beer cans strewn about. Consciously or not, Wallace here directly dramatizes the scene he laid for Larry McCaffery back in 1993, which I've already cited, wherein his generation of writers is likened to a bunch of kids in high school who have thrown a party while the parents are gone, only to feel, after a day or two, like they want the parents "to come back and restore some fucking order." Further evidence to support this linkage comes from Fogle himself, who remembers this shameful episode as "being the worst confirmation of the worst kind of generation-gap stereotype and parental disgust for their decadent, wastoid kids" (170). In this passage, as in dozens of others, Wallace invites us to view Fogle as representative of that generation of "decadent, wastoid kids"—Wallace's own generation, in other words—and the father as a walking embodiment of the preceding generation, who are described as "high-strung and tightly controlled." In this sense, then, the Fogle monologue is not just a conversion narrative but a generational study. Fogle's decadence, directionlessness, and nihilism also serve as objective correlatives for Glendenning's generational analysis of the decline in civic engagement. In his own representative role, the father, surveying the wreckage of his living room, raises his arm in mock despair and quotes the famous line from Shelley's *Ozymandias,* "Look on my works, ye mighty, and despair," thus echoing not only Glendenning's sense that the current state of American self-interested individualism might "bring us down as a country" but also Glendenning's magnanimous sense that, though from an older generation, he, too, must take some blame for the crummy state of things.

Obviously, the father's violent death on a train platform constitutes the second key "priming" event, for it is after that horrific episode that Fogle endeavors to buckle down and, in the wake of numerous transfers and changes of majors, complete his college degree. The scene itself is grisly enough: while trying to board a train, the father shoots out an arm to stop the doors from closing, only to find himself trapped by the clamped doors as the train begins moving and accelerating along the platform. Fogle is partly to blame, because his "directionless" "dawdling" as he and his father rush to the train have made them late. But the father, while jostling through the agitated Christmas-season crowd, also falls victim to general herd anxiety about missing trains, which Fogle connects back to "primal, prehistoric fears that you would somehow miss getting to eat your fair share of the tribe's kill, or be caught out alone in the veldt's tall grass as night falls" (199). Again, consciously or not—and here I vote for consciously— this latter passage echoes an earlier passage from the civics-debate § in which Glendenning describes paying taxes as similar to being stranded on a lifeboat, whereby "you have a duty to the others in the boat. A duty to yourself not to be the sort of person who waits till everybody is asleep and then eats all the food" (131).

Throughout the narrative, Fogle depicts his father as the quintessential "man in the gray flannel suit," right down to the hat and the gray flannel suit, part and parcel of the novel's extended and self-conscious parody of Hollywood depictions of 1950s corporate culture, now all the rage thanks to the *Mad Men* television program. This is an important point to keep in mind when considering the agent of Fogle's actual conversion, the Jesuit-priest accountant professor, referred to at one point, *pace* James Joyce, as "the fearful Jesuit" (215).[4] Like the father, the priest is dressed not in his robe but in "an archaically conservative dark-gray suit whose boxy look might have been actual flannel" (215). Also like the father, the priest appears to be "in that amorphous . . . area between forty and sixty" (217)—in other words, a member of the preceding generation.

Significantly, the first transparent the priest shows the class is a graph "representing the progressive marginal tax rate schedule for the 1976 federal income tax" (218). Wallace did not choose this graph at random, because 1976, in addition to being the year of the American Bicentennial, marked the last year in which the average—or effective—tax rate for the top 0.1 percent of wage earners was 60 percent, after which it declined to 52 percent in 1980 and then, after the Reagan tax cut, down to less than 40 percent by 1985–6, the year of the novel's setting, before reaching an all-time low of 35 percent in 1988. This means that the average tax being paid by top wage earners was already declining *before* Reagan decreased the top progressive marginal rate from 70 percent to 50 percent, and then to an another all-time low of 28 percent for 1988–90, before Bush, Sr, now unable to ignore the size of the debt accumulating under his watch, reneged on his "No New Taxes" and raised the marginal rate back to 31 percent, a process Bill Clinton completed when he raised the rate one more time to 40 percent in 1994, thereby, and in direct contradiction to all counter projections by Supply Siders, ushering in one of the most robust economic expansions of the postwar period, an expansion which ended with Clinton balancing the federal budget and getting impeached by the Republican majority in the House of Representatives (Piketty and Seaz 15–16).[5] The novel even includes a possible explanation for the decrease in *effective* tax rates prior to the drop in progressive marginal rates, per se, namely the Alternative Tax/Shelters provisions of 1976, 1978, and 1980 that are being enforced by the Immersive Group to which David Wallace has been mistakenly assigned. The narrator describes these provisions "as Congress's clever way of reducing a certain group's tax *burden* without lowering its tax rate—one simply allowed special deductions or provisions that exempted certain portions of income from the taxable base" (335). More specifically, Wallace's group has been charged with enforcing "certain special provisions that the '76 and '80 acts had put in place to keep extremely wealthy individuals and S corps from paying, . . . in effect, no tax at all" (335).

The priest's lengthy speech—what Fogle calls, curiously, his "hortation" rather than "exhortation"—has been justly singled out and celebrated in many of the book's early reviews, with particular attention paid to its pithy concluding line, "Gentleman, you are called to account" (233). Space does not permit me to paraphrase the speech in its entirety. The key passage for our purposes involves the priest's now famous definition of "heroism," which he defines as "enduring tedium over real time in a confined space" (229). As we've seen, James, too, speaks of "heroism" in his description of the religious experience, coupling it with "an appeal to earnestness." As if to underscore the Jamesian connection here, Fogle, when he hears the priest first mention "heroism," instantly recalls the reference to James's "moral equivalent of war" that he'd read when he first entered the class, and which he had misidentified as "biblical" (229). As with James, the specific "religiosity" of this moment is immaterial to its positive effect. Fogle, recalling his objections to the Christian girl's own conversion experience, recognizes that, in fact, the priest was addressing him least of all, since he wasn't even a member of the class. "Nevertheless," Fogle insists, "a feeling is a feeling, nor can you argue with results" (230).

Overnight, Fogle trades in all his Seventies "commercial psychedelica," cuts his hair, and buys a "dark-gray ventless wool suit . . . and bulky box-plaid jacket" (233). Serendipitously, he also learns of a new recruitment effort by the IRS to train agents in exchange for college tuition. The scene detailing his appearance at the IRS recruitment station marks the novel's most overt, and this case, comic, engagement with James, for the IRS facility shares the same storefront with a US Air Force recruiting office. What's more, the Service, Fogle tells us, "had recently instituted a program of recruiting new contract employees in much the same way as the new volunteer armed forces" (241). Throughout Fogle's punishingly dull discussion with the IRS recruiting agent, a loud speaker from the Air Force office next door blasts a continuous loop of the "'Off we go into the wild blue yonder' musical theme" (242). The implications are clear: Fogle's conversion to IRS agent is a Jamesian religious conversion to an entity—which Wallace refers to throughout the novel as "The Service"—that fulfills James's call, in his later essay, for a reification of martial virtues minus the bloodshed of actual war, values he outlines as "intrepidity, contempt of softness, surrender of private interest, obedience to command," the latter phrase recalling Glendenning's remark to Fogle that "Real freedom is the freedom to obey the law" (193). It is no accident that agents in the Service refer to a national office in DC as "The Three-Personed God" (108). Tragically, the IRS that Fogle—and, later, David Wallace—joins is being systematically stripped of its Jamesian aura and turned instead into a corporation, which, contra Governor Romney, isn't a person, let alone a Three-Personed God.

Of course, there's no way to know how Wallace might have brought these themes to their full fruition in the finished novel. Although it is true that many of the themes explored here get raised and complicated in later portions of the published manuscript, particularly in the second long "David Wallace" §, wherein David first arrives at the Regional Examination Center, it is also true that these same concerns tend to fall away in the latter portions of the existing manuscript. Again, this fact is no doubt a product of the unfinished status of the book. That being said, I genuinely believe that Wallace was writing a book about, among other things, taxes, civics, and the current impasse over tax cuts versus budget cuts, and that his hopes for the book were not just aesthetic but, in a very real sense of the term, political. Given the dismal state of our political discourse, and the lock-step adherence to Supply-Side economic policy in every wing of the Republican party, we will continue to hear a great deal of misleading talk about taxes, tax cuts, government spending and budget deficits, and we will also hear a chorus of plangent cries about how we as a country need to change the way we talk about these things. With *The Pale King*, David Foster Wallace was trying to do just that.

Notes

1   Brief but relevant autobiographical interpolation: In fall 1986, not long after David Wallace was allegedly wrapping up his stint as a wiggler at the Peoria Regional Examination Center, I happened to read his short story, "Late Night," later collected in *Girl with Curious Hair* as "My Appearance," in the pages of my roommate's copy of *Playboy* magazine, emphasis here on "roommate's copy." At the end of the story was an entry form for the magazine's annual "College Fiction Contest," which contest I subsequently entered. Alice Turner, the fiction editor there, and one of Wallace's earliest literary advocates, awarded my story a Third Place prize. On the strength of this recommendation, two years later I sent Ms. Turner another story, which she accepted for publication, and for which I was paid the highest fee I have ever been paid for a single piece of writing, the whole of which I included under "Wages and Tips" in my subsequent year's 1040 Tax form,

a major screw up on my part, I quickly learned, as I was supposed to have reckoned this money as self-employment income under the auspices of the 1099. In short, I was audited.

2   Lizza goes on to reveal that he talked to six of Bachmann's former colleagues, three of whom still work there, and all of whom said that "Bachmann was not on the job long enough to gain much experience." As Bachmann had two children during her four-year stint, she spent much of her time at the I.R.S. office on maternity leave. "Basically, the rest of us that were here were handling Michele's inventory," complained one colleague, while another said, "She was an attorney here, but she was never here" (Lizza 60). Only one of her cases went to court, specifically a 1992 suit brought against a Chippewa Indian who failed to report three years of income from Youth Project, Inc., a community-organization nonprofit dedicated to "social justice and peace." Cue Glenn Beck here on the issue of "social justice."

3   With one curious exception: on p. 139 a first-person narrator intrudes. Because the episode seems to be taking place in early 1980—as Glendenning and others all theorize about the possibility of a Reagan presidency, though at this time George Bush also appears to be in the running—the first-person speaker cannot be David Wallace. Conversely, Shane Drinion, whose nickname is X, or Mr X (for "Mr Excitement"), is present, and seems to be the clearest candidate for this first-person narrator, as his interpolations correspond to those he makes during Meredith Rand's lengthy account of her stay at Zeller.

4   Perhaps not coincidentally, Fogle's mother's new live-in lover is named Joyce.

5   See especially Panel B of Figure 3. For a listing of the progressive marginal tax rates from 1976–94, see http://en.wikipedia.org/wiki/Income_tax_in_the_United_States#1913_-_2010.

Works Cited

Adorno, Theodor. *Aesthetic Theory*. Ed. Gretel Adorno and Rolf Tiedemann. Trans. and ed. Hullot-Kentor, Robert. Minneapolis: University of Minnesota Press, 1997.

Alber, Jan, Stefan Iversen, Henrik Skov Nielsen, and Brian Richardson. "Unnatural Narratives, Unnatural Narratology: Beyond Mimetic Models." *Narrative* 18.2 (2010): 113–36.

Althusser, Louis. "Ideology and Ideological State Apparatuses (Notes towards an Investigation." 1971. *On Ideology*. London: Verso, 2008. 1–60.

Andersen, Tore Rye. "Pay Attention! David Foster Wallace and His Real Enemies." *English Studies* 95.3 (2014): 7–24.

Anderson, Sam. "David Foster Wallace's Unfinished Novel—And Life." Rev. of *The Pale King: An Unfinished Novel* by David Foster Wallace. *New York Times Magazine*, April 4, 2011. Web. December 20, 2011.

Arnheim, Rudolf. *The Power of the Center: A Study of Composition in the Visual Arts*. Berkeley: University of California Press, 1982.

Aubry, Timothy. "Selfless Cravings: Addiction and Recovery in David Foster Wallace's *Infinite Jest*." *American Fiction of the 1990s: Reflections of History and Culture*. Ed. Jay Prosser. New York: Routledge, 2008. 206–19.

—. *Reading as Therapy: What Contemporary Fiction Does for Middle Class Americans*. Iowa City: University of Iowa Press, 2011.

Bakhtin, Mikhail. *Problems of Dostoevsky's Poetics*. Ed. and trans. Caryl Emerson. Minneapolis: University of Minnesota Press, 1984.

Bal, Matthijs and Martijn Veldkamp. "How Does Fiction Reading Influence Empathy? An Experimental Investigation on the Role of Emotional Transportation." *PLoS ONE* 8.1 (2013). Web. February 7, 2013, http://www.plosone.org/article/info:doi/10.1371/journal.pone.0055341

Barth, John. *The Friday Book: Essays and Other Nonfiction*. New York: Putnam, 1984.

—. *Lost in the Funhouse: Fiction for Print, Tape, Live Voice*. New York: Anchor Books, 1988.

Barthes, Roland. 1968. "The Death of the Author." *Image, Music, Text*. Ed. Stephen Heath. New York: Hill and Wang, 1977. 142–8.

—. "Upon Leaving the Movie Theater." 1975. *Apparatus: Cinematographic Apparatus: Selected Writings*. Ed. Therese Hak Kyung Cha. Trans. Bertrand Augst and Susan White. New York: Tanam Press, 1980. 1–4.

Baskin, Jon. "Death Is Not the End: David Foster Wallace: His Legacy and His Critics." *The Point* 1 (2009): 33–45.

Benjamin, Walter. "The Storyteller." 1936. *Theory of the Novel: A Historical Approach*. Ed. Michael McKeon. Baltimore: Johns Hopkins University Press, 2000. 77–93.

Bennett, Jane. "Franz Kafka." *Dictionary of Existentialism*. Ed. Haim Gordon. Westport: Greenwood Press, 1999. 235–9.

Benstock, Shari. "At the Margins of Discourse: Footnotes in the Fictional Text." *PMLA* 98.2 (March 1983): 204–25.

Bergson, Henri. *Laughter: An Essay on the Meaning of the Comic*. 1911. Trans. Cloudesley Brereton and Fred Rothwell. New York: Macmillan, 1928.

Berlin, Isaiah. "Two Concepts of Liberty." *Four Essays on Liberty*. Oxford: Oxford University Press, 1969. 118–72.

Berman, Morris. *Coming to Our Senses: Body and Spirit in the Hidden History of the West*. New York: Simon, 1989.

Bidart, Frank. *Desire*. New York: Farrar Straus Giroux, 1997.

Bigelow, Patrick. "The Ontology of Boredom." *Man & World* 16.3 (1983): 251–65.

Boddy, Kasia. "A Fiction of Response: *Girl with Curious Hair* in Context." Boswell and Burn 23–41.

Boswell, Marshall. *Understanding David Foster Wallace*. Columbia: University of South Carolina Press, 2003.

Boswell, Marshall and Stephen J. Burn, eds. *A Companion to David Foster Wallace Studies*. New York: Palgrave Macmillan, 2013.

Bruhn, Siglind. *Musical Ekphrasis: Composers Responding to Poetry and Painting*. Hillsdale: Pendragon Press, 2000.

Buffett, Warren. "Stop Coddling the Super Rich." *The New York Times*, August 14, 2011: A21.

Burn, Stephen. "After Gaddis: Data Storage and the Novel." *William Gaddis, "The Last of Something": Critical Essays*. Ed. Crystal Alberts, Christopher Leise, and Birger Vanwesenbeeck. New York: McFarland & Co., Inc., 2010. 160–9.

—. "The Collapse of Everything: William Gaddis and the Encyclopedic Novel." *Paper Empire: William Gaddis and the World System*. Ed. Joseph Tabbi. Tuscaloosa: University of Alabama Press, 2007. 46–62.

—. *David Foster Wallace's* Infinite Jest: *A Reader's Guide*. New York: Continuum, 2003.

—. *Jonathan Franzen at the End of Postmodernism*. London: Continuum, 2008.

—. "Toward a General Theory of Vision in Wallace's Fiction." *English Studies* 95 (2013): 1–9.

Campbell, Joseph. *Myths to Live By*. New York: Viking-Penguin, 1972.

Carey, John. *The Intellectuals and the Masses: Pride and Prejudice among the Literary Intelligentsia, 1880–1939*. London: Faber, 1992.

Carlisle, Gregory. "Introduction: Consider David Foster Wallace." Hering, *Consider* (2010): 10–23.

—. "Liverpool Keynote Address on David Foster Wallace." Keynote Address Consider David Foster Wallace Conference, University of Liverpool, July 29, 2009, http://www.sideshowmediagroup.com/?p=97

Carriere, Jonathan S. A., James Allan Cheyne, and Daniel Smilek. "Everyday Attention Lapses and Memory Failures: The Affective Consequences of Mindlessness." *Consciousness and Cognition* 17 (2008): 835–47.

Carroll, Noël. "The Specificity of Media in the Arts." *Journal of Aesthetic Education* 19.4 (1985): 5–20.

Chait, Jonathan. *The Big Con: Crackpot Economics and the Fleecing of America.* Boston: Houghton Mifflin Company, 2007.

Chanen, Brian W. "Surfing the Text: The Digital Environment in Mark Z. Danielewski's *House of Leaves.*" *European Journal of English Studies* 11.2 (August 2007): 163–76.

Cheyne, James Allan, Jonathan S. A. Carriere, and Daniel Smilek. "Absent-mindedness: Lapses of Conscious Awareness and Everyday Cognitive Failures." *Consciousness and Cognition* 15 (2006): 578–92.

Cioffi, Frank. "'An Anguish Become Thing': Narrative as Performance in David Foster Wallace's *Infinite Jest.*" *Narrative* 8.2 (May 2000): 161–81.

Clark, Hilary A. "Encyclopedic Discourse." *Sub-stance* 21.1 (1992): 95–110. Print.

—. *The Fictional Encyclopedia: Joyce, Pound, and Sollers.* New York and London: Garland, 1990.

Clüver, Claus. "Ekphrasis Reconsidered: On Verbal Representations of Non-Verbal Texts." *Interart Poetics: Essays on the Interrelations of the Arts and Media.* Ed. Ulla-Britta Lagerroth, Hand Lund, and Erik Hedling. Amsterdam: Rodopi, 1997. 19–33.

Coe, Jonathan. *Like a Fiery Elephant: The Story of B.S. Johnson.* 2004. London: Picador-Macmillan, 2005.

Cohn, Dorrit. *The Distinction of Fiction.* Baltimore: Johns Hopkins University Press, 1999.

Cohn, Norman. *The Pursuit of the Millennium: Revolutionary Millenarians and Mystical Anarchists of the Middle Ages.* 2nd ed. New York: Oxford University Press, 1970.

Coover, Robert. *The Public Burning.* New York: Viking, 1977.

Crosland, T. W. H. *The Suburbans.* London: Long, 1905.

Culler, Jonathan. "Omniscience," in *The Literary in Theory.* Stanford: Stanford University Press, 2007.

—. *Structuralist Poetics: Structuralism, Linguistics, and the Study of Literature.* London: Routledge & Kegan Paul, 1975.

Danielewski, Mark Z. *House of Leaves.* Remastered Full Color Edition. New York: Random House, 2000.

de Man, Paul. "The Concept of Irony." *Aesthetic Ideology.* Minneapolis: University of Minnesota Press, 1996. 163–84.

—. "The Rhetoric of Temporality." *Blindness and Insight: Essays in the Rhetoric of Contemporary Criticism.* 2nd ed. Minneapolis: University of Minnesota Press, 1983. 187–228.

DeLillo, Don. *Underworld.* New York: Scribner-Simon, 1997.

—. *White Noise.* New York: Penguin, 1985.

Dennett, Daniel. *Consciousness Explained.* 1991. London: Penguin Press, 1992.

Derrida, Jacques. "Autoimmunity: Real and Symbolic Suicides—a Dialogue with Jacques Derrida" (with Giovanna Borradori). Trans. Pascale-Anne Brault and Michael Naas. *Philosophy in a Time of Terror: Dialogues with Jürgen Habermas and Jacques Derrida*. Ed. Borradori. Chicago: University of Chicago Press, 2003. 85–136.

—. *Writing and Difference*. Trans. Alan Bass. Chicago: University of Chicago Press, 1978.

Dewey, Bradley R. "Seven Seducers. A Typology of Interpretations of the Aesthetic Stage in Kierkegaard's 'The Seducer's Diary'." *International Kierkegaard Commentary vol. 3: Either/Or Part 1*. Ed. Robert L. Perkins. Macon: Mercer University Press, 1995. 159–99.

"Discussing Cruft." *Wikipedia*. Wikimedia Foundation, October 11, 2010. October 16, 2011.

Dreyfuss, Hubert and Sean Dorrance Kelly. *All Things Shining: Reading the Western Classics to Find Meaning in a Secular Age*. New York: Free Press, 2011.

Dulk, Allard den. "Beyond Endless 'Aesthetic' Irony: A Comparison of The Irony Critique of Søren Kierkegaard and David Foster Wallace's *Infinite Jest*." *Studies in the Novel* 44.3 (2012): 325–45.

Eco, Umberto. *The Open Work*. 1962. Cambridge: Harvard University Press, 1989.

Eliot, George. *Adam Bede*. New York: Harper & Brothers, 1859.

—. *Middlemarch*. 1872. London: Penguin Books, 2003.

—. "The Natural History of German Life." 1856. *Essays of George Eliot*. Ed. Thomas Pinney. London: Routledge, 1963. 266–99.

Elliott, Kamilla. "Novels, Films, and the Word/Image Wars." *A Companion to Literature and Film*. Ed. Robert Stam and Alessandra Raengo. Malden: Blackwell, 2004. 1–22. Print.

Eriksen, Niels Nymann. *Kierkegaard's Category of Repetition. A Reconstruction*. Berlin: Walter de Gruyter, 2000.

Evans, David H. "'The Chains of Not Choosing': Free Will and Faith in William James and David Foster Wallace." Boswell and Burn 171–89.

Fenske, Mark J. and Jane E. Raymond. "Affective Influences of Selective Attention." *Current Directions in Psychological Science* 15.6 (2006): 312–16.

Fest, Bradley J. "The Inverted Nuke in the Garden: Archival Emergence and Anti-Eschatological Aesthetics in David Foster Wallace's *Infinite Jest*." *boundary 2* 39.3 (2012): 125–49.

Fielding, Henry. *The History of Tom Jones, a Foundling*. 2 vols. Ed. Fred Bowers. Middletown: Wesleyan University Press, 1975.

Fishburn, Evelyn. "A Footnote to Borges Studies: A Study of the Footnotes." *Renscrituras: Texto y Teoría*. Ed. Luz Rodríguez-Carranza and Marilene Nagle. *Estudios Culturales 33*. New York: Rodopi, 2004. 285–302.

Fludernik, Monika. "New Wine in Old Bottles? Voice, Focalization, and New Writing." *New Literary History* 32 (2001): 619–38.

—. *Towards a "Natural" Narratology*. London and New York: Routledge, 1996.

Foster, Graham. "A Blasted Region: David Foster Wallace's Man-made Landscapes." *Consider David Foster Wallace: Critical Essays*. Ed. David Hering. Los Angeles: Sideshow Media Group Press, 2010. 37–48.

Foucault, Michel. *The Order of Things. An Archaeology of the Human Sciences*. London: Routledge, 2002.

—. "What Is an Author?" *Modern Criticism and Theory: A Reader*. Ed. David Lodge. Longman: New York, 1988. 196–210.

Franzen, Jonathan. "The Art of Fiction 207: Jonathan Franzen." Interview with Stephen J. Burn. *Paris Review* 195 (2010): 38–79.

—. "Farther Away." *New Yorker* (April 18, 2011): 80–94.

—. "Mr. Difficult." *How to Be Alone*. London: HarperCollins, 2002. 238–69.

Freud, Sigmund. *The Interpretation of Dreams*. Trans. James Strachey. New York: Basic, 2010.

Freudenthal, Elizabeth. "Anti-Interiority: Compulsiveness, Objectification, and Identity in *Infinite Jest*." *New Literary History* 41.1 (Winter 2010): 191–211.

Friedman, Thomas L. *The Lexus and the Olive Tree: Understanding Globalization*. Updated and Expanded Edition. New York: Anchor, 2000.

Frye, Northrop. *Anatomy of Criticism*. 1957. Princeton, NJ: Princeton University Press, 2000.

Fukuyama, Francis. *The End of History and the Last Man*. New York: Free Press, 2006.

Gallese, Vittorio. "The 'Shared Manifold' Hypothesis: From Mirror Neurons to Empathy." *Journal of Consciousness Studies* 8.5–7 (2001): 33–50.

Gardner, John. *On Moral Fiction*. New York: Basic Books, 1979.

Gass, William H. *Finding a Form*. New York: Knopf, 1997.

Genette, Gérard. *Narrative Discourse: An Essay in Method*. 1972. Ithaca: Cornell University Press, 1980.

—. *Paratexts: Thresholds of Interpretation*. Trans. Jane E. Lewin. New York: Cambridge University Press, 1997.

Giddens, Anthony. *Modernity and Self-Identity: Self and Society in the Late Modern Age*. Cambridge: Polity Press, 2004.

Giles, Paul. "Sentimental Posthumanism: David Foster Wallace." *Twentieth Century Literature: A Scholarly and Critical Journal* 53(3) (Fall 2007): 327–44.

Gladstone, Jason and Daniel Worden. "Postmodernism, Then." *Twentieth-Century Literature* 57.3–4 (2011): 291–308.

Gleick, James. *The Information*. New York: Pantheon Books, 2011.

Goerlandt, Iannis. "'Put the Book Down and Slowly Walk Away': Irony and David Foster Wallace's *Infinite Jest*." *Critique: Studies in Contemporary Fiction* 47.3 (2006): 309–28.

Goldberg, Yael K., John D. Eastwood, Jennifer LaGuardia, and James Danckert. "Boredom: An Emotional Experience from Apathy, Anhedonia, or Depression." *Journal of Social and Clinical Psychology* 30.6 (2011): 647–66.

Goldsmith, Kenneth. *Uncreative Writing: Managing Language in the Digital Age*. New York: Columbia University Press, 2011. Print.

Goodstein, Elizabeth S. *Experience without Qualities: Boredom and Modernity*. Stanford: Stanford University Press, 2005.

Grafton, Anthony. *The Footnote: A Curious History*. Cambridge, MA: Harvard University Press, 1997. Print.

Grøn, Arne. *The Concept of Anxiety in Søren Kierkegaard*. Trans. Jeanette B. L. Knox. Macon: Mercer University Press, 2008.

Guignon, Charles. *On Being Authentic*. London: Routledge, 2008.

Haraway, Donna. "A Manifesto for Cyborgs: Science, Technology, and Socialist Feminism in the 1980s." *The Norton Anthology of Theory and Criticism*. Ed. Leitch, Cain, Finke, Johnson, McGowan, and Williams. New York: W.W. Norton & Co., 2001. 2269–99.

Harvey, David. *A Brief History of Neoliberalism*. Oxford: Oxford University Press, 2005.

—. *The Condition of Postmodernity: An Inquiry into the Knowledge of Cultural Change*. Malden, MA: Blackwell, 1990.

Hayes-Brady, Clare. "The Book, the Broom and the Ladder: Philosophical Grounding in the Work of David Foster Wallace." Hering, *Consider* 24–36.

Hayles, N. Katherine. "The Illusion of Autonomy and the Fact of Recursivity: Virtual Ecologies, Entertainment, and *Infinite Jest*." *New Literary History* 30.3, Ecocriticism (1999): 675–97.

Healy, Seán Desmond. *Boredom, Self, and Culture*. New Jersey: Fairleigh Dickinson University Press, 1984.

Hecht, Eugene. *Optics*. 4th ed. New York: Addison Wesley, 2001.

Heffernan, James. *Museum of Words: The Poetics of Ekphrasis from Homer to Ashbery*. Chicago: University of Chicago Press, 1993.

Heller, Joseph. *Catch-22*. 1961. New York: Simon & Schuster, 1999.

Hering, David, ed. *Consider David Foster Wallace: Critical Essays*. Austin, TX: SSMG Press, 2010.

—. "Theorizing David Foster Wallace's Toxic Postmodern Spaces." *US Studies Online* 18 (2011). Web. December 7, 2011.

Herman, Luc and Bart Vervaeck. "The Implied Author: A Secular Excommunication." *Style* 45.1 (2011): 11–28.

Hoberek, Andrew. "The Novel After David Foster Wallace." Boswell and Burn 211–28.

Holland, Mary K. "'The Art's Heart's Purpose': Braving the Narcissistic Loop of David Foster Wallace's *Infinite Jest*." *Critique: Studies in Contemporary Fiction* 47.3 (2006): 218–42.

—. *Succeeding Postmodernism: Language and Humanism in Contemporary American Literature*. New York: Bloomsbury Academic, 2013.

Hutchison, Anthony. *Writing the Republic: Liberalism and Morality in American Political Fiction*. New York: Columbia University Press, 2007.

Iser, Wolfgang. *The Act of Reading: A Theory of Aesthetic Response*. 1976. London: Routledge & Kegan Paul, 1978.

Jacob's Ladder. Dir. Adrian Lyne. Scr. Bruce Joel Rubin. Carolco, 1990.

Jacobs, Timothy. "American Touchstone: The Idea of Order in Gerard Manley Hopkins and David Foster Wallace." *Comparative Literature Studies* 38.3 (2001): 215–31.

—. "The Brothers Incandenza: Translating Ideology in Fyodor Dostoevsky's *The Brothers Karamazov* and David Foster Wallace's *Infinite Jest*." *Texas Studies in Literature and Language* 49.3 (2007): 265–92.

James, William. "Circumscription of the [Religious] Topic." *The Writings of William James: A Comprehensive Edition*. Ed. John J. McDermott. Chicago: University of Chicago Press, 1977. 741–58.

—. "Experience and Religion: A Comment." *The Writings of William James: A Comprehensive Edition*: 740–1.

—. "The Moral Equivalent of War." *The Writings of William James: A Comprehensive Edition*: 660–71.

—. *The Principles of Psychology*. Vol. 1. New York: Holt, 1890.

Jameson, Fredric. *Postmodernism, or, The Cultural Logic of Late Capitalism*. London: Verso, 1991.

Johnson, B. S. *Aren't You Rather Young to Be Writing Your Memoirs?* London: Hutchinson, 1973.

—. *Christie Malry's Own Double-Entry*. 1973. New York: New Directions, 1985.

Jost, François. "The Look: From Film to Novel. An Essay in Comparative Narratology." *A Companion to Literature and Film*. Ed. Robert Stam and Alessandra Raengo. Malden: Blackwell, 2004. 71–80.

Kakutani, Michiko. "Maximized Revenue, Minimized Existence." Rev. of *The Pale King: An Unfinished Novel* by David Foster Wallace. *The New York Times,* March 31, 2011. Web. December 20, 2011.

Karnicky, Jeffrey. *Contemporary Fiction and the Ethics of Modern Culture*. New York: Palgrave Macmillan, 2007.

Keen, Suzanne. *Empathy and the Novel*. New York: Oxford University Press, 2007.

Kelly, Adam. "David Foster Wallace: The Death of the Author and the Birth of a Discipline." *Irish Journal of American Studies Online* 2 (Summer 2010a), http://www.ijasonline.com/Adam-Kelly.html

—. "David Foster Wallace and the New Sincerity in American Fiction." Hering, *Consider* (2010b): 131–46.

Kenner, Hugh. *Joyce's Voices*. Berkeley: University of California Press, 1978.

—. *Ulysses, Revised Edition*. Baltimore: Johns Hopkins University Press, 1987.

Kermode, Frank. *The Sense of an Ending: Studies in the Theory of Fiction with a New Epilogue*. 2nd ed. New York: Oxford University Press, 2000.

Kidd, David Comer and Emanuele Castano. "Reading Literary Fiction Improves Theory of Mind." *Science* 342.6156 (October 18, 2013): 377–80.

Kierkegaard, Søren. *The Concept of Anxiety. A Simple Psychologically Orienting Deliberation on the Dogmatic Issue of Hereditary Sin.* Trans. Reidar Thomte and Albert B. Anderson. Princeton: Princeton University Press, 1989. [abbreviated as *CA*]

—. *The Concept of Irony: With Continual Reference to Socrates; Together with Notes of Schelling's Berlin Lectures.* Trans. Howard V. Hong and Edna H. Hong. Princeton: Princeton University Press, 1989. [abbreviated as *CI*]

—. *Concluding Unscientific Postscript to Philosophical Fragments.* 2 vols. Trans. Howard V. Hong and Edna H. Hong. Princeton: Princeton University Press, 1992. [abbreviated as *CUP*]

—. *Either/Or.* 2 vols. Trans. Howard V. Hong and Edna H. Hong. Princeton: Princeton University Press, 1987. [abbreviated as *EO*]

—. *Fear and Trembling / Repetition.* Trans. Howard V. Hong and Edna H. Hong. Princeton: Princeton University Press, 1983.

Kirsch, Adam. "The Importance of Being Earnest." *The New Republic* (August 18, 2011): 20–6.

Klapp, Orrin E. *Overload and Boredom: Essays on the Quality of Life in the Information Society.* New York: Greenwood Press, 1986.

Klein, Naomi. *The Shock Doctrine: The Rise of Disaster Capitalism.* New York: Metropolitan Books, 2007.

Kleinknecht, Richard. *The Man Who Sold the World: Ronald Reagan and the Betrayal of Main Street America.* New York: Nation Books, 2009.

Koepnick, Lutz. "Reading on the Move." *PMLA* 128.1 (2013): 232–7. Print.

Konstantinou, Lee. "No Bull: David Foster Wallace and Postironic Belief." *The Legacy of David Foster Wallace.* Ed. Samuel Cohen and Lee Konstantinou. Iowa City: University of Iowa Press, 2012. 83–112.

—. "The World of David Foster Wallace." *boundary 2* 40.3 (2013): 59–86.

Kornacki, Steve. "The Market Meltdown and the Hopeless Politics of 2011." Salon.com, August 9, 2011, http://www.salon.com/2011/08/09/market_obama/

Kottke, Jason. "How to Read Infinite Jest." *kottke.org*, July 15, 2009. Web. August 31, 2011.

Krieger, Murray. *Ekphrasis: The Illusion of the Natural Sign.* Baltimore: Johns Hopkins University Press, 1992.

Kroeber, Karl. *Make Believe in Film and Fiction: Visual vs. Verbal Storytelling.* New York: Palgrave Macmillan, 2006.

Kuhn, Reinhard. *The Demon of Noontide: Ennui in Western Literature.* Princeton: Princeton University Press, 1976.

Lacan, Jacques. "The Mirror Stage as Formative of the Function of the I as Revealed in Psychoanalytic Experience." *Écrits: The First Complete Edition in English.* Trans. Bruce Fink. New York: W. W. Norton & Co., 2006.

Lanser, Susan. "The 'I' of the Beholder: Equivocal Attachments and the Limits of Structuralist Narratology." *A Companion to Narrative Theory.* Ed. James Phelan and Peter Rabinowitz. Malden: Blackwell, 2005. 206–19.

Lasdun, James. Rev. of *The Pale King: An Unfinished Novel* by David Foster Wallace. *The Guardian,* April 15, 2011. Web. December 20, 2011.

LeClair, Tom. *The Art of Excess: Mastery in Contemporary American Fiction.* Urbana and Chicago: University Illinois Press, 1989.

—. "The Prodigious Fiction of Richard Powers, William Vollmann, and David Foster Wallace." *Critique* 38.1 (1996): 12–37.

Lejeune, Philippe. "The Autobiographical Pact." 1975. *On Autobiography.* Ed. P. J. Eakin. Minneapolis: University of Minnesota Press, 1989. 3–30.

Lepenies, Wolf. *Melancholy and Society.* Trans. Jeremy Gaines and Doris Jones. Cambridge: Harvard University Press, 1992.

Lessing, Gotthold Ephraim. *Laocoön: An Essay on the Limits of Painting and Poetry.* 1766. Trans. Edward Allen McCormick. Baltimore: Johns Hopkins University Press, 1984.

Lewis, C. S. *An Experiment in Criticism.* Cambridge: Cambridge University Press, 1961.

—. *The Screwtape Letters.* 1942. New York: Macmillan, 1953.

Lipsky, David. *Although of Course You End Up Becoming Yourself: A Road Trip with David Foster Wallace.* New York: Broadway Books, 2010.

Lizza, Ryan. "Leap of Faith: The Making of a Republican Front-Runner." *The New Yorker,* August 15 and 22, 2011: 60.

Loewen, James W. *Lies My Teacher Told Me: Everything Your American History Textbook Got Wrong.* Tenth Anniversary ed. New York: Simon & Schuster, 2007.

Luhmann, Niklas. *Social Systems.* Trans. John Bednarz with Dirk Baecker. Stanford: Stanford University Press, 1995.

Luther, Connie. "David Foster Wallace: Westward with Fredric Jameson." Hering, *Consider David Foster Wallace,* 49–61.

Maloney, Edward. "Footnotes in Fiction: A Rhetorical Approach." Diss. Ohio State University, 2005. Print.

Marino, Gordon, ed. "Introduction." *Basic Writings of Existentialism.* New York: The Modern Library, 2004. ix–xvi.

Marx, Leo. *The Machine in the Garden: Technology and the Pastoral Ideal in America.* New York: Oxford University Press, 1964.

Max, D. T. *Every Love Story Is a Ghost Story: A Life of David Foster Wallace.* New York: Viking-Penguin, 2012.

—. "The Unfinished: David Foster Wallace's Struggle to Surpass *Infinite Jest.*" *The New Yorker* 85.4 (2009): 48–61.

—. "William Gass and John Gardner: A Debate on Fiction." 1978. *Conversations with William H. Gass.* Mississippi: University of Mississippi Press, 2003. 46–55.

McCarthy, Mary. *Ideas and the Novel*. London: Weidenfeld and Nicholson, 1980.

McCarthy, Tom. "David Foster Wallace: The Last Audit." Rev. of *The Pale King: An Unfinished Novel* by David Foster Wallace. *New York Times Sunday Book Review,* April 14, 2011. Web. December 20, 2011.

McDonald, William. "Kierkegaard's Demonic Boredom." *Critical Studies: Essays on Boredom and Modernity*. Ed. Barbara Dalle Pezze and Carlo Salzani. Amsterdam and New York: Rodopi, 2009. 61–84.

McGurl, Mark. *The Program Era: Postwar Fiction and the Rise of Creative Writing*. Cambridge: Harvard University Press, 2009.

—. "Zombie Renaissance." *n+1*, April 27, 2010. Web. October 23, 2013.

McHale, Brian. *Postmodernist Fiction*. 1987. London and New York: Routledge, 1996.

McLaughlin, Robert L. "Post-Postmodern Discontent: Contemporary Fiction and the Social World." *symploke* 12.1–2 (2004): 53–68.

Melville, Herman. *Moby-Dick, or, The Whale*. Introd. Andrew Delbanco. New York: Penguin, 1992.

Mendelson, Edward. "Encyclopedic Narrative." *MLN* 91.6 (December 1976): 1267–75.

— "Gravity's Encyclopedia." *Mindful Pleasures: Essays on Thomas Pynchon*. Ed. George Levine and David Leverenz. Boston: Little, Brown and Co., 1976. 161–95.

Metz, Christian. *Psychoanalysis and Cinema: The Imaginary Signifier*. Trans. Celia Britton et al. London: Macmillan, 1982.

Miller, J. Hillis. *Literature as Conduct: Speech Acts in Henry James*. New York: Fordham University Press, 2005.

—. *On Literature*. London: Routledge, 2002.

—. *Reading Narrative*. Norman, OK: University of Oklahoma Press, 1998.

—. *Speech Acts in Literature*. Stanford: Stanford University Press, 2001.

Mitchell, W. J. T. *Iconology: Image, Text, Ideology*. Chicago: University of Chicago Press, 1986. Print.

—. *Picture Theory: Essays on Verbal and Visual Representation*. Chicago: University of Chicago Press, 1994.

Moats, Michael. "Year of David Foster Wallace." *Fiction Advocate,* December 20, 2012, http://fictionadvocate.com/2012/12/20/yearofdavidfosterwallace2012/

Moore, Steven. *The First Version Draft of* Infinite Jest. *Online*, http://www.thehowlingfantods.com/ij_first.htm

—. *William Gaddis*. Boston: Twayne, 1989. Twayne's United States Authors 546.

Moretti, Franco. *Graphs, Maps, Trees: Abstract Models for a Literary History*. London: Verso, 2005.

—. *Modern Epic: The World-System from Goethe to García Márquez*. 1994. Trans. Quinton Hoare. New York: Verso, 1996.

Morris, Pam, ed. *The Bakhtin Reader: Selected Writings of Bakhtin, Medvedev and Voloshinov*. London: Edward Arnold, 1994.

Morrissette, Bruce. *Novel and Film: Essays in Two Genres*. Chicago: University of Chicago Press, 1985.

Morson, Gary Saul and Caryl Emerson. *Mikhail Bakhtin: Creation of a Prosaics*. Stanford, CA: Stanford University Press, 1990.

Nabokov, Vladimir. *The Annotated Lolita*. Ed. Alfred Appel, Jr. London: Penguin Classics, 2000.

Nagel, Thomas. *The View from Nowhere*. New York: Oxford University Press, 1989.

Nancy, Jean-Luc. *The Inoperative Community*. Ed. Peter Connor, trans. Peter Connor, Lisa Garbus, Michael Holland, and Simona Shaw. Minneapolis: University of Minnesota Press, 1991.

Nielsen, Henrik Skov. "Natural Authors, Unnatural Narration." *Postclassical Narratology: Approaches and Analyses*. Ed. Jan Alber and Monika Fludernik. Columbus: Ohio State University Press, 2010. 275–301.

Nørretranders, Tor. *The User Illusion: Cutting Consciousness Down to Size*. Trans. Jonathan Sydenham. New York: Penguin, 1998.

O'Donnell, Patrick. "Almost a Novel: *The Broom of the System*." Boswell and Burn 1–22.

Olsen, Lance. "Termite Art, or Wallace's Wittgenstein." *Review of Contemporary Fiction* 13.2 (1993): 199–215.

Palmer, Alan. *Fictional Minds*. Lincoln and London: University of Nebraska Press, 2004.

Parker, Ashley. "'Corporations Are People,' Romney Tells Iowa Hecklers Angry Over His Tax Policy." *The New York Times*, August 12, 2011: A16.

Percy, Walker. *The Message in the Bottle: How Queer Man Is, How Queer Language Is, and what One Has to Do with the Other*. New York: Picador-Farrar, 1975.

Pezze, Barbara Dalle and Carlo Salzani, eds. *Essays on Boredom and Modernity*. New York: Rodopi, 2009.

Phipps, Gregory. "The Ideal Athlete: John Wayne in *Infinite Jest*." Hering, *Consider David Foster Wallace*, 75–88.

Pietsch, Michael. "Sylvanshine." Message to Stephen Burn. September 10, 2011. E-mail.

Piketty, Thomas and Emmanuel Saez. "How Progressive Is the U.S. Federal Tax System? A Historical and International Perspective." Working Paper 12404, National Bureau of Economic Research, http://www.nber/papers/w12404, 15–16.

Pynchon, Thomas. *The Crying of Lot 49*. Philadelphia: J. B. Lippincott & Co., 1966.

—. *Gravity's Rainbow*. New York: Viking, 1973.

Quinn, Paul. "'Location's Location': Placing David Foster Wallace." Boswell and Burn 87–106.

Rahv, Philip. "The Cult of Experience in American Writing." *Literature in America*. Ed. Rahv. New York: Meridian Books, 1957. 358–72.

Raymond, Eric S. *The New Hacker's Dictionary*. 3rd ed. Cambridge, MA: MIT Press, 1996. Print.

Reagle, Joseph. *Good Faith Collaboration: The Culture of Wikipedia*. Cambridge, MA: MIT Press, 2010. History and the Foundations of Information Science 2.

Richardson, Brian. *Unnatural Voices: Extreme Narration in Modern and Contemporary Fiction*. Columbus: Ohio State University Press, 2006.

Rousseau, John-Jacques. *The Social Contract*. Trans. Maurice Cranston. London: Penguin Books, 1968.

Ryan, Marie-Laure. *Narrative as Virtual Reality: Immersion and Interactivity in Literature and Electronic Media*. Baltimore: Johns Hopkins University Press, 2001.

—. *Possible Worlds, Artificial Intelligence, and Narrative Theory*. Indianapolis: Indiana University Press, 1991.

Sager Eidt, Laura M. *Writing and Filming the Painting: Ekphrasis in Literature and Film*. Amsterdam: Rodopi, 2008.

Sargent, Greg. "The Plum Line: Bachmann on Why She Worked for the IRS: First Rule of War Is 'Know Your Enemy.'" *Washington Post* online edition, August 18, 2011, http://www.washingtonpost.com/blogs/plum-line/post/bachmann-on-why-she-worked-for-irs-first-rule-of-war-is-know-your-enemy/2011/03/03/gIQAmVD6NJ_blog.html

Sartre, Jean-Paul. *Nausea*. Trans. Lloyd Alexander. New York: New Directions, 2007.

Scholtens, Wim R. "Inleiding." Søren Kierkegaard. *Over het begrip ironie*. Amsterdam: Boom, 1995. 7–31. [Publication in Dutch]

Scott, A. O. "The Panic of Influence." *The New York Review of Books* 47.2 (2000): 39–43.

Sedgwick, Eve Kosofsky. "Melanie Klein and the Difference Affect Makes." *South Atlantic Quarterly* 106.3 (2007): 625–42.

Smith, Terry. *What Is Contemporary Art?* Chicago: University of Chicago Press, 2009.

Smith, Zadie. "Brief Interviews with Hideous Men: The Difficult Gifts of David Foster Wallace." *Changing My Mind: Occasional Essays*. London: Hamish Hamilton, 2009. 257–300.

Spacks, Patricia Meyer. *Boredom: The Literary History of a State of Mind*. Chicago: University of Chicago Press, 1995.

Staes, Toon. "Work in Process: A Genesis for *The Pale King*." *English Studies* 95.3 (2014).

Strecker, Trey. "Narrative Ecology and Encyclopedic Narrative." *Avant-Post: The Avant-Garde Under Post Conditions*. Ed. Louis Armand. Prague: Litteraria Pragensia, 2006. 281–98.

Svendsen, Lars. *A Philosophy of Boredom*. London: Reaktion, 2005.

Swigger, Ronald T. "Fictional Encylopedism and the Cognitive Value of Literature." *Comparative Literature Studies* 12.4 (December 1975): 351–66.

Tabbi, Joseph. "William Gaddis." *Conjunctions* 42 (2003): 405–6.

Taels, Johan. *Søren Kierkegaard als filosoof. De weg terug naar het subject.* Leuven: Universitaire Pers Leuven, 1991. [Publication in Dutch]

Thompson, Hunter S. *Fear and Loathing in Las Vegas.* 2nd ed. New York: Vintage, 1998.

Toohey, Peter. *Boredom: A Lively History.* New Haven: Yale University Press, 2011.

Tresco, Matt. "Impervious to U.S. Parsing: Encyclopedism, Autism, and *Infinite Jest.*" *Consider David Foster Wallace: Critical Essays.* Ed. David Hering. Los Angeles and Austin: Sideshow, 2010. 113–22.

Trilling, Lionel. *The Liberal Imagination: Essays on Literature and Society.* 1948. New York: Doubleday, 1957.

—. *The Liberal Imagination: Essays on Literature and Society.* 1950. New York: NYRB Editions, 2008.

Turner, Jenny. "Illuminating, Horrible Etc." Rev. of *The Pale King: An Unfinished Novel* by David Foster Wallace and *Although of Course You End Up Becoming Yourself: A Road Trip with David Foster Wallace* by David Lipsky. *London Review of Books* 33.8, April 14, 2011. Web. December 20, 201.

van Ewijk, Petrus. "Encyclopedia, Network, Hypertext, Database: The Continuing Relevance of *Encyclopedic Narrative* and *Encyclopedic Novel* as Generic Designations." *Genre* 44.2 (Summer 2011): 205–22.

—. "'I' and 'Other': The Relevance of Wittgenstein, Buber and Levinas for an Understanding of AA's Recovery Program in *Infinite Jest.*" *English Text Construction* 2.1 (2009): 132–45.

Verstrynge, Karl. "De autonomie van de esthetiek in Kierkegaards *Enten/ Eller.* Over ledigheid en verveling." *Algemeen Nederlands Tijdschrift voor Wijsbegeerte* 92.4 (2000): 293–305. [Publication in Dutch]

Wallace, David Foster. *Both Flesh and Not.* New York: Little, Brown and Co., 2012.

—. *Brief Interviews with Hideous Men.* Boston: Little, Brown & Co., 1999.

—. *The Broom of the System.* New York: Penguin Books, 1987.

—. *Consider the Lobster and Other Essays.* Boston. Little, Brown & Co., 2005.

—. *Fate, Time and Language: An Essay on Free Will.* Ed. Steven M. Cahn and Maureen Eckhert. New York: Columbia University Press, 2010.

—. *Girl with Curious Hair.* New York: W.W. Norton & Co., 1989.

—. *Infinite Jest.* Boston: Little, Brown & Co., 1996.

—. Interview with David Foster Wallace. *The Believer,* November 2003, 1.8: 85–93.

—. Interview with David Wiley. *The Minnesota Daily.* February 27, 1997, http://www.badgerinternet.com/~bobkat/jestwiley2.html

—. Interview with Michael Silverblatt. *Bookworm.* KCRW. April 11, 1996, http://www.kcrw.com/etc/programs/bw/bw960411david_foster_wallace

—. Letter to Bonnie Nadell. July 5, 1989. TS. Bonnie Nadell's Papers. Harry Ransom Humanities Research Center, Austin *The Pale King*. Boston: Little, Brown & Co., 2011.

—. "List of Top Ten Books." *The Top Ten: Writers Pick Their Favorite Books.* Ed. J. Peder Zane. New York: W.W. Norton & Co., 2007. 128.

—. *Oblivion: Stories.* New York: Little, Brown and Co., 2004.

—. *The Pale King: An Unfinished Novel.* New York: Little, Brown and Co., 2011.

—. *A Supposedly Fun Thing I'll Never Do Again.* Boston: Little, Brown and Co., 1997.

—. *This Is Water. Some Thoughts, Delivered on a Significant Occasion, about Living a Compassionate Life.* New York: Little, Brown & Co., 2009.

Warren, Rosanna. *Fables of the Self: Studies in Lyric Poetry.* New York: W.W. Norton & Co., 2008.

Wehner, Peter. "The GOP's Philosophical Straightjacket." *Commentary* online, August 12, 2011, http://www.commentarymagazine.com/2011/08/12/gop-taxes-straightjacket/#more-763748

Welsh, Ryan. "Ekphrasis." Winter 2007. *The University of Chicago: Theories of Media: Keyword Glossary,* http://csmt.uchicago.edu/glossary2004/ekphrasis.htm

Wilson, Christopher P. *White Collar Fictions: Class and Social Representations in American Literature, 1885–1925.* Athens, GA: University of Georgia Press, 1992.

Wilson, Timothy D. *Strangers to Ourselves: Discovering the Adaptive Unconscious.* Cambridge, MA: Belknap-Harvard University Press, 2002.

Wittgenstein, Ludwig. *The Philosophical Investigations.* 2nd ed. Trans. G. E. M. Anscombe. Malden, MA: Blackwell Publishers, 1958.

—. *Tractatus Logico-Philosophicus.* Revised ed. Trans. D. F. Pears and B. F. McGuinness. New York: Routledge, 1974.

Woloch, Alex. *The One vs. the Many: Minor Characters and the Space of the Protagonist in the Novel.* Princeton: Princeton University Press, 2003.

Wood, James. "Human, All Too Inhuman." *The New Republic* (July 24, 2000): 41–6.

Zunshine, Lisa. *Why We Read Fiction: Theory of Mind and the Novel.* Columbus: Ohio State University Press, 2006.

Notes on Contributors

Marshall Boswell is Professor and Chair of the Department of English at Rhodes College. He is the author of two works of literary scholarship: *John Updike's Rabbit Tetralogy: Mastered Irony in Motion* (2001) and *Understanding David Foster Wallace* (2004). He is also the author of two works of fiction, *Trouble with Girls* (2003) and *Alternative Atlanta* (2005). With Stephen Burn, he is the coeditor of *A Companion to David Foster Wallace Studies* (2013).

Stephen J. Burn is the author or editor of five books, including *Jonathan Franzen at the End of Postmodernism* (2008) and *Conversations with David Foster Wallace* (2012). His essays, reviews, and interviews have appeared in *Contemporary Literature*, *Modern Fiction Studies*, the *New York Times Book Review*, the *Paris Review*, the *Times Literary Supplement*, and the *Yale Review*. He is a Reader at the University of Glasgow.

Ralph Clare teaches twentieth- and twenty-first-century American literature at Boise State University. He has essays forthcoming on Richard Powers (*Critique*), William Gaddis (*Studies in the Novel*), and Kurt Vonnegut (*Critical Insights on Kurt Vonnegut*). His current book project is *Fictions Ltd.: The Corporation in Postmodern American Fiction, Film, and Popular Culture*.

Allard den Dulk is Lecturer in Philosophy, Literature, and Film at Amsterdam University College. He studied history and journalism at the University of Groningen and philosophy at VU University Amsterdam. He was Lecturer in Modern Philosophy and Aesthetics at VU before moving to AUC. He has published articles on philosophy, literature, and film. In 2012, he finished his dissertation, "'Love Me Till My Heart Stops': Existentialist Engagement in Contemporary American Literature," a philosophical analysis of the fiction of David Foster Wallace, Dave Eggers, and Jonathan Safran Foer. Parts of this dissertation and more information can be found at www.allarddendulk.nl.

Bradley J. Fest received his MFA in poetry from the University of Pittsburgh, where he is now a Visiting Instructor and PhD candidate studying nineteenth- through twenty-first-century American literature. He is currently working on his dissertation, "The Apocalypse Archive: American Literature and the Nuclear Bomb." An essay on David Foster Wallace's *Infinite Jest* will appear this fall in *boundary 2*, and an essay on nuclear criticism in the collection *The Silence of Fallout: Nuclear Criticism in a Post-Cold War World* is forthcoming. His poems have appeared in *Spork, Open Thread, BathHouse, Flywheel,* and elsewhere. He blogs at *The Hyperarchival Parallax.*

Adam Kelly is Lecturer of American Literature at the University of York. Previously he was an Irish Research Council CARA Postdoctoral Mobility Fellow at Harvard University and University College Dublin. He has published articles on American literature in journals including *Twentieth-Century Literature, Critique, Philip Roth Studies,* and *Phrasis,* as well as in various essay collections. His first monograph, *American Fiction in Transition: Observer-Hero Narrative, the 1990s, and Postmodernism,* was published by Bloomsbury in 2013. He is currently working on a second project entitled "Twenty-First-Century American Fiction and the New Sincerity."

David Letzler lives in Queens, New York, and is a doctoral candidate at the CUNY Graduate Center. In addition to the essay in this issue, he has an article out this fall in the *Wallace Stevens Journal,* as well as a piece in next year's forthcoming collection *Of Pynchon and Vice.*

Philip Sayers is a PhD student in the English department at the University of Toronto. He works on contemporary American fiction and on literary theory, including psychoanalytic theory, structuralism, and poststructuralism. Before moving to Canada, he read English as an undergraduate at Fitzwilliam College, Cambridge. He then studied comparative literature in University College London's MA program, where his thesis was titled "Film in and Around the Novel: David Foster Wallace's *Infinite Jest.*" It is from this project the chapter in this issue was developed. He intends to continue his research on David Foster Wallace.

Toon Staes is affiliated with the Department of English Literature of the University of Antwerp, where he works as a doctoral fellow of the Flemish Research Foundation (FWO). He has published on contemporary American literature and narrative theory. Together with Luc Herman, he is currently editing a special issue of *English Studies* on the posthumous publication of David Foster Wallace's *The Pale King.*

Andrew Warren is Assistant Professor of English at Harvard University, specializing in Romanticism. His first book project, currently under reader review, is entitled "Populous Solitudes: the Orient and the Young Romantics." He has also recently found himself thinking about narrative technique, and he has written forthcoming articles on Ann Radcliffe and

James Joyce for *The Eighteenth Century: Theory & Interpretation* and the *James Joyce Quarterly*, respectively. This particular piece was inspired by a course he teaches at Harvard, "David Foster Wallace & Environs."

Conley Wouters is a PhD student in the English Department at Brandeis University, where he teaches undergraduate writing seminars on rap music and, beginning in spring 2013, David Foster Wallace. He works on contemporary American fiction and is interested in digital humanities, the encyclopedic novel, and the intersection between politics and technology in the American novel.

Index